Little Melton

The story of a Norfolk village

Edited by Anne Carter

Design by Stewart Cable

Researched and written by members of the Little Melton History Group;
Anne Carter, Jayne Cable, Stewart Cable, Annetta Evans,
John Evans, Alan Mann, Hugh Waghorn.

First Edition September 2003

ISBN 0-9545571-0-7

Published by Little Melton Community Trust

Little Melton

This book is dedicated to the memory of
Robert (Bob) Burton Brett
1937 - 2001

the Contributors...

After her husband Claude died in 1996, **Anne Carter**, grandmother of six, was looking for a cottage in a friendly rural community near Norwich, and was lucky enough to discover Little Melton. After war service, she studied at Bristol University, before being appointed way back in 1949 as one of Norfolk's earliest Probation Officers, later working in education. Anne holds certificates in both local history and genealogy, and has had several articles and books published on these subjects. She loves children, (having been involved with Girlguiding, Norfolk, for nearly half a century), as well as the countryside, her garden and her church, and hates apathy, injustice, red tape and plastic tomato sauce bottles.

Jayne Cable is the only contributor who can claim to be truly a Little Melton person, being born here just a few years ago! Having grown up here and attended both the current and previous Little Melton schools, she went on to be educated at Wymondham College and is now an Office Manager. Jayne and Stewart's children, Laura and Jamie, also attended Little Melton's Playgroup and School. Apart from four years living elsewhere she is truly a village *'mawther'*.

Stewart Cable was born *'next door'* in Great Melton where he grew up, being primarily schooled in Hethersett, he also attended Wymondham College, where he met Jayne. He now works for himself, as a Consulting Design Engineer, specialising in scenery and lifting equipment for performing Theatres and Concert halls here, and around the world. He is also an amateur artist and, at the time of this book's publication, the chair of Little Melton Parish Council.

North Norfolk-born **Annetta Evans** has lived in Little Melton since 1965. On retirement, after working as a Bio-Medical Scientist for nearly 40 years, she fulfilled her ambition to study for a part-time degree in History at the University of East Anglia and is now working towards an M. A. in the Centre of East Anglian Studies there. She is also involved in yacht racing management at a local sailing club, is secretary of the Norwich Charity Christmas Card Shop and can often be seen walking her chocolate Labrador Tarka through the village.

John Evans has worked as a teacher in Norfolk since 1987. Originally a city boy from London who always wanted to live in a village, John finally made it when he moved to Little Melton in 1998 and was delighted to have the chance to make a small contribution to a book about its history.

Alan Mann is a native of Norwich. He was educated at the City of Norwich School before embarking on a career in banking, in which he remained until early retirement in 1993. Happily married to Pam, their move to the village coincided with the year of his retirement. Since then Alan has been busy on many fronts and has written several books about his musical idol Buddy Holly. An active member of several clubs, he has been involved with the Priscilla Bacon Lodge on a voluntary basis since 1995, and currently works there part time as driving co-ordinator for the Day Care Unit. He stoically awaits imminent qualification for his bus pass.

Hugh Waghorn is a Deputy Principal in the motor industry, and lived in Little Melton for 3 years from 1998, when he and his wife Jasmine much enjoyed village life, regularly attending All Saints church. Having always been very interested in history in general, he was keen to find out more on discovering that there was a slight connection between the explorer Captain James Cook and Little Melton, particularly as he has a brother living in New Zealand.

Contents

**reface**

reface

You and I are yesterday's answers,
The Earth of the past come to flesh,
Eroded by time's rivers,
To the shapes we now possess.
Greg Lake.

Early in 1999 a small group of enthusiastic volunteers got together to plan celebrations for the arrival of the new millennium. We received a grant of £1000 from the village's Parochial Charity to get us started. Many different projects were planned, this book being one of them. One of the first to be completed was a village calendar featuring old photos of the village and its folk. These were sold and made a profit enabling the group to plan further activities. Commemorative mugs were printed and distributed free to children under 16 in the village. Another small group began to stitch and embroider a beautiful banner to mark the millennium. This now hangs in the church. A village party was planned for old year's night 1999, there was a big bonfire and fireworks and lots of food and drink. A great time was had by all who attended. Now into the millennium, another planned project has just been completed, the millennium garden, adjacent to the village hall. Planned as a celebration it has unfortunately taken a more subdued status, now combined with a memorial to the late Bob Brett, whom you will discover later in these pages.

The most ambitious project was this book and thanks to the hours of research and hard work by the 'History Group' it is now a reality. The Little Melton of today is very different from the one you will read about here. It is no longer a poor farming community but an affluent suburb of Norwich. There has been significant development in the village over the last few years, there are approximately 400 homes here now and very few have farming connections. We have a thriving and happy First School which continues to achieve excellent OFSTED reports. At present the school has around 80 pupils, we have three full time teachers and a headmistress who splits her time between administration and teaching. There is also a popular Pre-school which is full to capacity. The village had until recently, the choice of two shops both selling essentials plus a few treats! Sadly only one now remains. There is a large pub with a play area for children, known as The Village Inn, but like many places in the village it has a fascinating history that is not at all obvious when looking at its modern facelift. There are some particularly good stories relating to the war years including famous visitors.

We are lucky to have a superb village hall in which many groups meet including the Meltonians (a group for our older residents), a social badminton club, tennis coaching for the youngsters and various church groups. The village homewatch scheme aims to prevent and reduce crime in the locality. A network of telephone links ensures that important information is passed to street co-ordinators who in turn make sure that residents are kept informed. We also have a wonderful children's playground, the result of lots of hard work by a small group of parents.

We have a beautiful little church which is well supported by its congregation and an active friends organisation who plan to ensure that the historical wall paintings will be preserved for future generations of the village to enjoy.

Small though it is Little Melton also boasted until recently, its own railway set in woodland. Little Melton Light Railway or 'Bob's train' (as many of us know it) used to run once a month for charity and has raised thousands of pounds for good causes. Sadly Bob died in July 2001, but to find out more about him and the railway, keep reading!

Little Melton Mothers' Union Banner

▋ntroduction

Times change, and we change with them.

Harrison 1577 A.D.

Norwich was an immensely important city in its early days, second in size only to the great metropolis of London, while the surrounding county of Norfolk was the most densely populated part of England, with its 660 ancient parishes and 969 medieval churches. This book is an attempt to tell the story of just one of those ancient parishes.

The small rural community of Little Melton lies about five miles south west of Norwich, and has no particular claim to fame. No earth-shattering events have been recorded here by the group of local historians who have been seeking out its past, but its quiet and often impoverished lifestyle is worth the telling, if only to record something of a way of life that has gone for ever.

'Do Different' is Norfolk's motto, so our story is told back to front! The preface gives a brief description of the village as it is today, and this is followed at intervals by stories of this and that, snippets about curious local facts that span the centuries, occasionally humorous, sometimes sad, always asking the question 'Did you know that?'

No attempt has been made to relate a chronological history, as this can be so very boring! Instead we have tried to concentrate on specific matters like farming, schooling, the church, the poor law, war service, the history of housing and parish management since earliest times, and, of course, the light railway. These detailed chapters sometimes end with tales told by a few of our senior residents, recalling people and events within living memory. We ask for understanding should mistakes occur, or should your particular interest not be included, but we are all amateurs, with a limited amount of time at our disposal.

This book started as a millennium project, but research is a lengthy process, and we hope the result has been worth the wait. We thank the many people who have helped us with its production and with gathering the facts, and hope that you will get as much fun from reading it as we have from writing it.

In particular, we are very grateful to the staff of the Norfolk Record Office; the Norwich Studies Library; the Public Record Office at Kew; the library of Emmanuel College Cambridge; Hethersett Library; Jan Allen and Andrew Rogerson of the Norfolk Archaelogical Unit at Gressenhall; George Gleadhill for the use of quotes from his publication - *Comparison of conditions at Little Melton and Colney School in the first ten years as a Board School 1875 - 1885 and under LEA control 1904 - 14; and* Mrs Clements for permission to examine the School records;

as well as the many long-suffering people of Little Melton, for without your unstinting help, this book could never have been produced.

Aerial view of School Lane c.1987

Chapter One

ere there dinosaurs?

I'm not frightened of Fierce
Animals in the Ordinary Way.

A. A. Milne – Winnie-the-Pooh

Sadly, no fossils of dinosaurs have been found here, nor can we boast a massive cache of more than 38,000 flint implements or Roman coins like those found at Great Melton. No buried hoards of golden torcs have been discovered within our parish boundary but, slowly and surely over the past hundred years or so, evidence has been found of human life within the confines of our small parish, dating back to the Old Stone Age or Palaeolithic Period. There are now more than twenty archaeological sites where flint tools, metal implements, coins, pieces of pottery and other artefacts, deliberately discarded or accidentally dropped by our ancestors, have been discovered, dated and catalogued.

The story begins in the Old Stone Age, the Palaeolithic Period, an immensely long time span archaeologically-speaking, classified as lasting from 500,000 B.C. to 10,000 B.C.! It was during this period that the first men, women and children we would recognise as looking anything like ourselves were travelling in nomadic groups in Northern Europe. They were following and hunting migrating herds of animals, and at the same time were gathering wild cereals, fruit and nuts to add variety to their diet. It may have been as long ago as 400,000 B.C. that these groups first came to Norfolk, as it was relatively easy to get here. There was no North Sea or English Channel to cross! Fossil evidence from the Old Stone Age reveals that the area was populated by rhinos, straight-tusked elephants, mammoths, deer, wild pigs, horses and beavers, all living in an environment dominated by pine and birch woodland. The tools that these ancient people used to kill their prey, and skin and prepare the carcasses for eating, were fashioned from the plentiful deposits of flints found in East Anglia. Flint remained the principal material for tool making until the first metal, bronze, was introduced in about 2,300 B.C. One large flint could be painstakingly worked on to produce as many as ninety different tools. It is the finding of these worked pieces of flint, surviving either as the core of the stone or the pieces that were chipped off by the flint-knapper, that give us evidence of human life here. As the millennia passed, the tools became better adapted to the tasks they were made for, and these differences enable archaeologists to categorise them into different time periods. The first catalogued archaeological find in Little Melton is credited to Miss A. Crabbe, the teacher of the Infants Class at Little Melton and Colney School. It was in 1907 she, or perhaps one of her pupils, picked up in a cornfield, what turned out to be a Palaeolithic hand axe. The exact site was not recorded but the axe is now in the Norwich Castle Museum. I wonder if Miss Crabbe used it as a visual aid next day in school to illustrate an object lesson on 'Our Primitive Ancestors!'

The Old Stone Age ended as a massive ice sheet covered the Northern Hemisphere. When the ice melted, (around 8,000 B.C.), nomadic tribes again roamed Eastern England, but the huge mammals they once hunted had disappeared, and the animals they hunted now were smaller mammals, wild oxen, elk, deer and wild boar. Britain was still joined by land to Continental Europe. Eventually the melting ice sheet led to a rise in sea level, the North Sea and English Channel formed, and people who came here now arrived by boat and were more inclined to settle, first along the sea coasts and then along the river banks. Once settled, they grew barley and primitive forms of wheat and domesticated cattle, sheep, pigs and goats for their milk, meat, skins and hides. They still collected apples and other fruit and nuts growing wild. The differences in the appearance of the flint implements they made, together with the change in lifestyle from nomadic Hunter-Gatherers to settled farmers, has led archaeologists to call this period, the Neolithic or New Stone Age.

Palaeolithic oval hand axe.

It is this period in history that has given us by far the largest number of archaeological 'finds' in the parish. Flints of all shapes and sizes are often noticed after ploughing has disturbed the soil. On a dozen or more sites, flint implements in the form of scrapers of varying sizes, core-stones, hammerstones (used to put the initial pressure on the stone to make the desired shape), whetstone hones (used to polish the flints and grind the edges to a razor-sharpness) and the short flakes of flint, painstakingly chipped off by the tool-maker to make broad-bladed knives have been found. The fact that very great care was lavished on some Neolithic axe-heads, in order to attain a highly polished smooth surface, has led archaeologists to speculate that these flints may have had some ritualistic or symbolic significance, especially as they have been found in long barrows, the burial chambers of Neolithic man. Were they perhaps his most highly prized material possession, buried with him to enable him to clear woodland, build shelter for himself and hunt for his food in a next life?

Around 2,300 B.C. a technological revolution occurred throughout Western Europe. Knowledge of the production and use of bronze, a mixture of the metals tin and copper, is thought to have worked its way across the Continent and over to Britain. It may have arrived via already well established trade routes and been brought by people known as Beaker people, (because their characteristic pots were tall and slender, made by coiling sausage-shaped lengths of clay round and round on a base). The advantage of being able to use metal for the first time in tools and weapons was enormous, but it would be wrong to think that the use of flint died out overnight. As with most things in our history of technological innovation changes occurred gradually. As the Bronze Age progressed, moulded axe-heads with a hollow socket at the neck end, allowing a wooden haft to be securely fitted, were being produced in our village. These were very similar in design to our present-day axes, and a very far cry from the hand-held rough oval flints of the Old Stone Age.

In the early 1990s archaeologists got the opportunity to look beneath the ground in Little Melton. This was a rare and exciting event. Most of the earlier 'finds' had been recovered from on or very near the surface of the ground. It was the construction of the Norwich Southern By-Pass that allowed this glimpse of prehistory at a deeper level. In keeping a 'watching brief' on the great swathe of land that was disturbed to the east of the village, the Norfolk Archaeology Unit confirmed the existence of a Bronze Age settlement in the parish. The remains of a Bronze Age hearth with metal working debris still in it, sherds (fragments) of characteristic Beaker-pottery and of other Bronze Age vessels and even a bronze chisel were unearthed. The effort to mine these two metals, to transport them to this area, their scarcity and the time and effort needed to make the objects, meant that the tools were constantly being melted down for re-use, and this in turn has reduced the likelihood of finding vast numbers of Bronze Age implements in any area. This is in contrast to the reason for the rarity of finding great numbers of examples of the next metal used, iron. Many of the tools and pots made of iron have simply rusted away! Iron was being used in Norfolk by about 650 B.C. but the use of bronze did not die out. It continued to be used for high-status goods especially jewellery, coins, decorative and domestic pots, and its aesthetic qualities are still appreciated today. As with bronze, iron was thought to have been introduced by traders from Europe who brought the raw material and technology to Britain along pre-existing trade routes. Distinctive pottery from the period has been found throughout modern France, Germany, Denmark and Central Europe, indicating that these links continued in the Iron Age.

With the coming of the Iron Age to East Anglia we find the first people identified by personal names in our history - members of the British tribe of the Iceni. The Iceni was the dominant tribe in Norfolk, Suffolk and Cambridgeshire when the Romans arrived as a conquering army in A.D.43. Their capital was at Thetford, and the Icenian king at that time was Antedios, (his name is known from silver coins found in that area). The Romans allowed him to continue his rule and the Icenian territory to become a client state of Rome. The Romans probably regarded this status as being a prelude to eventual incorporation into the Roman Empire. It suited them to allow tribes who appeared to be relatively successful at governing themselves to continue to do so for a time. However, only three years later they started to introduce repressive measures against the Iceni and commenced a programme of fort construction in Icenian territory. In retaliation the Iceni started to do battle against the Romans, who further retaliated by building a fort on a very important Icenian site at Saham Toney. An uneasy truce must have ensued for a time, for the Iceni were able to rebuild their early capital, Thetford.

Trouble next erupted on the death of a succeeding king, Prasutagus, in A.D.60. In his will the king had named the Roman emperor, Nero, as joint inheritor of

A 'Bury' type early silver coin of the Iceni c 40 BC

his kingdom with his two daughters. Rome, however, immediately rejected this arrangement. It ordered the confiscation of all the royal land, flogging the king's widow, Boudica, and treating her daughters in a degrading way. Loans made by Rome to the Iceni were called in, and the financial management of the province was taken over by Rome. Hatred of the Romans by the aristocracy and by the ordinary citizens (whose young men were compelled to serve in the Roman army) ensured that Boudica had no difficulty in raising a huge army against the Roman aggressors. In the course of the conflict three very important new Roman towns, London, Colchester and Verulamium (St.Albans) were all but destroyed before a final battle, (thought to have been at Mancetter in Warwickshire), brought utter defeat to the Iceni and their allies, the Trinovantes tribe from Essex. From then on, Romans were to dominate East Anglia until the recall of their legions in A.D.410 to defend Rome itself from invasion. The Icenian kingdom ceased to exist. Rome established a new centre of control for the area and named it Venta Icenorum, 'the market place of the Iceni', (now Caistor St.Edmund), only about five miles as the crow flies from Little Melton. This has helped to ensure that the name of the tribe that had fought so fiercely against them under the warrior queen Boudica has survived. It is from the period of Icenian influence that the earliest coin found in the village can be dated. It is known as a 'Bury type' coin, is made of silver and shows on one face the attractive and stylised figure of a lively, prancing horse. It is thought to date from before the reign of Boudica and her husband. The Iceni were the first British tribe to add lettering to their coins and stamped the letters E, C and E prominently on them. Sherds of pottery also from the Iron Age have been found in at least two locations in the parish, but as yet no iron tools surviving the two millennia have been discovered. Fragments of pottery known as 'grey and red ware' found here, also indicate that the village may have been home to people in the Roman period. A bronze coin and a silver coin, (positively identified as being minted in the period A.D.330 to 337 showing a ship on one side), have also been found. A pottery loom-weight, a bronze brooch and bell, and lead and bronze metal-working debris, (all identified as being produced in the Romano-British period A.D.43 to A.D.409), add to the evidence that there was a settlement here in the period when Britain was part of the mighty Roman Empire.

In A.D.410 the recall of the Roman legions and administrators to Rome, to help defend it against the Germanic tribes that were attacking it from the north, meant that Britain was left to fend for itself against the Northern Europeans that had been harassing its eastern seaboard during the Roman occupation. With the departure of the Romans, raiding parties and slow infiltration gave way to larger scale settlement, and the people who were to give our area its name, 'the Angles', came in large numbers. Sherds of pottery from both the Middle Saxon (A.D.651-850) and Late Saxon Periods of history (A.D. 851-1065) have been found in Little

Melton over the years, and in the 1980's a fragment of a bronze Coptic bowl dating from the Middle Saxon period was found here. Some of the Late Saxon pottery has been identified as Thetford-type Ware which was produced in large quantities in Thetford itself, (where a number of kilns were found grouped together on one excavated site), and also in Norwich and other rural locations in Norfolk. The Middle Saxon Ware found in the village has been identified as Ipswich Ware, made in that town from about the 640s, and found throughout East Anglia. Like Thetford Ware it was fired in kilns rather than in bonfires.

By the Late Saxon period another invader from Continental Europe was leaving his mark on Norfolk. The most recently reported archaeological 'find' from the village is a copper alloy stirrup terminal, decorated in Scandinavian Viking Ringerike style, and described in the literature as 'extremely beautiful'. We will never know if the high-status individual who owned this work of art lived in the parish or was just riding through, when his stirrup broke! It might even have started its journey here in another finder's hands. After nearly a millennium its aesthetic qualities can still be recognised.

It must have been around this time that the origins of the Village Name came into being. James Rye, in his book 'A Popular Guide to Norfolk Place Names' (The Larks Press 1991) describes the name MELTON as meaning 'Middle Enclosure'. It is derived from MAELTUNA being a mixture of the Old Norse 'METHAL' meaning 'MIDDLE' and Old English (Anglo Saxon) 'TUN' which means an enclosure, settlement or farm. As we hear later in the book, the 'LITTLE' or at the time of the Domesday census 'PARVA' prefix was given to distinguish us from a more prominent neighbouring 'enclosure'.

We have reached 1065, the last year in which Norfolk can be described as 'Anglo-Saxon', for the following year the descendants of Scandinavians who had settled in Northern France came to the shores of England with a vengeance...

A Viking Longhouse, which could have once stood in our village, would have housed the entire community including the animals!

> *It has long been an axiom of mine that the little things are infinitely the most important.*
>
> Sir Arthur Conan Doyle.

id you know that ...

... the first suggestion that a Village History be written was made in the Parish Magazine of February 1978?

Let's hope that it's been worth the long wait!

... our Village of Little Melton has a connection with the famous explorer, Capt. James Cook?

James Cook was born on the 27th October 1728 in the small Yorkshire village of Marton and baptised in the village church a week later. His father, James senior, had a reputation for being a steady and industrious man and worked hard in a regular job for a local farmer in Marton. James junior, naturally lived with his parents and at the age of eight was already helping his father around the farm with hedging and ditching, etc. The family had an excellent local reputation which was rewarded by an offer from Thomas Skottowe, the lord of the manor of Great Ayton, Yorkshire, a few miles away from the village of Marton, to join his estate as Bailiff, a highly respected job for James senior. Moreover, Thomas Skottowe was both shrewd and kind enough to recognise special qualities in the young James and paid for him to attend the local village school.

Thomas Skottowe was the eldest son of Thomas and Elizabeth Skottowe of Little Melton and he became lord of Great Ayton manor through the right of his mother. His parents, Thomas and Elizabeth Skottowe were part of the well known Norfolk family and both have memorials in our village church. Thomas Skottowe's memorial is on the north wall of the chancel and Elizabeth is remembered by a black marble slab in the chancel floor.

Thomas Skottowe junior must have visited his parents in Norfolk from time to time and since he held both James Cook senior and junior in very high regard, it is very likely that they would have travelled with him on some occasions as part of the lord's entourage. Hence, James Cook junior, later to become Capt. James Cook, may well have visited Norwich and possibly Little Melton between the years of 1736 and 1745.

In the summer of 1745, James junior was apprenticed to William Sanderson, a shopkeeper in Staithes, North Yorkshire, and further in the

Autumn of 1746 was apprenticed to John Walker of Whitby, a shipowner and master mariner. It was during his second apprenticeship that he found his 'sea legs', learnt navigation, how to read a chart, etc. By April 1750 he completed his apprenticeship and in December 1752 passed his exams to become a ship's mate. He enjoyed this rank for some 2 - 3 years and at the age of 27 years was offered his own ship. However, James turned the offer down. These were dangerous times at sea and if war should break out again with France, he would be a prime target for the press gangs of the time. So, James decided he would do better to volunteer to join the Royal Navy and so, in June 1755, he signed on at Wapping and joined a ship of the line, HMS Eagle. From there, James went on to become the renowned explorer and on the 7th October 1769 sighted New Zealand for the first time and then Australia in April 1770.

Captain James Cook

Chapter Two

 **n the Map**

All that mankind has done, thought, gained, or been,
it is all lying in magic prescription in the pages of books.

Thomas Carlyle

On the 14th October 1066 an event occurred on the south coast of England that changed the face of the country for ever. One day of fierce and bloody fighting was to give us a new royal dynasty and nobility, foreign leaders in the Christian church, different styles of art and architecture, a new system of government and even a different official language! The effects were to be felt even here in Little Melton, where the Anglo-Saxon social order was swept away, and that of the Norman French imposed. The event was the Battle of Hastings when William, Duke of Normandy, defeated Harold Godwin, Earl of Wessex, who had succeeded, rightly or wrongly, to the throne of England on the death of Edward the Confessor in January 1066.

Twenty years later documents appeared that give us the first detailed evidence of the existence of Little Melton. These documents, Domesday Book and Little Domesday Book (which covered the eastern counties) are unique in Medieval Europe for the information they give on the economic resources and social structure of William's conquered territory. They provide us with a rich insight into everyday life in Norfolk, where then, as now, agriculture was the predominant activity in rural parishes. Each county or 'shire' was divided into administative units or 'Hundreds' as they were known. We learn that like our near-neighbours, Great Melton, (called Meltuna in the Book), Hethersett (Hederseta) and Colney (Coleneia) we are in the Hundred of Humbleyard or Humiliart.

We cannot be certain when hundreds came into being, but their position and importance in the administration of pre-Conquest England was probably well-established by the 10th Century. Little Melton and its neighbours are described as being in the holdings of Godric the Dapifer or Steward, at the time of the Domesday Survey. Godric is just one of sixty-three individuals (all male) listed as 'landholders' in Norfolk in 1086, the year of the Survey. The list is headed by King William himself but William was not just a landholder. He worked on the premise that he was ultimately the owner as well as overall ruler of the country. As such, he was to confiscate large estates and bestow them on the soldiers and other supporters who had enabled him to conquer England. William's two half brothers Odo, Bishop of Bayeux in Normandy, and Robert, Count of Montain, were to be given substantial landholdings in Norfolk and elsewhere. Odo was also to act as Regent when William was in Rouen, the capital of his Duchy of Normandy.

13

An extract from the Bayeux tapestry

However, Odo eventually overreached himself by attempting to buy the Papacy and William had no option but to punish him by imprisonment. We know little of Godric the Dapifer, our new landlord, other than what Domesday tells us.

He had landholdings in many different hundreds in Norfolk and a few terse words, - the English translation of which is *'when Earl Ralf forfeited'* - indicate that Godric was not the first Norman to acquire land in the Meltons after the Conquest. There had been, in fact, three different landholders here since the time of Edward the Confessor, which must have been very unsettling for the people living here then. William the Conqueror had originally bestowed these lands on one of his noble supporters, Ralf Guader or Wader, (a half-Breton and half-Norman follower), whom he had made Earl of East Anglia and whom he had entrusted with the construction of the first Norman castle on the present site in Norwich. It was here at the castle, a little later on, that Ralf was to marry his wife, Emma. Not content with the honours heaped on him, Ralf, in 1075, with the help of Emma's brother Roger, Earl of Hereford, and Waltheof, Earl of Northumbria, mounted what turned out to be the last serious insurrection of William the Conqueror's reign. Ralf and Roger are even said to have plotted the rebellion during the marriage celebrations! What must have been particularly galling to William when he discovered the plot was that the co-conspirators, Emma and Roger, were the children of one of his closest confidants.

Back to the Domesday Survey itself! Such were the instructions given by William to those entrusted with the collection of data for Domesday Book that we are lucky enough to find out what the economic situation was, not only in the year of the Survey, but also for three different periods in the 11th Century: at *'the time* of King Edward' (Edward the Confessor, regarded by the Normans as the last legitimate King of England) at 'the time King William gave it' (immediately after the Conquest) and 'as it is now' (in 1086 - the year of the Survey). No contemporary documents survive which tell us exactly how the information was collected, but a 12th century one from Ely Abbey gives us some indication of the thoroughness with which the investigation was carried out. King William wished to know for every large administrative unit - the Hundred - the answers to the following questions: who the landholder was and what were the names of the manors in each one? how much land there was in total? how much land was arable and under the plough as 'ploughlands'? how much was woodland, pasture or meadow land? how many ploughs and ploughteams (2, 4 or 8 oxen depending on the heaviness of the soil) were in the possession of the lord of the manor and how many his tenants had? Whether there were any fishponds or mills? (These would have been watermills in this period.) How many animals there were on the lord's land other than oxen? how much land had been added to the manor or how much lost since King Edward's time? how much appreciation or depreciation in value had occurred in the three periods? and what the taxable value of the manor was in 1086? This last sum seems to have been worked out on the principle that every holding had to contribute a stipulated number of pence to each 20 shillings (£1) for which the Hundred was liable. It was levied annually and the rate could vary, like our Council tax! The money raised was used to form part of the royal revenue and also to help maintain a standing army and navy. It was the responsibility of the lord of the manor to collect it from his tenants and to submit it to the king's collectors of taxes in the shires, (the sheriffs and their officers) who then transported it to the royal coffers. The significance of all this information being in the hands of the monarch for the first time ever was not lost on the native population, and its nickname of 'Domesday' or the Day of Judgement stuck! The potential for fiscal change was easy to see, but the survey was also seen as putting the seal of 'fait accompli' on the massive take-over of land from Anglo-Saxon hands into Norman ones. William, nowadays regarded by historians as an efficient ruler as well as a ruthless administrator, may also have had a third reason for wanting to be in possession of so much information about the resources of his conquered kingdom. 1085 had seen the rumblings of new threats of invasion from Denmark, and he needed to have an accurate record of the available manpower and food-producing potential of each manor.

What can we find out about Little Melton from its Domesday Book entry? We are told first of all that 'in the time of Edward the Confessor' Meltuna Parva was in the hands of Edwin, a thegn, (an Anglo-Saxon administrator), and that he had two carucates of land, (these are areas of ploughed land of varying size) in the manor with two ploughteams to work them. Edwin had intended to leave part of his estate at Meltuna Parva to the Abbot of St. Benet's Abbey at Holme on the River Bure, his will written some time between 1030 and the Conquest still survives! St. Benet's was the earliest monastery established in Norfolk but many founded in former centuries were no longer in existence after being sacked or deserted. St. Benet's itself had ceased to exist for a time having been sacked by Danish invaders but was re-founded in 1016 by the Danish King Cnut, when he became King of England, as an act of atonement for the savagery of his Viking forebears. So Edwin was hoping to strengthen the establishment of a fairly new foundation by his bequest, not realising that his manor would soon cease to be his to give! His will vividly illustrates the importance of the Christian religion in the hearts and minds of late Anglo-Saxon society. He intended the gift to the Abbey to be an act of thanksgiving for *'the good gifts God had given me in this life'*, and he also made provision for the freeing of all his men after his death *'for the redemption of my soul and forgiveness of my sins'*. In addition, he left ten acres of land to the church at Little Melton, giving us evidence that a church already existed in Little Melton by the mid-11th Century.

St. Benet's Abbey ruins c.2002

Domesday also tells us that there were three acres of meadowland in Godric's newly acquired manor. This was the most valuable land of all. It provided summer pasture for grazing animals and hay for winter feed. The lord's land was also the home of one cob and five head of cattle in Edwin's time, but by Domesday the stock of animals had been increased by the addition of fifteen pigs and ninety sheep. Consequently the value had increased from 40 shillings before the Norman Conquest to 60 shillings 'when King William gave it' and to £4 in 1086. Edwin's manor had also been home to a number of tenant farmers - Domesday describes them as twelve freemen, who had been attached in 'patronage and fold-rights' - and they between them had half a ploughland and three acres of meadowland. Their numbers of animals are not specified but the value of their part of the manor was 20 shillings in 1086. Lower down the economic scale on Edwin's manor, when it was bestowed on Godric, were three smallholders (or bordars) and one slave. The presence of different types of peasants in Godric's manor, freemen, bordars and slaves, helps to illustrate the different classes of society which had evolved in the Anglo-Saxon period and which, broadly-speaking, carried over into the Norman administration and well beyond. Historians are still debating the precise details of how each had evolved and what each one's function was in the manor. The lowest stratum consisted of the slaves, or servi. They are thought to have done the majority of the manual work on the lord of the manor's land, their main job being looking after the oxen and ploughing. Although subservient to their master and mistress, and unable to buy or sell goods or change their allegiance or dwelling without permission, they may nevertheless have had some rights by this time. They may, for instance, have been able to cultivate a small amount of their own land, and had small amounts of free time in which to work for pay, and some may have amassed enough to buy their freedom eventually. They probably also had an annual allowance of food from their master. By the middle of the 11th century the numbers of slaves is thought to have fallen in England, partly in deference to the teaching of the Christian religion, (hence Edwin's will), and partly because it made better economic sense to make them self-supporting.

Slightly up the economic and social scale in Little Melton were three bordars, or smallholders, who may even have once been slaves themselves. Bordars usually possessed a small amount of land, possibly five acres or so, but were obliged to work on the lord's land as well as their own on a regular basis, though probably less often than the servi. Next mentioned are twelve freemen. Again the precise status and definition of a 'freeman' in the period is not completely clear. All men, high and low, were beholden to the next tier in the hierarchy and ultimately to the King. It is likely that freemen also had to perform regular services to the lord but less onerous ones than the bordars. These may have been in the form of some sort of labour; they also almost certainly had to pay a rental for their land. One of the services was known as 'fold-rights' and referred to the tenant grazing his animals on the demesne land, (belonging to the lord of the manor), so

Norman mounted knight

that he himself had the benefit of the manure produced! We know from Domesday that this is one of the services the twelve freemen rendered in Little Melton to their lord, and, in return, they expected a considerable degree of protection and 'commended' themselves to him for this purpose. To further complicate the picture of land occupancy in the village, Domesday reports that *'in the time of King Edward'* there was a smaller manor held by a *'certain freeman also a thegn'* who had one ploughland and one ploughteam, and that this manor was partly in Melton Parva and partly in Meltuna (Great Melton). Its valuation was included in the valuations of the other two by 1086. We are not told the name of the other thegn but one historian has speculated that he may have been Edwin's brother, Wulfric. He too was to have his land ownership taken from him and given to Earl Ralf and eventually to Godric the Steward. This part of the Domesday entry introduces us to another member of the complex feudal hierarchy, as this smaller manor was home to three villagers, or villeins, who appear to fit into a slot between bordars and freemen in the order of things, having more land and rights than a bordar but probably less than a freeman. Between them the three villeins possessed half a ploughteam, perhaps sharing a team with a group of villeins in another manor. We are even told the dimensions of the parish of Little Melton, 10 furlongs long and 5 furlongs wide. The furlong, then as now, was 220 yards, so the village was roughly one and a quarter miles long (from east to west) and a little over half a mile wide (from north to south), very similar to its present day size. The tax assessment in 1086 was worked out to be eight and a quarter pence, the same as Colney's.

It becomes apparent that Domesday was in no way a census of the population, and it is not possible to use it to get an accurate figure for the number of people living in Little Melton in 1086. Whole sections of the community, such as the wives and children of the bordars, freemen and villeins are not mentioned at all, and historians have no idea of the size of families in this period in history. We know that by 1086 there was a church in the village, but no priest is mentioned in the Survey. At this time the clergy were allowed to marry, so he too might have had a wife and children. Occupational groups such as metal-workers, carpenters and smiths receive no mention in Domesday.

Taking these various factors into consideration some modern scholars of the medieval period believe that we can get a rough idea of the population by applying a multiplier of at least five to the number of males mentioned. This gives a combined population of around a hundred people living in the two manors held before the Conquest by Edwin and Wulfric. This figure supports the theory of the historian who examined Edwin's will in detail. He believes that the presence of both Norse and Anglo-Saxon elements in the name of the village indicates fairly extensive settlement in the area by the 11th Century. The various items of pottery and other artifacts from the Romano-British and Anglo-Saxon periods found at the western end of the parish also support the view that people had lived in the area for hundreds of years before the Norman Conquest.

The Great Domesday and the Little Domesday books.

Whatever I do, and whatever I say,
Aunt Tabitha tells me that isn't the way;
When she was a girl (forty summers ago)
Aunt Tabitha tells me they never did so.

Oliver Wendell Holmes

Did you know that ...

... Ringwood Close is named after Mr. James Ringwood, who died in 1961? He was Clerk of the Parish Council for 46 years, and was a shoemaker. He was the last to make footwear by hand-sewn methods in what was at that time the malthouse, being part of the old 'Rose and Crown' (the Village Inn). He assisted with 3 football and cricket teams that used to play on the field opposite the church.

... Gibbs Close is named after Mr. Frank Marston Gibbs, who will, amongst other things, be remembered for his long presidency of Little Melton Social Club, which he formed on 1st October 1936? Meetings were held in the Church Room on three nights a week, and activities included billiards, darts, cards, socials, concerts, dances, whist drives, and football and cricket. The club motto was 'Service Not Self'. At the start, in addition to the President, there were 6 Vice-Presidents who were Mr. W. Clements, Canon N. Paine, Mr R. Hayes, Mr E.A. Clarke JP, Mr H.E. Clarke, and Mr W. Lack. The Secretary was Mr William Loftus Potter and the treasurer Mr F. King. The Committee members were Messrs H. Kinch, J. Payne, F. Wilkinson, W. Sparrow and J. Codling. In 1945, prisoners of war on their return home were invited to partake in all club activities free of charge, and it was agreed that a Roll of Honour should be erected in the Church Room in memory of the 9 members who had lost their lives in the war. The club continued until the early 1950s.

... in the 1930's and 1940's Mr. Eden sold Pork on Great Melton Road? There used to be a slaughterhouse there, in which he killed the pigs, and Miss Violet Mace, who lives today at Babur Cottage, Watton Road, remembers in her youth, asking his wife if she might turn the handle of the sausage machine; and long before, in the 1880s and 1890s, there used to be a tin shed on the forecourt of Crossways Stores in which Mr. William Bailey also slaughtered pigs for sale. He was the proprietor, listed as both grocer and butcher in early documents.

... in the 76 years between 1814 and 1900 no less than 423 burials are entered in the burial register of Little Melton, of whom 159 were children under 14 years of age, a large proportion of these being infants.

... Mr. Ambrose Woods was our local undertaker, carpenter and handyman? He died in 1981 aged 92, and from the July Parish Magazine of that year we learn that he spent his working life, as well as several years of retirement at Crossways, Little Melton. His obituary said that *'as a German prisoner in the first world war, he became skilled at carving with only a penknife, and no-one could build a stair-case better than he. Single-handed, he would descend 100-foot wells to dismantle, repair and re-build the pumps; slate a roof, decorate houses inside and out, dig graves, build chimneys, repair agricultural machinery, make oak coffins to measure, lay drains, make ladders, install plumbing, and undertake at funerals with quiet dignity and efficiency, among other accomplishments'.*

...that the Lych-gate was designed in 1946 by Mr. Howard of Blofield? He had done much of the earlier church restoration work in the 1930's, when Canon Paine was vicar here.

The Lych-gate, All Saints Church Little Melton c.2000

... for nearly 50 years Mr Percy Garrod, a skilful D.I.Y. enthusiast and engineer, has lived a life of almost total self-sufficiency in Little Melton? He moved to the village with his wife, all the way from Bawburgh in 1955. Formerly a cabinet maker, craft teacher, musical instrument restorer and journalist, Percy put all these skills into use once he had settled into his cottage near the Watton road, with its half acre of garden. On moving in, he found that the electricity board had failed to provide the necessary power to his property, so he turned his hand to building his own generating windmill to supply all the current he needed for lighting, only relying on the mains for cooking and heating water. This he drew from his well, or collected in containers from the heavens, so allowing dual plumbing for hard and soft water. For good measure, he added an old-style chemical lavatory, recycled waste through his vegetable garden, made most of his own furniture, hung his own paintings on the walls, wrote books and articles for the press, and in earlier days milled his own home-grown wheat with which his wife used to make delicious, crusty bread. Somehow he also found time to play a full part in village life, serving on the parish council, and helping in a score of other ways. In his nineties he is still called upon to play his violin on special occasions, wherever and whenever required, most recently in Bawburgh.

...on Friday October 6th 1950 Mr. Percy Garrod wrote a piece for the Norwich Evening News detailing the delights of 'The Over-Sixties Harvest Home' (otherwise known as *'High Jinks over High Tea'*) held at the Church Room at 6 pm. *'It all came about as a result of the parson making an initial contact with a number of farmers of the village, and they, in addition to giving certain financial assurance, induced members of their families and friends to take an active part with them in the organisation of the whole affair'*. There was feasting, singing and a conjuror doing a magic show, but *'the real cream of the fun came later, when a number of the gentlemen fell victim to the task of dressing some of the ladies – or, to be more correct, over dressing them – for which copious supplies of newspapers and pins were well in evidence. Thus did Little Red Riding Hood, Madam Butterfly and a host of other ingenious creations come through their ordeal intact, apart from an occasional tear of the papers and the other kind of tear brought on by almost uncontrolled merriment.'*

Chapter Three

Village Government

THE MANOR OF LITTLE MELTON, THE CHURCH VESTRY AND THE PARISH COUNCIL

'O let us love our occupations,
Bless the Squire and his relations,
Live upon our daily rations,
And always know our proper stations.'

Dickens – The Chimes.

Tucked away in the archives of the Norfolk Record Office, there are no less than 12 books or *'gatherings'* (bundles of papers) dating from 1650 to 1845, relating to the Manor of Little Melton. The minute books give details of the court by court proceedings, and the rental books give the names of tenants, the size of their holdings, and the fines and rents they had to pay. The trouble is that the writing is often almost impossible to decipher, and even worse, much of it is in Latin. From 1733 the stewards of the court, who were normally lawyers, were permitted to record proceedings in their native tongue, and during the Commonwealth from 1649 to 1660, all legal documents were also in English.

It has been a major task to transcribe and translate this material, but it has been worth it both for the sheer pleasure of handling the original parchment documents, and also because they throw so much light on the workings of this small agricultural community. In addition, they give us the names of people who lived here long ago, which is important in the absence of our early parish registers which have sadly not survived.

By the seventeenth century the main court and leet of the manor of Little Melton was nearly always held annually on or around St. Luke's Day, 18th October, under the Walnut Tree on the Lower Green, (near Manor Farm) before adjourning to someone's house. Special courts were also held when there was any particular extra business to discuss. The village crier would go round all the outlying properties, announcing the time and place of the court, and summoning all tenants to attend. The steward would then swear in two juries from amongst the tenantry, one for the court and another for the leet. Full notes were made of the business transacted, these being later transcribed by the steward into the court books, and it has been interesting to compare the rough notes with the books themselves, where both have been kept together. Afterwards, the lord might

Extract from the 1652 Manorial Book

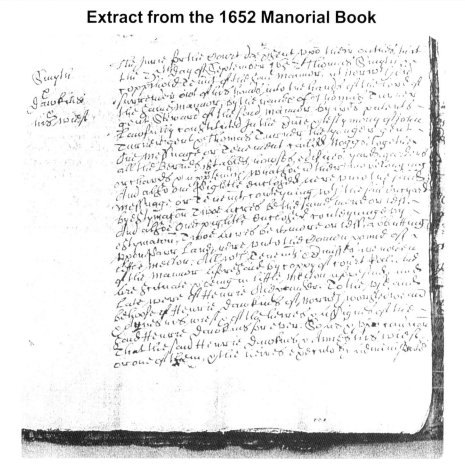

Transcript of Manorial Book Extract above;

Smyth and Dawkins and his wife.

The jurie for the Court doe present upon their oathes that the 25th day of September 1652 Thomas Smyth coppihold tenant of the said Mannor, at Norwich, did surrender out of his handes into the handes of the lord of the same mannor, by the hand of Thomas Turner Gent, Steward of the said mannor, by letters patentes Lawfully constituted in the presence and testemony of John Turner Gent and Thomas Turner the younger Gent, One messuage or Tenement called Nogges, together with all the Barnes, Stables, howses, edifices, yardes, gardens owthouses and appurtenances whatsoever thereunto belonging. And also one Pightle enclosed nere unto the said Messuage or Tenement conteyning with the said orchard by estymacion Two acres be it more or less, abutting upon Parr lane nere unto the Common Pound of Little Melton: All which tenements and premisses are holden of the Mannor aforesaid by coppy of court Roll, And are situate and being in Little Melton, And late were of Henrie Alexander. To the use and behoofe of Henrie Dawkins of Norwich, worsted weaver, and Annes his wife and of the heires and Assignes of the said Henrie Dawkins for ever.

reward his steward, his crier and jurors with a good dinner, one in 1720 consisting of *'A tub of ale, plum puddings, beef and turnips, two geese and apple pie'*, and often there was money for tobacco and pipes as well.

From medieval times, every manorial court played a key role in the life of the community it served, for it was here that tenants were admitted to their land holdings by the lord, or his steward, and here that fines were collected when occupancy changed. The leet court (which was often held at the same time as the manorial court) was also the responsibility of the lord, and was mainly concerned with the enforcement of bye-laws, the punishment of minor crimes, and with the appointment of village officers, such as haywards and constables. Attendance at both courts was compulsory for all tenants of the manor, those absenting themselves without leave being subject to a fine. Early manorial records, where they still remain, stretch right back to the twelfth and thirteenth centuries. These show how the local unfree peasantry had to work almost entirely at the will of the lord, sowing his corn, ploughing, harvesting and looking after his animals, in return for their own few tenanted acres. After the great plague of the mid 14th century, when the Black Death had decimated the working population, (as it did in this village), labourers were in short supply, and money rents started to take the place of feudal services, though this was a slow process. At this time the beginnings of copyhold tenure came into existence, each tenant holding his land by copy of court roll, a system that only came to an end in 1922. (A few fifteenth century documents do exist for Little Melton but these have not been studied in any depth).

A Medieval Ploughteam

In Little Melton manor the court rules decreed that it was always the **youngest** son who inherited the property, **not** the oldest as is more often the case. This system of tenure is called 'Borough English' and existed until 1924. Many families, of course, wanted their inheritance to go to their eldest son, and got over the difficulty through a technicality, formally 'surrendering' their property at court to the use of their last will and testament. It must be remembered that the lord held all copyhold manorial property from the king, houses, outbuildings and land, and the word 'surrender' features in every entry. It means *'to give up an estate to the lord of the manor'* (Oxford English Dictionary), or to give it up *'to the use of a will'* in this instance.

A small fine was paid to the lord when a tenant surrendered to his will, so many did not bother with this. For example, as late as the first half of the eighteenth century no less than 11 youngest sons inherited in a period of 36 years, meaning that many were 'infants' in law, being under 21 years old. When this happened a guardian was admitted to the property, and two fines were payable, one on admission of the guardian, and the other on admission of the youngster when he finally came of age. In one particular case, at a court in 1664, the death of Marian Mollet was announced, and it was reported that Robert Mollet, her 'infant' son, was next heir to the property. He was then duly admitted under the guardianship of John Cobb, and three years later, on reaching his 21st birthday, was admitted in his own proper person, small fines being paid on both occasions. It was quite a lucrative business to be lord of the manor! However, it was not totally one sided, for land often stayed with a particular family for long periods when youngest sons succeeded each other at a time when life expectancy was far less than it is today.

In some courts, fines were at a set rate *'according to the custom of the manor'*, but in Little Melton they were always *'at the will of the lord'* which meant that if he so wished, he could favour one tenant, and penalise another. A light-hearted note was struck in 1709 when Mr Thomas Skottowe fined John Carter junior, *'a Bottle Clarett'*. In 1712, Richard Rackham was admitted to a good-sized property on the death of his mother, and was only fined £6, Mr. Skottowe commenting *'I favoured him by reason his mother gave it to him with many legacies to pay'*. In 1724 when Sir Benjamin Wrench (an eminent Norwich doctor) held the manor, Jeremy Revans was admitted to 2 acres on the surrender of Richard Gay, and was only fined 15 shillings, (half the usual rate). The steward noted *'A moderate fine, he being the lord's particular friend and patient'*.

Each year the leet court chose someone to act as 'Hayward' or 'Field Master' for the next twelve months. This was a task allotted in rotation, according to the occupancy of each copyhold farm. It was a responsible job, involving the management of the common fields, the supervision and repair of manorial and parish fences, and care of the common stock of animals. The hayward was also empowered to lock up stray cattle in the village pound, keeping them there until a fine was paid to retrieve them. It is good to find that 71 School Lane, Little Melton, is named 'The Pound', just to remind us of where the old enclosure used to stand.

Every tenant had to take his turn as village constable for the year, two men being elected to carry out the task at each sitting of the leet court. It was not a pleasant job, but was usually accepted with resignation and a shrug of the shoulders, until one particular day in 1653, when Edward Garrard was elected. He *'peremptorily and obstinately refused to take the oath to serve'* and the steward fined him forty shillings *'for which contempt'*. This was a considerable sum of money in those days, perhaps eight times the weekly wage of a labourer.

The misdemeanours brought before the leet court were infrequent and not too serious. For example, in 1654 the jury reported that *'Henry Lynn did break the Lord's Pound'* (which presumably meant that he attempted to rescue his own horse or cow from the lockup without payment, and perhaps damaged the building in so doing). He was fined 8 shillings. In 1697 Jacob Alexander, gent, was in trouble on two counts. One of his houses had been damaged by fire, and roof repairs on another 'Domus' had been carried out in thatch, where it had previously been tiled. He was ordered to repair both immediately. Much later, in the eighteenth century, John Mayes was also in trouble twice, for in 1767 he was fined and prevented from stopping up a 'driftway' through his yard to an adjacent field, and four years later was fined *'for running cattle and sheep on the common of Little Melton, without right'*.

The manor books provide much miscellaneous information from time to time. For instance, the first mention of the surname 'Lofty', (very familiar in this locality) seems to have been way back in 1662 when Edward Lofty (sometimes spelt 'Loftey') was on the court jury. From other entries we also discover that there was 'a Smith's Shop' presumably a Blacksmiths in the village owned by Thomas Davy in 1691 and Thomas Rackham in 1694.

A Weaver at work (from late 17th century engraving).

We probably should have had little knowledge of the woollen trade that was carried on in the village for some years had it not been for these court books. In 1654 a master worsted weaver of Norwich named Henry Dawkins set up shop here, with his wife Anne, and lived at a house named Noggs, which features in the chapter called 'House Histories'. The Norwich Apprenticeship Records point out that one of his apprentices was Henry Band (or Bawd), son of Robert Bawd, a village husbandman, while the court books show that Henry Dawkins' grandson Nicholas Rackham continued in the business in Little Melton till his death in 1728, so weaving went on here for at least three-quarters of a century.

The following year of 1729 also saw the death of John Mills, a wealthy woolcomber, who had run a large enterprise in the village, probably centred at Greycot, (today's Grey Cottage on Green Lane), where the large barn would have provided excellent storage for huge amounts of wool. His inventory survives and shows that his 'Fleece Wool' was valued at £120 and *'Wool already at Spinning'* at no less than £161.16s. 3d., his assets totaling over £365. He must have employed many local men in his combing shop, and many women and children as home-workers, spinning away for all they were worth. Mr Mills' name does not occur in any of the court books, so he was never a copyholder, and Greycot was the only freehold house of substance in the village then, supplied as it was with both barn and outbuildings. The full inventory of John Mills is shown in Appendix D.

From the Settlement Examinations carried out under the Poor Law, and now held by the Record Office, we know that weaving in Little Melton was not limited to the Dawkins, the Rackhams and the Bawds. For example, William Fox worked here at this self-same trade in the late 1700s, but by the early 1820s and 1830s, after the industrial revolution had put hand-loom weaving in jeopardy, his son, another William Fox, aged 32, Robert Parish, aged 25, and George Brand, aged 33, were all out of work weavers who had now fallen on hard times.

Manors were rather like country estates, and were bought and sold just as any other commodity, often spreading over village boundaries. There were many different manors in our neighbourhood, so tenants often held land from different lords, all of whose courts they had to attend by law. In addition to Little Melton manor, there was the manor of Melton-Hall, which Thomas Batchcroft held on his death in 1501, (though later in the early seventeenth century the two were amalgamated), and there were also the manors of Hethersett Cromwells, Hethersett Woodhall, Great Melton Peverells, Great Melton Hacons, and Colney East Hall, to mention just a few. The 1817 Enclosure Map of Little Melton shows that most of these manors held land within the bounds of our parish at that time, so ownership was complex.

So far as Little Melton Manor is concerned, we know that the tenants assembled annually on Little Melton Green, before dispersing to someone's house where the court was to be held, and one of the rentals lists the venues over a twenty year period. In 1691 the court met at *'Woollards'*, and in 1697 at *'Martyn Buck's house'*, (neither of which has been identified), while for the years 1699, 1702 to 1704, 1712 and 1713, Thomas Skottowe, (lord from 1696 to 1720), entered the words *'the court was held at my owne house'*, and in 1708 and 1710 *'at the Manor House'*. The inconsistency in wording is probably of little importance, and almost certainly means that Mr Skottowe lived at the Manor House during most of the time he held the lordship. In 1707 the court took place at *'the Alehouse'*, which is almost the earliest reference we have that there was such a welcome place in the village!

In medieval times, as well as occupying themselves with the management of life on earth, manorial lords were much concerned with life after death. Many built their own churches to the glory of God, making bequests or appointing priests to pray for their souls, and the souls of all the departed. For example, as late as 1501 when Mr Batchcroft died as lord of the manor of Melton-Hall, he left money for the repair of Earlham Bridge, giving orders that a stone was to be erected there, beseeching all passers by to pray for the souls of his wife and himself, his parents and friends. From his will we know he did actually live at Melton-Hall, and from other records relating to the Evans-Lombe estate we know that the hall stood on the site of The Grange, close to our church. Manorial lords almost always built their churches near their homes, for convenience if for nothing else, so it is almost certain that All Saints, built about 1300 on the site of two previous churches, was erected by the lord of the manor of Melton-Hall nearby. This is why the church is so far from the main part of the village of today.

The Grange & Church c.1995

Who held the lordship then? The great Norfolk historian, Francis Blomefield, wrote that in 1228 William de Bek held it from the heirs of Montchensy, and that William de Hereford held it in 1280. Members of the important Montchensy family (Norman barons who came over with William the Conqueror) held the main manor of Little Melton at this time, too, so they may also have had a hand in its building. Perhaps their actual names no longer matter now, but we owe these benefactors of long ago a large debt of gratitude, for the church they erected still remains with us today in the 21st century. The graceful arcading of the nave, the simple Y-shaped windows of the chancel, and the unique paintings on the walls have made it *'a place of great architectural interest'*, which today is listed as a II* building.

With care (and luck) one can trace the history of houses from the manor court books too, which is an exciting and interesting project in itself, particularly when linked with the later Enclosure Award and its map of 1817, and the Tithe Redemption Apportionment and map of 1842. Some of these 'House Histories' are given in the chapter of that name, for those who are interested.

As time went on, the manorial courts became increasingly focused on one thing only, the surrender and transfer of land, and so a different kind of village government began to develop, that of the parish 'Vestry'. By the late 16th and early 17th century, each church had already established its own 'Vestry' within its own parish, headed by a network of officials, churchwardens, overseers of the poor, surveyors of the highways and constables. Gradually, with parliamentary approval, these were to become self-governing units, under the direction of the locally appointed and powerful Justices of the Peace. This is exactly what happened in Little Melton, though our local manorial courts continued to function until the mid 19th century, but were no longer of such great importance.

What is meant by the 'Vestry'? To many today it conjures up the picture of a dusty old room in the parish church where vestments, books and other paraphernalia are kept, but its older meaning is different, being very simply 'the governing body of a parish'. Little Melton had what is known as an 'Open Vestry', a general meeting of ratepayers which carried out the civic functions of the parish, and which had authority over the expenditure of the church rate. These ratepayers appointed their own officers annually, chief among them being the churchwardens.

The origin of the post of churchwarden is lost in antiquity. He was (and he or she still is) totally responsible for the management of church property and income, and for representing the views of parishioners in parochial and collective matters. The appointment of his 'side-kicks', the overseers of the poor, dates back to 1601, these men having had an important role to play for over three centuries, charged with the unenviable task of caring for the 'paupers' of the parish, as they were known, and with raising the rates on which to support them. Surveyors of the highways were first appointed in 1555, when the Highway Act was passed, their job being to attempt to keep the parish roads and tracks in good repair, (an almost impossible assignment), while the parish constables, previously chosen by the leet court, under the old manorial system, were now to be chosen by the 'Vestry'.

No early Vestry minutes survive for Little Melton, but the Town Books kept by this body from 1809 to 1831 are now on microfilm in the Norfolk Record Office. In 1814 the churchwardens were Edward Heath, of Church Farm, and the Rev. T.S. Buckle of Hethersett, who owned Elm Farm, Little Melton. The Constables were T.S. Buckle, John Girling (Manor Farm), Samuel Hipperson (Valley Farm), and William Cooper (Home Farm). The Overseers were Thomas Davy and William Cooper.

In that same year the Vestry was busy selling a house and garden to Mary Hempstead for the sum of £110. This was in the occupation of John Pettit, and had formerly belonged to the parish of Little Melton. (On the Enclosure map of 1817 this cottage used to be near today's 'Maytyme', near the crossways on School Lane). In 1819 Pettit had presumably not been paying the rent due to Mrs Hempstead, for the Vestry meeting held at the Parish Church resolved *'that instructions be given to Messrs. Taylor and Hales, Solicitors, Norwich, to bring an action for Double Rent against John Pettit, the occupier of the house sold to Mary Hempstead on 8 Nov 1815, the expense of legal proceedings being paid by the Overseers of the Poor.'*

Two entries for Jan 29th 1821 read *'Pair of Handcuffs 3 shillings'* and *'Constable's Staff 3 shillings'*, so the village had its problems even then, and Poor Law documents at the Public Record Office at Kew, also paint a picture of lawlessness, rather reminiscent of today. In June 1836, John Girling of Manor Farm, Little Melton, in his role as Guardian of the Poor for the parish, attended a weekly meeting of the board at the Swan Inn, St. Peter's, Norwich, where he reported that a reward was being offered for the apprehension of William Buck, on the charge of attempting to murder John Conyngham, Relieving Officer, who had been robbed of £12 in silver and a watch, and nearly murdered.

Over the next decade the Vestry deliberations probably continued much as before, but as there are no minutes remaining between 1831 and 1865, we are somewhat bereft of information. By this latter date, the Union Workhouse at Swainsthorpe had been in operation for over twenty years, and the office of Poor Law Guardian had been added to the list of officials elected by the Little Melton Vestry each year.

A school exercise book, lodged at the Norfolk Record Office, contains the Vestry minutes from 1865 to 1919, each page written out in exquisite copperplate Victorian and Edwardian script. We can pick up the story again at the meeting of 10th August 1865, when the Vicar, the Rev. J.C. Barkley, was in the chair. One interesting entry reads as follows: *'Allotting the sittings in the north side chapel of the church, which with the sittings in the south aisle have lately been altered, we agree:*

> *Pew No 1 to Mr Aldred* (of Church Farm)
> *Pew No 2 to Mr Utting* (of Manor Farm)
> *Pew No 3 to Mr Barrell* (the miller)
> *Pew No 4 to Mr Aves* (farmer)
> *Pew No 5 to Messrs Forster & Hipperson* (farmers and builders)
> *Pew No 6 to Miss Girling* (shopkeeper who lived at Grey Cottage)
> *Pew No 7 to Mrs Reynolds and family*
> *Pew No 8 to Messrs Long & Sparrow*
> *Pew No 9 to the servants.'*

This was signed by J.C. Barkley, vicar, and John Aves and Henry Hipperson, Church Wardens. (Please note that the words in brackets have been added by the writer who comments that such sittings were abolished years ago, today's worshippers being encouraged to sit wherever they like).

Meetings were held annually, but often little is noted except the names of those taking office, all, as earlier in the century, being leading men in the village. On 22nd March 1866, for instance, Mr T.D. Aldred and Mr Henry Hipperson were appointed overseers for the ensuing year; Henry Hipperson and Joseph Miller Aldred surveyors of the highways; John Utting guardian, and John Aves and Henry Hipperson churchwardens. The Aldreds, father and son, tenanted Church Farm, (employing 6 men, 5 boys and 2 women), Henry Hipperson was a master builder (employing no less than 40 men and 4 boys), John Utting held the Manor Farm, (employing 7 men and 1 boy), and John Aves was a farmer and sheep-dresser who lived near the Turnpike (today's B1108 Watton Road), employing his son Thomas.

However, no less than four meetings were held in 1872, with a number of matters under discussion. In January it was reported that the materials for repair of the highways allotted under the 1817 Enclosure Act were exhausted, and money was needed for the purchase of other land as a gravel pit. (The old pit was just off Rectory Lane near its junction with Great Melton Road). It was hoped that the Rev. Henry Lombe of Great Melton might buy the old pit, which adjoined his land, to enable this to be done. In April it was agreed that the rents of the Town Lands and Town House should go that year towards the provisions of the 1871 Elementary Education Act, and in November the Vestry voted unanimously against the recent Parish Constables Abolition Act, saying that *'the parish of Little Melton specially requires the services of resident parish constables'*. In April 1887 there was much discussion about the commemoration of Queen Victoria's Golden Jubilee, and in April 1889 it was agreed that application for the road from the school (on the boundary with Colney) to Great Melton to become a 'Main Road' should be forwarded to the County Surveyor.

Queen Victoria

Little Melton is to be congratulated on having a complete record of Parish Council deliberations from its very first meeting in 1894 to date. Eight heavy, leather bound Minute Books of foolscap size, each measuring 30cm by 22cm (12 by 8½ inches), and 4cm (1½ inches) thick, are still in existence, all in excellent condition. They make interesting (if time consuming) reading. Of course, it is only possible here to give a random selection of some of the issues raised by the Little Melton Parish Councillors over the years, but these detailed, hand-written records of twentieth century life are well worth preserving for posterity. Book One contains the minutes of the Parish Council for a whole forty year period from 1894 to 1934 and Book Two covers the thirty-two year period from 1934 to 1966, but as the members struggle with an ever increasing burden of bureaucracy, the minutes get longer and longer, the last three books just covering five years apiece.

On 4th December 1894, Mr William Diaper of Manor Farm chaired the inaugural meeting, which was held at 7.30 pm at the 'Board School'. There were ten nominations, the seven men with the most votes being chosen as councillors.

James A. Ottaway, labourer, had 22 votes; Joseph Carter, farmer, and William Carter, carpenter, each had 21; Samuel Barrell, miller and Henry Creasy, market gardener, had 18; William Bailey, grocer, had 17, and William Mitchell, labourer had 12. The three men not elected were John Childs, labourer, James Goward, carter, and Thomas Sparkes, pensioner.

At the next meeting a fortnight later, Mr. Charles Sharp was chosen as Chairman and Clerk of the council, and it was decided to hold meetings on the first Tuesday of each month. On the 1st January 1895 it was agreed that two oil lamps should be purchased for use by the councillors, and on February 5th a decision was made to pay Mr Eden a shilling a month to clean the school room after council use.

Until the Local Government Act of 1894 it had been the duty of the Parish Vestry to appoint the Parish Constables and the Overseers of the Poor, but now it was the task of the Parish Council to do this, and each year men were duly chosen to carry out this unpaid work. In order to aid continuity, a salaried post of 'Assistant Overseer' was created, and Mr Charles Sharp accepted this position, receiving £5 per annum for his work. In June 1895 Mr William Carter was appointed Vice-Chairman, and Hugh Gurney Barclay Esq, of Colney Hall, was elected Treasurer to the Council.

Samuel Barrell was churchwarden at this time, and an important figure in village life. Reading between the lines, he must have had doubts about the wisdom of handing over the powers of the long established Vestry, (of which he was a leading member), to this newfangled civic Parish Council, and, although a councillor, was reluctant to co-operate fully. On 11th June 1895 there is a plaintive entry in the Council Minutes saying *'How are we to get possession of the Parish Land Books, now in the hands of Mr. Barrell, Churchwarden?'*, and the following month, the Council was actually considering taking legal proceedings. Nothing further is minuted, however, so good sense must have prevailed.

Matters under discussion over the years centred on the appointment of the various parish officers, the maintenance of the two Parish Cottages near the crossways on Great Melton road, the rentals of the allotments and parish land, and the distribution of profits from this 'Town Land Money' to parishioners at Christmas, deliberation over matters put forward by the Henstead Rural District Council, (Little Melton having its say through its one Rural District Councillor, who for many years from May 1895 was Mr Richard Hill), and the vexed question of keeping the parish water courses and drains cleared out and clean. Parish meetings were held in the Spring of each year, when the new Council was elected, but gradually Council meetings began to be held at less frequent intervals, only being called when there were specific matters to discuss.

In March of 1896 the Rev. A. G. Green was appointed chairman for the coming year, with Mr Charles Sharp vice-chairman, and the Rev. Green also acting as clerk. A Deed Box was then bought to house the parish documents, which is probably why we still have this almost unique record of early proceedings. In October 1897 the Parish Room was let to the council, which now met here instead of in the school, and shortly afterwards it was agreed that coal and kindling be purchased to provide members with a fire on such occasions, and that Mrs Hill be paid 6d a night for cleaning duties. (Mr Eden had had a shilling for his work at the school - a blatant example of sex discrimination!) Each page of each Minute Book is numbered in large printed letters, and one wonders why pages 34 to 37 of the first book have been removed, covering the period April to October 1898. Was skulduggery afoot, or was it simply a matter of too many crossings-out, which spoiled the symmetry of beautifully kept minutes?

The Parish (or Church) Room, prior to conversion to a house in 2002

In March 1898 William Bailey was elected District Councillor, a post he held until his death in 1916, while in April 1899 the Assistant Overseer's annual salary was increased from £5 to £7 10s 0d. with Joseph Barrell appointed to the post. In 1900 William S. Carter became Chairman of the Parish Council, holding this position until he left the neighbourhood in 1911, and in 1903 Richard Hill was appointed Manager to Little Melton Provided School. In 1911 and 1912 Mr James Ringwood was Chairman, and Mr Charles Bilham Vice-Chairman, whilst from 1913 to 1918 the Rev. E. S. Upcher took over the chair, with Mr Bilham to assist him. In 1914 a letter was sent to the District Council saying that '6 houses are required for the working class of this parish' but these did not materialise for many years.

Very little is written in the minutes about the war, though in 1916 the Parish Cottages were not only to be insured for fire, (insurance cover increasing from £150 to £200), but also for loss or damage by aircraft, at an annual additional premium of four shillings. By this time Mr Ringwood had become Clerk to the Council and Assistant Overseer, and in December 1916 his wife was asked to carry on these duties, during the absence of her husband who had been called up for military service, and she kindly consented to do this. In 1917, a letter was circulated from the Food Controller to parishioners re the need for the cultivation of vegetables, and the Parish Council agreed to supply labour to soldiers' wives to help with the necessary gardening, although this would have to be paid for. Sadly there was no distribution of the 'Town Land Money' to parishioners in December 1918, just after the end of the war, 'because of extra expenses and the increase of Rates and Tithes', while in 1919 the possibility of joining forces with Colney and Bawburgh in the erection of a War Memorial was rejected. Later, Little Melton erected one of its own. Mr William Bailey of Home Farm (apparently no relation of Mr William Bailey, grocer and butcher, and former District Councillor), had first become a parish councillor in 1916, and in 1919 he was elected Chairman with Mr T.H. Loomb as Vice-Chairman, the Rev. Upcher being thanked for his past services, both as District Councillor and chairman.

Peace was to be celebrated with a tea and sports for all the village children. Mrs Loomb at 'The Cold Blow' was asked to supply ham, cake, bread and butter, the cost not to exceed one shilling per head, and a sports committee was formed. Little is written in the minutes about 'Peace Day' itself, but it was obviously a great success, and a bill of £4. 1s. was duly paid to Mrs Loomb, which must have meant that 80 or so children had had a good day out.

Application for the rental of allotments outstripped the supply, so these were sub-divided from half acres or quarter acres into ten or twenty rods apiece. In 1921 Mr F. Allcock was allotted 10 rods on appeal, he explaining 'that he had nowhere to empty the night soil, as he has no garden adjoining his house convenient for that purpose.' By 1922 Mr W.J. Bailey (son of William Bailey, the late District Councillor) had vacated his rental of 3 acres of parish land, which was sub-divided as follows: Russell Lofty to hire ½ acre at 15s. 0d. per annum; Mr H. Kinch 1 acre at £2 p.a.; Albert Eden ¼ acre at 7s. 6d. p.a.; A. Woods ¼ acre at 7s. 6d. p.a.; Mr. G. Woodgett ¾ acre at £1. 2s. 6d. p.a. and Mr F. Allcock ¼ acre at 7s. 6d. p.a. At this time Mr. William Bailey was still firmly in the chair, having been assisted by Mr. C. Sparkes as Vice-Chairman from 1922-24 and Mr J. Daniels from 1925-1928, (when he left the village), Mr. W. Davy being elected in his place.

At the Annual Parish Meeting of 17th March 1920, the Clerk to the Council presented the Charity Accounts, which were received and adopted. This is the first time that such accounts are mentioned, (later minutes often stating that the names of the recipients were then read out), and seems to herald an administrative change, because a few years later the annual election of Parish Overseers was to come to an end. Mr Richard Hill and Mr Charles Bilham had held this office from 1913 to 1926, being re-elected time after time, but no further elections to these posts followed after this date. It seems that the office of Overseer was abolished by the Rating and Valuation Act of 1925, (to take effect from 1st April 1927), care of the poor being transferred to the local authorities shortly afterwards. So ended no less than three hundred and twenty five years of parish support for the less well off, Overseers having first been appointed in 1601. The election of Parish Constables followed for a few years longer, the last two nominated in Little Melton being Mr. Herbert Rudd and Mr. C. Skerrit on 28th May 1929.

Celebrations outside the 'Rose & Crown' during the 1925 carnival

In 1926 there is the first firm decision by the District Council to erect four cottages in Little Melton, on a site near the school. (These are presumably 89 and 91 School Lane adjoining 3 and 4 Green Lane). On 14th April 1927 the Parish Council looked at all urgent housing applications, and suggested the following as suitable applicants: Mr. William Mallett, Mr John Lake, Mr John Burcham and Mr Edward Joy, and all were accepted by the R.D.C. and duly moved in. One parishioner, Mr. B. Cullum was unhappy about this, as he had two children and was living in one bedroom accommodation but, though sympathetic, the Parish Council was unable to help him. The following October the Rural Workers Housing Act was passed, and the councilors were asked if any more houses were needed in the village, if so how many, and whether there were cases of over-crowding or houses in a dilapidated condition? This was discussed in depth, and a decision taken that no further housing was needed for the present.

The clearance of water courses in the parish caused something of a headache, and in 1931 the clerk reported that he had been approached by the Sanitary Inspector to Henstead R.D.C. with regard to the disposal of surface water for three cottages lately purchased by the district council, situated to the west of the allotments. (These were later referred to as the Armes Cottages, built between 1817 and 1842, on what is now Burnthouse Lane and demolished in the 1960s). The district council asked for permission to lay pipes across the allotments owned by the Parish Council, in order to carry the water from the cottages to the ditch on the north side of the allotments. Permission was given.

In 1933, the clerk was instructed to write to The Eastern Omnibus Company to ask for a bus service for the village, buses only being available occasionally on the Watton and Hethersett main roads, at an inconvenient distance for parishioners. It was stressed that 20 new Council Houses had recently been erected, (on Braymeadow Lane), and there was a great need for public transport. The United Omnibus Company replied that *'they could not see their way to provide a more convenient bus service at present'*. That same year, in June 1933, proposals were made by the County Council to abolish Henstead Rural District Council, and the Parish Council was much against this proposition. The previous year 'The Rights of Way Act' had come into existence, and in January 1934 the Parish Councils were asked to mark all footpaths on the local maps provided by the R.D.C., and this was duly carried out.

Book Two starts with the minutes of the Annual Meeting on 5th March 1934, followed by those of a Parish Council Meeting in April when Mr William Bailey was elected chairman and Mr. W. H. Davy Vice-Chairman, as before. King George V's Silver Jubilee was discussed, a house to house collection taken, and tea and sports for children from the ages of 4 to 14 was enjoyed again, with Canon Paine, the vicar, giving a Jubilee mug to each child.

Henstead Rural District Council had been enlarged and was now Forehoe and Henstead R.D.C., one of its first tasks being to enquire as to which roads needed to be scheduled under the speed limit. Little Melton suggested that the road leading from the school to the four crossways be recommended for consideration. In 1937 the Coronation of King George VI was celebrated with tea and sports for children, but this time with sports for adults as well, and Mr E. A. Clarke was kind enough to offer 'Jubilee Meadow' for this purpose once more. A ladies committee was formed to arrange the tea, and an all male committee managed the sports.

There was still great enthusiasm to serve on the council, and on 15th March 1937 no less than 15 men offered to serve as councillors, the 7 with the

King George V

most votes being chosen, viz: Messrs. Harry Kinch, Edwin Alfred Clarke, Frank Marston Gibbs, Frederick Henry King, Reginald Barlow Hayes, William Loftus Potter and Robert George Quantrill. Mr Kinch was to be the new Chairman, with Mr F.M. Gibbs as Vice-chairman, and there was much discussion about repairs to the Parish Cottages, which were costing more and more money. In September '37, Mr W.R. Gould became the tenant of No 1 cottage, Mrs. Warr having given notice that she was leaving. Mrs. Warr's father, the late Joseph Symonds, had been an earlier tenant, living there from before 1894 until his death in 1916, so members of just one family had been in occupation for some forty-five years.

On 14th Dec 1938 the first meeting of the Trustees of the Poors' Land Charity was held, the Trustees being Messrs. William Bailey, farmer, and Charles Bilham, market gardener. From the minutes, it seems that this committee was now responsible for the allocation and upkeep of allotments, and for the disbursement of the profits made from the parish land, the Trustees having taken over part of the work done earlier by the Overseers. That Christmas the Poors' Land Charity gave 9d to each eligible child and adult in the village, and 2s a head to all widows and widowers.

In 1940 Mr H. Kinch was still Chairman, but as Mr. Gibbs had resigned from the council, Mr R. Hayes was elected as Vice-Chairman, and the following year Mr. F King and Mr E. A. Clarke took over these posts. Again, as in the previous war, there is little mention of the conflict in the minutes, except over the all important matter of food production, in which the Norfolk War Agricultural Committee and the R.D.C. Food Control Committee were involved. The Parish did have an Invasion Committee, however, with Mr E. A. Clarke as Chairman until 1943, when he resigned due to pressure of extra work at Elm Farm and magisterial duties. There was also a War Savings Committee with Mr. C. Carter as secretary.

No longer, now, are the Parish Council minutes full of decisions as to which allotment should go to which applicant, as this was now the business of the Trustees, but the management of the Parish Cottages remained with the Council itself. In 1941 the tenant of cottage 2 had died, after living there for nearly fifty years. She was Mrs. Hannah Symonds, widow of the late James, the same family having tenanted the property since before 1894. There were several applicants for the cottage, Mr. W. Burcham finally being offered the tenancy at a rent of £7.10s. per annum, an increase of 40% from the previous rent of £5.10s p.a. Mr. Burcham was also to have the 1/2 acre of land that went with it.

In 1942 Mr F. H. King resigned from the council, and Mr E. A. Clarke took his place as Chairman, with Mr Kinch as his Vice-Chairman. Mr Herbert Eagle of Grange Farm was co-opted to fill the vacancy. Under the Public Health Act of 1936 the R.D.C. had analysed the well at the Parish Cottages and had found the water unfit for drinking, so the Parish council agreed to have it relined. In 1945 Messrs H. Rudd and J. Herwin became Chairman and Vice-Chairman respectively, and there was another attempt to get a bus service for the village. No 1 Armes Cottages, Burnthouse Lane, became vacant that year, (a property owned by the R.D.C.) and the Parish Council suggested Mrs. R. Hemmings of the Council Houses as tenant.

At the Annual Meeting in 1946, 10 men offered themselves to fill the 7 places, and the Councillors chosen were Messrs. Robert Eagle, Herbert Eagle, Thomas Herwin, William Potter, Herbert Rudd, William Barley and Robert Quantrill, with Mr Quantrill taking Mr Herwin's place as Vice-Chairman to Mr Rudd. The first moves towards obtaining land for a Recreation Ground were put forward, with much support from all concerned. As the war was over, 'Peace Day' celebrations were discussed, but with little interest, so plans were later abandoned. In 1947 Mr Herbert Eagle became Vice-Chairman, and Mr Herwin resigned, having left the village, Mr. James Nash of Manor Farm being elected in his place. In 1948 Mr W. J. Dunham of the Norfolk Playing Fields Association addressed the meeting, and there was considerable enthusiasm. Even more moves were made towards increasing the bus service, now operating on Wednesdays and Fridays, but without result.

1948 was a year of slight emancipation for women, as Mrs. M. I. Quantrill was appointed the first woman manager of the school, and Mrs.

World War II poster

Hemming, the caretaker, was paid a whole shilling a night, to clear up and clean after council meetings! In 1949 Mr J. Nash was appointed Vice-Chairman to assist Mr H. Rudd, and the clerk's salary was increased to £6 per annum. There were complaints about a stench from the Sewerage Disposal Plant, and this was to be looked at.

The Playing Field at last came into existence in 1950, leased from the Great Melton and Marlingford Estate Company, but no organised games were to be allowed on Sundays. 1952 saw the appointment of Mr James Nash as Chairman, and Mr H. Rudd as Vice-Chairman. The parishioners seem to have been particularly generous at this period, agreeing to support a number of charities, with house to house collections for the British Empire Cancer Campaign, the Royal National Lifeboat Institution and the Norfolk Voluntary Association for the Welfare of the Physically Handicapped.

1953 saw the Chairmen changing places, Mr H. Rudd now being assisted by Mr J. Nash. To celebrate the Coronation of Queen Elizabeth II, there was a United Service on the Playing Field, tea and sports for schoolchildren once again, and tea for Old Age Pensioners. In 1955 Mr W. Potter was elected Chairman, with Mr Nash as Vice-Chairman. The village was still not on main sewerage, and the collection of night soil was a major problem, the R.D.C. being contacted with some urgency.

Chairmanship changed again in 1956 with Mr W. Barley and Mr W. Potter filling the two posts.

In 1957 the District Council offered to buy the Parish Cottages on terms to be agreed, but their suggested price of £150 for both land and houses was considered far too low, and was rejected. The following year Mr Nash took the chair, with Mr L. Herwin to assist him, and Mr James Ringwood resigned as clerk, due to ill health, after having served the council for 46 years. A gift and cheque were presented to him, with many expressions of thanks, and the post was advertised, Mr R. P. Garrod taking over the clerkship for a short period.

In 1959 the cost of repairs to the Parish Cottages came to the large sum of £29.16s with this succinct entry *'Nothing to be done until means of raising money is found'*. Mr F. H. King had made an offer to buy a portion of parish land as a means of raising the money, but a petition containing 31 names was produced in protest against this. It was then suggested that the entire property - cottages and gardens - be offered for sale and advertised in the local press. A parish meeting was held, and 15 people voted for the sale, with 4 against. Eventually, the cottages were sold in 1962, the Council receiving something in excess of £900 after all costs had been paid. The money was invested in 5% Defence Bonds.

From 1961 Mr T. Jones became Parish Clerk, and was much involved in discussions (and endless letter writing) over on-going complaints that the public footpath between Mill Road and Watton Road had become ploughed up and was almost impassable. In addition, Mr. Jakes was reported as having been seen carrying a gun on the allotments, and was to be told to stop this at once. In 1964 Mr. Garrod made glass-fronted oak notice boards for the village, which were much appreciated, as before this, parish notices had had to be affixed to posts or gates.

That same year the Parish Council had to deal with a major upset, when the R.D.C. was using the pit opposite the stores as a tipping site for household rubbish. Satisfactory negotiations were reached eventually, but not until 80 people had affixed their names to a petition, for feelings were running very high. Building was going on apace, population was increasing, and a motion was carried that pavements were now needed on the village roads, and that consideration should be given to the imposition of a 30 m.p.h. speed limit. Throughout this whole period Mr. Nash continued as Chairman, with Mr Potter elected as Vice-Chairman in 1966, the five other councillors at this date being Messrs. Broughton, Garrod, Herwin, Hickling and Moore.

At the Annual Parish Meeting in March '67 the village highway names were discussed, the following being recommended to the District Council, School Lane, (rather than 'The Street' as it had been known earlier), Great Melton Road, Braymeadow Lane, Mill Road, Burnthouse Lane, Rectory Lane and Green Lane.

Mr Hickling was concerned as to the need to help the elderly and handicapped with meals on wheels, nursing equipment and the prevention of hypothermia, so Mrs. Broughton (senior), Mrs Flower, Mrs Marjorie Gould, Mrs Harcourt, Mrs Hickling, Mrs Sandford, Mrs Sewter and Rev. F. J. Willson agreed to form a panel to find out current needs. This splendid 'self-help' theme is evident throughout all these books of minutes, showing that when problems need to be tackled, local people have almost always come forward, most willingly, to offer their services. The question of the need for a Village Hall was raised, and a special committee was established to look into this, while finally, the R.D.C. reported that the Armes Cottages on Burnthouse Lane had been condemned, and were to be demolished.

At every Annual Parish Meeting it has always been the custom to receive reports from the various statutory and voluntary groups in the village, and in April 1969 these were the Poors' Charity, the Playing Field Trustees, the Football Club, the Youth Club, the Village Association, the Village Hall Committee, Little Melton School, the Pre-School Playgroup, the W.I. (with a membership of 50), the Panel for the Care of the Elderly and Handicapped, and the British Legion. By 1971 the Wives Circle and the Luncheon Club had been added to this list.

Mr Garrod and Mr Potter resigned from the Council in 1970 and their long service was duly appreciated. Until this time all Councillors appear to have been men, but this year saw the first election of a woman, Mrs. Flower of The Pightle.

The Chairman, Mr. Nash, told the Annual Meeting that there were now more pensioners than school children in Little Melton, 45 houses being without piped drainage, of which 23 were occupied by pensioners, 18 of whom were more than 70 years old. This was the year, too, when there was much concern over the future of The Rose and Crown, with the possibility that it might be entirely demolished, its 3.5 acres being used for housing, or that the pub itself might be kept, and the new school built on part of its land. The latter idea was much more acceptable to the parishioners, and was what happened in due course.

On 30th Sept '71 the first of many meetings was held, attended by the locally elected County Councillor and the Norfolk County Planning Officer, in order to explain future plans for housing development, the 38 villagers present being told that *'It was desirable that expansion of the present village of rather more than 500 people should be limited to natural growth.'*

In February 1972 the Parish Councillors stood in silence, in token of respect to the late Mr. James Nash, who had so admirably served the village for so long. Mr Cyril Harris was elected chairman in his place, with Mr. Norman Nash (James' son) as vice-chairman. By October, Mr. Edward Evans-Lombe had given consent to football games being played on the Playing Field on Sundays, provided they did not coincide with church services. Throughout these years the minutes of the meetings of the Trustees of the Poors' Charity had been included in the Parish Council Book, but from February '73 they were to be kept separately.

By 1973 the new school had just begun to be built, and the Council agreed to investigate the possibility of using the old building for parish purposes, when it became available. This year also saw the election of new Councillors, who were Messrs. Cole, Harcourt, Nash, Potter, Richardson and Tobyn, with Mrs. Hickling as the one woman member. County structure had changed, and the new South Norfolk District Council was set up, replacing the old Forehoe and Henstead R.D.C., Mr Humphrey Back and Mr Wiles were elected to represent Little Melton and Hethersett on this body. Both played a useful part at future Parish Council meetings, which they attended regularly. One step forward in 1974 was that Parish Councils would now be informed of all local planning applications, previously something of a sore point. The old Post Office near the crossways at the end of School Lane closed, the new Post Office being sited next to the garage at the other end of the village. Bureaucracy was also setting in, it now being necessary for Parish Clerks to attend day courses on their work. There was a bright side to this, however, as the Little Melton Clerk's salary was now raised to £100 per annum. This was the year, too, when mention was first made of the Norwich Southern Bypass being likely to be built, the A47.

In March '74, no less than 79 people attended a special public meeting to protest against the steep increase in rate demands, although the village still had no sewerage. The leader of Norfolk County Council attended, and was given something of a rough passage. There was deep resentment at the unfairness of these increased charges, and letters of protest were written to the Prime Minister, Mr. Harold Wilson, as well as to the leader of the Opposition, Mr. Edward Heath, our local M.P., Mr John McGregor, the Secretary of the Environment, the Anglian Water Authority, the Chief Executive Officer of the Norfolk County Council and the South Norfolk District Council. By 1975 local charges for the emptying of septic tanks were slightly reduced, so perhaps the clerk's efforts did have some little effect eventually.

The new school opened for children on 3rd June 1974, with a formal opening on 15th May the following year, the Council now agreeing to hire the old school as a Community Centre, at an annual rental of £104. The first Parish Council meeting was held there on 19th May '75, when Mr Nash was again elected Chairman, with Mr. Percy Harcourt as Vice-Chairman. The centre consisted of two classrooms, with a kitchen, cloakroom, toilet facilities, central heating, and a paved area to the front and rear. A grant application was made for improvements to this newly styled 'Old School Hall'. Later, in January '76 at a special public meeting, 53 people voted in favour of the purchase of the old school at the price of £2,000, only 2 voting against the motion. Later that year a licence was granted, and further applications were made for grant aid, £600 being offered by the Norfolk Education Committee.

The Rose & Crown 1976

By August 1975 Mrs. Edith Mary Hambling had ceased her tenancy of the Public House from Watney Mann, and a petition from 247 customers to save the pub was made, the matter being featured, with a photograph, in the Eastern Daily Press on 27.8.75. Despite this, the building was offered for sale, with benefit of licence, and was boarded up. By 1976, to everyone's relief, an announcement was made that Mr David Bales would probably open it as a Free House by the autumn. Other good news was that there was now an improved bus service in the village, buses running four times a day in each direction. Sadly, in April '76 Mr. W. L. (Curly) Potter resigned after 39 years service, and was thanked by the council in an appropriate manner.

In March 1977 Mr. A. A. Flower relinquished the clerkship, after holding the post for 11 years, and five candidates were interviewed to take his place, Mr. Richard Sinclair of Little Melton being the successful applicant. Twenty five years later, Mr. Sinclair's flowing hand still adorns all the Minute Books of the Parish Council, making them both informative and a pleasure to read.

The Silver Jubilee was celebrated with children's parties, organised by Mrs. Hickling, and Strawberry and Cream teas were provided for the elderly and handicapped. Jubilee Crowns were given to local children, 193 being listed to receive these, paid for by local fund raising efforts. On Sunday 24th July a Cathedral Service of Thanksgiving was held at Norwich Cathedral, two councillors attending.

Throughout these years the question of heavy lorries from Brooks' factory passing through the village was a constant concern, as was the sewerage issue. In 1978 there was a smell from ditches around Brooks' factory, but new meat processing premises were soon to be opened, with an up to date drainage system, which would lead to a vast improvement. There was, (and still is), a high water table in Little Melton, and houses had to have their septic tanks emptied frequently. Indeed, the tanks at the school needed emptying two to three times a week, and those at the Village Inn, every day.

Mr Norman Nash continued as Chairman through the seventies, with Mr. P. Harcourt mentioned from time to time as Vice-Chairman. On 1st May 1980 Mr Williams became Vice-Chairman, while in 1981 Mr Dicks took over this post. In May '81 a special meeting was held to discuss the development of the village. The District Planning Officer for South Norfolk gave some interesting statistics, taken from the ten yearly census returns. In 1901 there had been 81 houses in the village; 87 by 1931; 125 by 1951; 135 by 1961 and 251 by 1981, Little Melton's population then being 660. As occupancy was now only 2.6 persons per house, it was likely that population would decline by approximately 10% over the next ten to fifteen years if new properties were not built. Mr. Nash formally put forward a resolution that five dwellings per year for the next 5 years could be allowed, and this was carried. In February 1985 the first large scale proposition for development was put forward by Mr. T. Grady, who envisaged 50 new properties being built in the six to seven acres off Braymeadow Lane. There was strong local feeling against this, one parishioner remarking that he did not want Little Melton 'to become another Hethersett'.

Book Five starts in April 1985 with the good news that at last the sewerage system in the village was in place. Later that year the Senior Planning Officer for Norfolk County Council warned that now that Little Melton was connected to main drainage, the Norfolk Structure Plan could well be altered, 'limited estate development' being likely to change in favour of greater development. The writing was already on the wall, however, as Mr. Grady had, two months earlier, put in an application to build 19 houses and an estate road off Braymeadow Lane. This was subsequently refused, as was his wish to build 62 further properties there in 1987. The probable likelihood of the stopping up of School Lane was also discussed, following the building of the Norwich Southern Bypass. At this time Mr Nash ceded the chairmanship to Mr. M. Dicks, with Mr. R. James being Vice-Chairman.

The main event at the end of 1985 was the decision of the Village Hall Committee to seek approval in principle to the erection of a new Village Hall on the playing field, at a proposed cost of £85,000 to £90,000. A letter was written to the Evans-Lombe Estate for approval. Some months later an offer of £37,500 was made to purchase the freehold of 'The Old School Hall', but this was considered premature and was rejected. At this time Mr James resigned from the Council, so Mr. N. Nash was elected Vice-Chairman in his place. In 1987 Mr Back of Hethersett resigned as a South Norfolk District Councillor, an office he had held for 14 years, and he was thanked for the support he had given to Little Melton during this period.

By May '87 the site north of the village playing field had become the property of the Parish Council, and a year later approval was received for the erection of the new Village Hall. The decision was then taken for the sale of 'The Old School Hall', Mr. N. Nash and his brother Mr. W. Nash kindly giving a small area of land to the rear, to make it sizeable enough for the later erection of two houses on the site. The sum of £112,000 was raised by an auction in December, and it was considered that this, together with grant aid, might well cover the cost of the erection of the new building, estimated to be between £120,000 and £150,000. Work eventually began on the site on 2nd August 1989.

The 7th May 1990 was the wonderful day on which the new and spacious hall was opened in style by Keith Skipper, a fete being held at the same time. All those long hours of work and worry by the Village Hall Committee had at last paid off, with the completion of the fine badminton or dance hall, balcony, committee room, seated bar area, kitchen, store rooms, cloakrooms and toilets, all under one water-tight roof, and available for local residents of all ages to enjoy. No better

Little Melton Village Hall c.2000

tribute can be paid than that of Peter Wakeford two years later, when he said *'The Village Hall is a remarkably good facility, heavily utilised, although initially some had said its location was less than satisfactory'*.

By March '91 Mr 'Curly' Potter had died, and a letter of sympathy was sent to his widow. In May the first woman Chair of the Parish Council was elected, Miss Jean Durrell, with Norman Nash as Vice-President. The Council now consisted of Miss Durrell and Messrs P. Broughton, W. Chamberlain, N. Duffield, N. Nash, G. Tomlin and P. Wakeford. High on the list of their concerns was the consideration of the proposed development on the 'Greenacres' site, with its high density of dwellings and the inevitable destruction of many trees and shrubs. There had been some burglaries in the village, and Police Superintendent Peter Fraser was asked to address a meeting on 15th September '92. He said that there had been an 105% increase in crime in Norfolk in the last ten years, and only a 17% increase in manpower over the same period. A Home Watch scheme was suggested.

On 2nd November '93 is an entry recording that children from the 1st School, Little Melton had attended the Norfolk Show in Victorian costume, and that their behaviour had been exemplary. In May '94 three Overseas Fellows studying at Birmingham University were present at the Parish Council meeting, to learn how such proceedings should be conducted in their own countries. At this period Jean Durrell resigned, after three years in the chair, and Norman Nash was chosen in her place, with Norman Duffield as Vice-Chairman.

In March '95, Norman Nash and Jean Durrell both offered their resignations from the Council, Norman having served for 25 years, with some 14 years as Chairman, and Jean for 14 years, with 3 as Chairman. Both were heartily thanked, and the following month a presentation was made to Mr Nash. Two months later, at the Annual meeting, the Trustees of the Poors' Charity reported a change of name to the more fitting Little Melton Parochial Charity, with envisaged changes in their constitution to facilitate a wider use of funds. Mr Norman Duffield was then elected Chairman with Mr George Gleadhill as Vice-Chairman, and in December, the Council stood in silent tribute to Mr Wakeford, who had done so much for the village, and had sadly died following a heart operation.

In 1996 A Mini Recycling Centre was set up outside the Post Office, and rubbish left by gypsies was eventually cleared from a site near the Norwich bypass on School Lane, no less than 6 lorry loads of old tyres having to be removed, as well as tins, glass etc. In January of the following year, seventy residents attended a meeting at which the South Norfolk Council's consent to the erection by Persimmon Homes of 58 dwellings with garages was presented as a fait accompli, and in February '98, the Parish Council agreed the suitability of the road names put forward by South Norfolk Council as being Greenacres for the main spine, with Broadoak, Poplar, Elm, Larch and Birch for the closes.

A Millennium Committee was set up in late 1998 to consider suitable celebrations, members working hard to achieve this, with great success. Their projects were outlined to the Council, but the minutes do not refer to these in detail. A magnificent party was held in the Village Hall to see in the Millennium year, much enjoyed by the many people who attended. Later, Mrs Jo Buxton was thanked for the major part she had played in all these arrangements.

In January '99 Wimpey Homes made application for 15 dwellings on land south east of Gibbs Close, the Parish Council being told that this had already been approved in the local plan. Other smaller housing developments were also allowed, the Parish Council feeling, on occasions, that their wishes were often being ignored by higher authority, and on 16th March '99 it was announced, to everyone's relief, that no further development would be carried out until 2006, other than that already approved. Messrs Duffield and Gleadhill retired in 1999, and Mr. David Perrin was elected to the Chair, with Stewart Cable as Vice-Chairman.

Later that year, Mr Cable reported that the huge sum of £26,000 had been raised by the Apple Appeal for the refurbishment of the Children's Playground. The Apple Appeal was set up in 1995 by three village mothers, Jayne Cable, Rose Spaul and Sharon Kean, who subsequently left the village and was replaced by Sharon Livick. Despite many cynics they were to achieve a tremendous feat, with immense hard work, generous help from many villagers and the grants from the Parochial Charity and South Norfolk District Council, another superb village amenity was finished with due congratulations from the Parish council upon this magnificent achievement.

The village playground being enjoyed by Mark Carter, one of the editor's grandchildren, in 2002

In 2001 Mr Cable took over as Chairman with Mr Perrin as Vice-Chairman. Monthly deliberations continue today, many local people freely giving both time and energy to ensure the well-being of the parish, and we owe a debt of gratitude to them all, both past and present. One final comment might be summed up in that well known phrase, *'The more things change, the more they are the same'.*

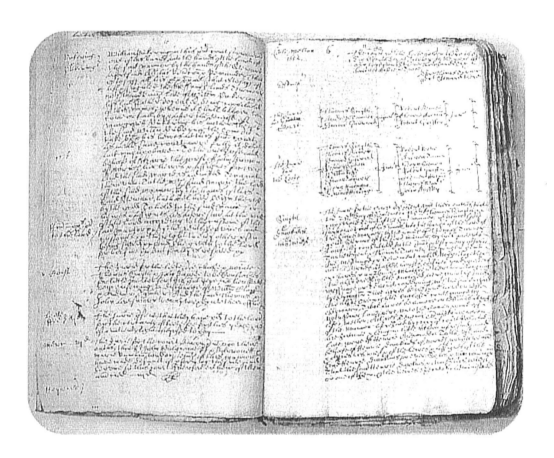

An original Manorial Record book for Little Melton
(MC 1861/23 865X9 p10 & p11)

*Strange to see how a good dinner
and feasting reconciles everybody.*

Samuel Pepys.

id you know that ...

   ...the well-known Diarist, The Rev. James Woodforde, employed Eliza Claxton of Little Melton as his 'Cook Maid' from 1778 to 1784?
   The Rev. Woodforde was rector of the Norfolk village of Weston Longville for twenty-seven years until his death in 1803, being most famous for his meticulous records of the enormous meals served at the parsonage house. *'A plain dinner'* on March 8th 1780 consisted of *'some hash Mutton, a plain sewet Pudding and a couple of Rabbits rosted'*, while on June 8th 1781, entertaining the local squire and his wife, the rector wrote *'I gave them for dinner, a Couple of Chicken boiled and a Tongue, a Leg of Mutton boiled and Capers and Batter Pudding for the first Course, Second, a couple of Ducks rosted and green Peas, some Artichokes, Tarts and Blancmange. After dinner, Almonds and Raisins, Oranges and Strawberries. Mountain and Port Wines. Peas and Strawberries the first gathered this year by me. We spent a very agreeable day, and all well pleased and merry.'* Eliza must have played an important part in the preparation of such feasts. The diary entries about her are as follows:
'Oct 14 1778 sent Cary's cart with one of my horses by Ben to Little Melton about 4 miles beyond Easton after my new maid this afternoon and she returned about 6 o'clock. Her name is Eliza Claxton about 40 years of age but how she will do I do not know as yet but her wages are £5.15s.6d. per annum but out of that she is to find herself in tea & sugar. She is not the most engaging I must confess by her appearance that she makes.'
'Jany 7 1782. To my senior maid Elizabeth Claxton paid also this morning a year's wages due the 6th instant £5.15.6.'
'Oct 11 1784 After breakfast I paid my maid Eliz: Claxton who leaves me today 3 quarters wages being £4.7.0. She breakfasted here and left us about 11 this morning.'

   ...Mr. Custance, the Squire who features in James Woodforde's diaries, once owned land in Little Melton? and that it was almost certainly he who recommended Eliza Claxton to the Parson? John Custance Esq.

Parson Woodforde (from a painting in Weston Longville Church)

bought the Weston Longville estates in 1726, and appeared before Little Melton Manor Court in 1743, when he became the copyhold owner of a house and 4 ¾ acres of land here, (on the surrender of Thomas Clarke). He had married Sarah, daughter of John Hambleton Esq., and as was the fashion then, he named his eldest son after her. This son, Hambleton Custance, inherited the Little Melton property on the death of his father in 1753. Hambleton and his wife, (born Susannah Press), had two sons, naming the elder boy John after his grandfather, and the younger boy Press, after his mother.

In 1757, on Hambleton's death, Press Custance was admitted to the Little Melton holding. He was still a small child, but it was always the youngest son who had the right of inheritance in this manor. In 1772 Press surrendered the house and land to his elder brother John, the squire who features in so much of the Woodforde diary.

Much later, in 1817, our Enclosure Award shows several acres as belonging to *'Press Custance as trustee for the poor inhabitants of Melton Parva not receiving parochial relief'*. In other words, he was one of the early trustees of what later became known as 'The Poors' Charity'. By now he must have been elderly, but the strange thing is that he is not listed in Burke's 'Landed Gentry' like the rest of his family. Is this, perhaps, because in his youth he was something of a black sheep?

On June 18th 1780 Parson Woodforde noted *'I read Prayers and Preached this afternoon at Weston. My Squire and Lady at Church. Press Custance's Woman at Church and in my Seat also.'*

The following day there is this entry *'My Squire called on me this morn' and talked to me a good deal about his Brother's Mistress sitting in my Seat yesterday and whether she had leave, and also that she strutted by them in a very impudent manner coming out of Church - and stared at Mrs Custance.'*

Despite their annoyance, the squire, the parson and Press Custance seem to have remained on friendly terms, while only a year earlier, at the christening of Mr John Custance's eldest son, Hambleton Thomas, on April 11th 1779, *'the Gossips'* were Sir Edmund Bacon as proxy for Sir Thomas Beauchamp, Mr Press Custance and Lady Bacon. (Strange as it may seem Gossip is the old English word for Godparent)

...Little Melton had a Cup Winning Football team? Before the second world war, Little Melton had a thriving football team. As well as those from the village, the team was made up from men who came from the surrounding area, Marlingford and Earlham to name just two. One member, Les Williamson (second row, far right in the photograph) remembers biking to matches and not bothering about the weather, all playing in five inches of snow

Little Melton Football Club 1937/38 season

with their boots frozen to their feet. There were not enough team shirts for this photograph, so some wore ordinary white shirts. Other members of this team were Bob Quantrill, Jimmy Chamberlain, Curly Potter, Dudley Warnes, Peter Lee and Victor Warnes. Many of the young men went to fight in the war and never returned and the team never reunited.

Winning the Cup came after the re-creation of the Little Melton Football Team in 1955. The team was under the wing of the Little Melton Social and Sports Club who would run the village playing field and various fund raising dances and whist drives. During their first few years the team went from strength to strength culminating in winning the Norfolk Junior Cup in 1957. The team continued into the 1970's under the chairmanship of Mr. Hayes and the financial control of the Treasurer, Curly Potter, until unfortunately, interest waned and support faded along with players enthusiasm.

Little Melton Football Club 1968/69 season
Back row, left to right - R. Hambling (Sec), A. Brighton, K. Clarke,
B. Chamberlain, B. Read, W. Chamberlain, B. Buck.
Front row, left to right - I. Jones, M. Dunton, D. Harvey, G. Angus (Treasurer),
D. Perrin (Capt.), F. Reynolds.

The Little Melton Cup winning team 1957, celebrating their victory with supporters in the 'Cold-Blow'

*1 - Cutty Matthews; 2 - R. Thurtle; 3 - Tony Eastwick; 4 - Donny Elvin;
5 - Harry Chamberlain; 6 - B. Jakes; 7 - Milly Matthews; 8 - Curly Potter;
9 - K. Goldsmith; 10 - Dick Bell; 11 - L. Clarke;
12 - Cedric Bell; 13 - M. Matthews.*

Chapter Four

arming

On Inclosures
'Tis bad enough in man or woman
To steal a goose from off a common;
But surely he's without excuse
Who steals the common from the goose.

Anon.

In the days before detailed maps were commonplace, every field, enclosure and footpath had a local name, familiar to every villager. Some of the more interesting names that have been found in Little Melton manorial books, land deeds and church *'terriers'*, (schedules of church property), are given here:

Apple Tree Pightle,	*Foxnel Field,*	*Middlecroft,*	*Sowerland Furlong,*
Braymeadow,	*Goreys,*	*Newood,*	*Stam Furlong,*
Brockoles,	*Gravel Pit Close,*	*Oaky Pasture,*	*Stanneymeare,*
Church Field,	*Greengate Way,*	*Over Beck,*	*The Stoun Furlong,*
Clay Hill,	*Greenway Close,*	*Park Lane,*	*Thornes,*
Cockes Meadow,	*Hacking,*	*Pinnacle Furlong,*	*Upper Clay Close,*
Coulsey Field,	*Helve & Hatchet,*	*Procession Meere,*	*Upper Green,*
Crow Close	*High Close,*	*Redhills Row,*	*Vicarage Pightle,*
Dead Furlong,	*Home Croft,*	*Rogers Close,*	*Wrongland,*
Dove House Meadow,	*Kittes Acre,*	*Rooks Nest Furlong,*	*Yoxland.*
Dowes Hill,	*Land Grave Furlong,*	*Rowe Furlong,*	
Fir Close,	*Lower Clay Close,*	*Snoreshill Field,*	
Fleet Meadow,	*Lower Green,*	*Snow Hill Field,*	

Many of these names tell their own story but some are meaningless to us today, even with the help of dictionaries of archaic words. *Brockoles* could be where badgers lived, of course, but it was often applied to a field where cattle were particularly apt to break out. *Cockes Meadow* might have been a place where poultry were free to roam, or more probably was where woodcock used to *'rode'* or perform their special homing flight in the breeding season. Goreys apparently isn't as dreadful as it sounds, but means a slushy, muddy place, *'gorey'* expressing the thin, wet part of the mire. *Hacking* sounds very hard work, as a hack was a strong pick-axe or mattock, and *Helve and Hatchet* also sounds tough going, though *'to throw the helve after the hatchet'* sometimes meant *'to be in despair'. Land Grave Furlong* is a puzzle, for in Lincolnshire a Land Grave sometimes meant a potato hole, but did it have the same meaning here? A meere was a boundary, and *Procession Meere* was the name given to the old division between Little Melton and Bawburgh which later became the turnpike, and is now the traffic ridden B1108. *Greengate Way* used to lead from today's Mill Road to the Watton Road, past our Village Hall, which is referred to sometimes by senior inhabitants as 'Billy's Loke'. The very up-market sounding *Park Lane* was the road adjoining Little Melton Green, near the Manor House. *Rooks Nest Furlong* is a nice one, as it was usually seen as a sign of prosperity when rooks were building near a house. *Wrongland* and *Sowerland Furlongs* are both very expressive, (wrongland can also mean misshapen), but the all time favourite must surely be *Snoreshill Field*, as one can just imagine what went on there on a hot summer's afternoon!

Edwin Clarke using horsepower on Elm Farm c.1940

Possession of land has always been a sign of status, particularly so in the Middle Ages, when the well-to-do invested most of their wealth in this way. During the twelfth century, a bitter dispute over land ownership occurred in Little Melton, the details being found, somewhat surprisingly, in the records of St. Benet's Abbey, on the River Bure. Never before or since has our village been so famous!

It happened like this. In 1066 Edwin, the Anglo-Saxon owner of our village, had promised to give his lands to St Benet's Abbey, on the River Bure, after his death. This was not to be, however, as William the Conqueror ousted Edwin, eventually appointing his powerful Norman steward Godric in his place. Godric and his wife then gave Little Melton to the Abbey *'for their souls after their death'*, stating that their son, Ralf de Montchensy, was to hold these lands during his lifetime.

Another of Godric's sons was Hubert de Montchensy, who in due course inherited the manor from his brother. There was much in-fighting during the turbulent reign of King Stephen (1135-1154), and Hubert decided to claim the lands as his own, saying that the Abbey had no right to them. For a while all was seemingly lost to St. Benet's, but during the time of Abbot William II, in 1155/56, Hubert was fined twenty marks (£6. 13s 4d) and was forced to give back the land to the Abbey, for which he was to pay 10 shillings a year rent. This was on the direct order of King Henry II himself, and in the presence of the Archbishop of Canterbury! Letters from these eminent personages abound in the Abbey records, the original Latin having now been transcribed and printed, with English summaries.

Let's now return to more modern times, by jumping no less than seven centuries, a huge time span, during which the back-breaking toil of the agricultural year must have continued in its regular pattern, season by season.

By the early eighteen hundreds, most cultivated land was fenced off into small fields, (often known as 'closes'), but in some villages, as here, there were still a few sizeable stretches of open arable or 'common field'. This was a relic of the age-old method of husbandry, when each man worked a number of scattered strips of land, rather than having a concentrated holding in one place. It seems that some ninety acres of this type of 'field land' were still being farmed in this way in Little Melton before the Enclosure Act came into force. In particular, 'Church Field', surrounding All Saints, consisted of several different 'closes' at that time, as well as considerable areas of 'strips', the latter varying from a quarter of an acre or less in size, to a couple of acres or so. This was by now an outdated method of farming, not only wasteful both of land and time, but also preventing all attempts at crop experimentation. The local Enclosure Awards followed as a result, Hethersett in 1800, Little Melton in 1817 and Great Melton in 1819, each one leading to an extensive redistribution of land.

Whatever the rights and wrongs of enclosure, many smaller men felt themselves hard done by, for until then most families had had the right to keep animals on the commons, some geese perhaps, a pig or two, or maybe a goat or cow, as well as the privilege of taking dead wood, turf and bracken for firing. These were valuable assets when life was hard, and were now to be done away with. The accompanying sketch map is an attempt to show the lay-out of the village at the time the Enclosure Award came into being, when Little Melton had no less than five commons.

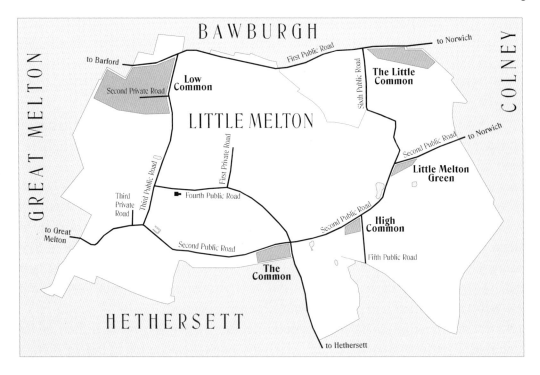

The Common of six acres lying south of Great Melton Road as far as Hethersett Beckhythe. This was open land, with no building of any kind.

The Little Common of nine and a half acres off the Watton road, where Vine Cottage and the Little Melton Light Railway used to operate.

High Common of about four acres, opposite today's Village Inn, on the Elm Farm side of the road.

Low Common of about twenty-eight acres in the north west corner of the village, near Valley Farm, adjoining Bawburgh's west boundary, close to the Watton Road.

Little Melton Green of about an acre and a half fronting the Manor House on the corner where School Lane and Green Lane meet. The Green once boasted a fine Walnut tree, under which the tenants of the manor used to forgather for court hearings on St. Luke's day, a century or so earlier. There was also a pound in which to lock up straying cattle, and a large pit for water. Today's modern house named 'The Pound' stands near the old site, while its neighbour, 65 School Lane, has a large underground garage where the pit once stood. The original village green had three gates, each blocking the road leading off it, and there was a further gate across the highway at the junction of Burnthouse Lane with Hethersett.

In Little Melton, an Act of Parliament was *'passed in the 54th year of the Reign of his present Majesty, King George the Third'*, entitled *'An Act for Inclosing Lands in the parish of Melton Parva'* which can still be seen in the Norfolk Record

Office. Few copies of original acts still exist, so this is an interesting document, and tells us that the Commissioner appointed was a Mr Elisha de Hague, whose first task was to set out the parish boundaries. He starts *'in the south fence of Lake's Meadow, belonging to Mr. Edward Heath, where the parishes of Little Melton, Great Melton and Hethersett join, and from thence along the middle of the said lane, to the north-west corner of Blind Pightle, late belonging to John Luke Iselin'* and so in an anti-clockwise direction until the whole parish has been circuited. All sorts of transient landscape features are mentioned along the way, such as hedges, gaps in hedges, fences, boundary trees and even *'a crab bush'* on one occasion.

The Commissioner's next task was to *'set out and appoint the six carriage roads and highways, and three private roads'* in the village. The first public road was part of the turnpike from Hingham to Norwich; the second was the whole of today's Great Melton Road with School Lane; the third was Rectory Lane, linking the B1108 with Great Melton Road; the fourth was Mill Road; the fifth led south from School Lane to Braymeadow; and the sixth was today's Green Lane. The first private road was the old 'Greengate Way', part of today's Mill Road after it turns the sharp corner to the Village Hall; the second led off Rectory Lane to Valley Farm; and the third went north from Great Melton Road, just after its junction with Rectory Lane, and led to the public gravel pit set out for the use of the surveyors of the highways, with which to keep the roads in good repair. These are all marked on the previous 1817 map.

Next, Mr de Hague was ordered to sell *'the commons and waste grounds towards defraying the costs of obtaining the Act and of carrying it into execution'*, and through these sales he obtained £1,192.10s in all, so enabling him to allot the land in proportion to the many claims made by previous occupants and owners. It is interesting to see how much money the commons were fetching at this time, for some of the land was in very poor condition, sometimes marshy and undrained, and almost always badly overgrown. Two pieces making 13 ¾ acres in all went to John Girling for £515; one piece of 7 ¾ acres to Edward Heath for £365; two further pieces totalling 6 acres to Thomas Hubbard for £255; one acre (being part of the village green) to Jehosophat Postle Esq., of Colney Hall for £47; and a quarter of an acre, (the remaining part of the village green) to James Copeman for £10.10s.

There follow the names of twenty three applicants who successfully claimed allocations of land, both freehold and copyhold. These were Elizabeth Girling, William Howard, Rev. Edward Frank (lord of the manor), Thomas Davy, John Reynolds, John Leeder, the three daughters of the late George Hayward, James Copeman, William Copeman, James Wortley, William Lofty, William Davy, Ann Davy, Sarah Forster, Rev. Thomas Starling Buckle (of Elm Farm), Edward Heath (of Church Farm), the Master and Fellows of Emmanuel College,

Cambridge,(who held the advowson of All Saints Church), the Mayor, Sheriffs, Citizens and Commonalty of the City of Norwich (as trustees for Hospital Farm), Press Custance (for the trustees of the poor), Rev. James Dunn (Vicar), Elizabeth Thompson, William Duckett and William Cooper. The largest allocation of 216 acres was to Edward Heath of Church Farm, and the smallest of 1 acre with a cottage to William Duckett.

Each allocation is described in full, that for William Cooper stating that he 'Claims a messuage, barn, outbuildings and 17A 1R 11P of inclosed land, and 7 acres of field land, in the occupation of himself; of which the messuage and 16A 1R and 0P are copyhold of the manor of Little Melton, and the remainder is freehold. He also claims divers walnut and elm trees growing upon the common in front of the said premises. He likewise claims to be entitled to a right of common of pasture for all his commonable cattle (levant and couchant thereon) upon all the commons and waste grounds with the said parish of Melton Parva, at all times of the year.' (Mr. Cooper's farmhouse was called 'The Grove' and dates from the early seventeenth century, today known as No. 64 School Lane, home to Dr. and Mrs. Beeby).

All those who had been allotted land had to fence their properties to the exacting standards set forth in the Act. Ditches had to be dug 'perpendicularly' to a depth of three feet, and were not to be less than four feet and a half wide at the top, while the summits of their adjoining banks were to be planted with good 'white thorn layer, and half hurdles, or a stake bound hedge or thorns.' These instructions together with the names of the proprietors were duly read out in church, as required by law, both because this gave added solemnity to the proceedings, and because the church was normally the only building large enough to hold all the assembled villagers.

Following the Enclosure Award, land in Great Melton was exchanged with land in Little Melton for the use of our Poor Law Trustees. It is said that Little Melton did rather well out of this, the allocation in our own village being of better quality. This is the origin of 'The Town Land' which the parish still owns today.

What crops were being grown in Little Melton at this period? The usual four-course rotation of the time, (long before the Dutch had introduced sugar beet to Norfolk), can be seen from the proceedings of the parish vestry meeting dated March 1815, in which it was agreed that *'the Town Land lying in the parish should be let to the best bidder for the term of four years from the following Michaelmas, and to be farmed in the manner following:*

First year – Corn.

Second year – Turnips, to be muck'd for with 12 loads per acre of good muck, not less than 8 heaps per load.

Third year – Barley or Oats and to be lay'd down with clean seeds.

Fourth year – To be fed or mown for hay.

To be let free of Town Charges. Rent to be paid 11 Oct. annually to Overseers of Poor'.

At the same meeting John Childs agreed to give 56s. per acre for it. Signed Thos S. Buckle (Clerk), churchwarden. The marks of William Cooper and Thos. Davy, overseers. While Wm. Howard, John Girling, William Allbin, and Sam Hipperson, Constable, all signed their names.

Elizabeth Girling was tenant of the Manor Farm at the time of the enclosure award, when her son John was actually farming the property. He also held land of his own in the village, and a map of 1822 shows his main crops as being wheat, turnips, peas and carrots.

Very few farmers' inventories remain for Little Melton, but three are perhaps worth mentioning. Way back in the summer of 1606 a husbandman named William Abell had died, and his farming goods were valued at:

A gelding - 26s. 8d.

3 'neates' (cows) and one calf - £6.6s.8d

3 sheep - £3.6s.8d.

2 sows, a 'shott' (a weaned pig under a year old) and another pig– 26s.8d.

12 geese – 3s.4d.

6 hens – 3s.4d.

3 acres of winter corn - £3

6 acres of barley - £3.6s.8d.

3 flitches of bacon – 15s.

The full inventory of William Abell is shown in Appendix D.

When Thomas Rose, yeoman, died in 1613 his goods included 2 cows, a heifer and a weaned calf valued at £5, plus 2 hogs worth 16s.

A hundred years later, John Carter had been farming in Little Melton for most of his lifetime, and died in 1725. He too was a yeoman with a large family, and had a barn adjoining his house, as well as a dairy, backhouse, corn chamber, stable and carthouse. Laundry was done in the backhouse, where there were several washtubs, and a cheese press. Beer was brewed in the buttery, which contained one half barrel, four firkins and a sieve, while butter and cheese were made in the dairy, where milk bowls and pails, churns, cheese vats, wooden scales and 'butter pints' were in common use. Because his death had occurred in June, no corn was stacked in the barn, but his livestock included:

2 horses and a mare valued at £5.

5 cows and a bullock £12.

a sow, a hog and two small pigs £2.

a cart, 'a plow', a pair of harrows, a 'plow line' and cart-rope, £4 together

There were also two sedge-collars for the horses (leather for this was probably still too expensive), halters, two saddles and a bridle and pair of steps, worth 6s in all,

Plus a spade, a shovel, a muck-fork and a stable-fork 3s

with 'lumber' 10s.

Agriculture has always been the mainstay of the village, but mechanisation has revolutionised its methods, abolishing the backbreaking toil of days gone by. Today a few skilled men operating the latest farm machinery can carry out the work in less than half the time that it used to take a whole army of men and boys. For example, in 1851, only a century and a half ago, there were no less than 67 agricultural labourers living here, while forty years later in 1891, this number had only decreased to 54.

There were ten farms in Little Melton in 1851:

Name of Farmer	Acreage	Name of farm where known	Number of people employed
Thomas Aldred	282	Church Farm	5 men & boys
Frances Rudd	180	Manor Farm	10 men
Samuel Hipperson	96	Valley Farm	3 men
Wm. Hipperson	45	Hospital Farm	1 man & 1 boy
Thomas Forster	40	Elm Farm	2 men
John Coggle	25		1 man (his son)
John Gaff	17	Steward's House	Himself
James Webster	13	Greycot	1 man
Edmund Eden	7		1 man (his son)
Robert Clark	6		Himself
Total	711		24 men & 6 boys

This meant that of the 67 agricultural labourers living in Little Melton, 37 of them would have had to find work outside the village, walking to and from their place of employment daily, often over long distances. Of the full-time labouring boys, one was a 9 year old, one was 10, one was 11, one was 13, and two were 14. Many younger children, (both boys and girls) also worked part time in the fields, stone-picking and crow-scaring, harvesting fruit and carrying milk, in addition to looking after their baby brothers and sisters while both parents were out at work.

Mr Norman Nash, son of the well-known and respected Mr James Nash, has contributed this oral history about agricultural developments in the parish. He says: *"I was born at Cringleford. Manor Farm, Little Melton was owned by the Barclay Estate at the time, and later on my father applied for the rental here. When we moved into the Manor House in September 1940, when I was 11, we took over from the previous tenant who had been here fifty years, and started off with 10 or 12 cows with 1 cowman and 6 horses.*

The Manor House, like most farmhouses, was fairly big. Cringleford was also fairly big, two families had lived there, my grandparents and my parents. My father and mother moved in when they married. They lived there from 1926 until 1940. Each family had rooms of their own but they shared a great big kitchen.

The Manor House in Little Melton, the farmhouse, had 5 bedrooms and bathroom. It was very chilly, you see. There was no central heating. The two front rooms were hardly ever used except at Christmas time. We lived in the kitchen and the little sitting room at the back. You had an open fire, the same as you did in the cottages, and you got roasted one side of the room and in the big kitchen there was an Aga cooker which was used to heat up water. We had a low sink for soft water with a little hand pump which was used for washing. Outside there was a well which had a pump, and we had a boy who worked for us and he used to pump the water into the tank in the attic for use for the rest of the day. It would take about three hundred pumps to get it up there. Heating was through the open fire. In the

Viscount 'Turnip' Townshend.
One of the Norfolk farmers who perfected the
four-course crop rotation system.

bedrooms there was no heating at all, like a lot of these cottages which had places in them for fire, but they were never used.

On the farm we had all out-buildings, the corn barn and the cow houses. There was the stable, the cart shed in there, an orchard, apple trees and so on. There was the pond where the cows and the horse drank.

The farming community around here was behind the times when we arrived. There was tremendous change during the war because they wanted as much food as they could get and we were pioneers, in a way, in getting the first tractor here. We used to have to plough up the meadows to produce the food. Of course the difference between then and now is tremendous.

The fields were mixed farming, with the meadows. The land was rotated on the old Norfolk four course rotation, with sugar beet or roots like mangolds and swede, followed by barley, then ley (grass and hay), and then wheat and back to sugar beet. There used to be as much weed in the fields as crop, like the fields in Poppy Land in north Norfolk, until they started developing the sprays, but that was not until the end of the war.

You see there was mostly a strong community feeling around then, some 'them and us' feeling, but mostly people were together. When we were young, everyone was in the harvest field, and there used to be the 'Holdya boys'. The corn was collected in sheaves and this was forked up onto the carts. There was someone loading or pitching on the sheaves or shocks as we used to call them, and there was a boy on the horse making sure that the wagon didn't move at the wrong time. He would call out 'Holdya boys' to make sure everyone held on tight, as the horse moved to the next lot of sheaves. If it went off, and you didn't shout,

'Modern Technology' at Elm Farm together with the traditional 'Tea Break'
(E. A. Clarke far left) c.1950

the man on the wagon would be standing there and go over the back, or he'd be swearing at you. So you see, at that time anyone could give a helping hand. There'd be children running around with sticks chasing the rabbits for food. Even at Cringleford, when I was nine or ten, I used to help at harvest on the stacks or help with the animals.

When I left school in 1943, I left at lunch time, the first job I did was I helped father with a new binder. They came from Canada in bits, and I helped him put it together to start the harvest. At the time we had one cowman, four labourers, 180 acres, now one hand will do a lot more than that.

I left school at 14 and went into farming. I'd be straight out at 7 a.m. The cowman and horseman would start earlier at about 6 o'clock to milk the cows and get milk ready for the lorry. They'd use 10 gallon churns and there was a stand there by the roadside. We'd wheel them out and they were picked up at 8'ish. We'd look after young stock, get the horses ready.

You see things were done by the horse as well as tractor then. There was feeding the bullocks, and that was hard work. Getting the swedes cut up and putting them in a two bushel skip. It was normal to keep an old sow. I even used to help keep them before I went to school. The farmer's wife looked after the poultry and she kept the egg money.

This was my favourite time, when I had just left school at 14 to the time I was 22, because I enjoyed working on the land. Later, when I was milking cows seven days a week, I didn't enjoy it so much. I enjoyed it most at harvest time. It was hard work, but it was the gathering in, everyone working together. Also this was the time when you were looking towards the money you were going to get. We had the old binders. If something stopped working, we'd tie it up with the binder twine and make it go. You felt more involved.

Of course on the farm we did well for food during the war. We had pigs, we'd make our own butter and we used to kill a pig and the chickens, so we didn't go short. After I left school, I went back a year later to see them. I did a talk about farming and the first thing they asked me was 'Do you have plenty to eat?' because everyone was still rationed, eggs and so on. We did have a healthy diet.

When I first came here to Little Melton there was nowhere near as many houses and everyone knew everyone. There was Ken Sewter who in 1938 moved here. He had the house opposite Manor House. His neighbour was the pub, the Rose and Crown, known as the Cold Blow. Everyone knew it as that because when it was an off-licence you got cold when you had to wait outside to get your drink. Then there were the old cottages in Great Melton Road. The farms were Clarkes at Elm Farm...then there was the midnight milkman who delivered his milk at night...that was Herbert Woodgett at Willow Farm.

Herbert Woodgett (Great nephew of Captain Woodgett of the Cutty Sark) c.1935

There was Herbert Eagle at what is now the Grange, Church Farm. By the new Persimmon Estate there was a Market Garden. Along both sides of Braymeadow Lane there were market gardens by Rose Cottage, with lettuces and the like. Another character was Jimmy Ringwood who has Ringwood Close named after him. He was Clerk of the Parish Council for donkeys years… and of course there's Swanns, which has always been a shop, run then by Mr. King.

We always had the school here. I went down there myself for a while, and then on to Avenue Road School, when I had to cycle 16 miles a day to get there and back. There were a lot of children in the village. There were big families, one couple had eight children, another had ten, but many had five or six children. There were the Council Houses down Braymeadow Lane that were built in the 1930's, known as 'Tin Tack'. The Mill Road ones were built after the war, in 1945 and '46.

And there was Barclay who owned our land, and he was a bit of an eccentric. He used to wear an eye shield all times of the year, and you could hear him half a mile away shouting at some men. He was alright, although once he suddenly got the idea that we weren't farming properly, so he gave us notice. He said he saw some rubbish. But that blew over, and later my father managed the farm at Colney for him.

Crossways Stores (Swann's) c1971

Little Meltons first 'estate' - the local authority houses at the end of Braymeadow Lane, known as 'The Ring' or to longer term residents - 'Tin-Tack'. c.1940

The people were mostly rural people with agriculture employing over half of them. Of course, some went to Norwich, but I suppose there was 20 houses in Little Melton with half a dozen or more connected with farming. They weren't educated people, but they had a kind of common sense, they were often very shrewd.

During the war when the blitz was on Norwich I wasn't very well, I had yellow jaundice, but we had got to the stage when you didn't take much notice of the air raid sirens. We'd be upstairs in bed and the shout of 'Sirens' went up, and then 'It's gone' 'All right' 'All clear's gone', and that's all we'd bother about. But when they had this blitz going on, it was different. Father was a special constable, and he and I went to have a look to see Norwich going up, the flames and things, the fires.

One day, Norwich looked as though it was alight from one end to another. We went up there the following day after they had used explosive bombs as well as the incendiaries, and you had a job getting through Norwich with the damage done. People used to come out here at night from Norwich and sleep here at Little Melton, sleeping under the billiard table at the farm or in the barn. They'd come out afraid of the bombing and go back the next day.

Then this particular night, a little after the blitz on Norwich, I was on the road in Little Melton when the school was bombed. There were five of us stood there, and we saw these flares go over, and the next thing we knew was that there was this bang, bang, bang, you see, and we dived. All except father, and he just stood there looking to see what was happening down School Lane. There was a string of eight bombs, and he was trying to look to see where they landed. You see my grandparents lived in the last house before the school. Well, we rushed into our house and found one or two windows broken, and my brother had been blown across the room. Mother was worried, saying 'Oh where have you been?'

Then we went down to the school, and we were one of the first down there. The roof was down off the school. The cottages there were badly damaged. There was this old boy in one of them, and we tried to get him out, and he was in bed and he wasn't going down until they had found his pipe. When school lessons started again, half the children had to go to the Church Room in Mill Road, and the other half were in the Clubhouse behind the pub. They were taught like that for a while. Some bombs landed on our fields, but why they did it is a bit of a mystery. Maybe it was the greenhouses, and the bomber saw the reflection from them, and thought it was a target.

Farming was struggling financially up to the war in the 1930s, but during the war the country wanted the food and you were helped a lot. The prices helped, and for ten years after the war farming did very well. Nearly everyone had cows then. It was that monthly cheque that came in for the cows that paid the wages.

Bomb damaged Litle Melton school (1943) with pupils;
(left to right) D. Glister, M. Joy, W. Warnes & B. Yallop)

My mother used to write these books with records of what happened to the money. Some money was spent on the blacksmith down at Colney whilst we had horses. Then there was Pinkstones – that was for medicines. Birbeck was the Land Agent who was paid £125 for half a year's rent. Stanleys was the vet, and the oil was from Goffs. Baxters was the feed merchants used for cattle food.

My father used to take the calves to the Cattle Market in Norwich almost every Saturday in the 1940s, but things were changing. With the coming of the tractor, of course, the horses were no longer needed, so the horse-man, who'd been with us since moving here, tried driving the tractors, but didn't like it, and left in 1952. I mean the horse-man had been important. The sugar beet were horse hoed, with a boy leading the horse and a man steering the hoes between the rows to kill the weeds. Then they were hand hoed, leaving one plant every 9 inches or so. Often people would come evenings to earn extra money. Harvesting sugar beet was hard and sometimes miserable work, pulling them up, knocking the soil off them, cutting the leaves off, throwing them into heaps to be loaded by hand onto a tumbril and carted to a big heap beside the road, for a lorry to take to the factory.

We had foot and mouth disease in 1951. They killed a lot of animals as a precaution, sheep from the surrounding farms and cattle. They bulldozed them off to bury them in a field on the farm. We had to scrub everywhere out and get things disinfected. It was funny, because my brother went off on 14th November to the army, and on the 15th we got foot and mouth, and then my son was born on the 16th. They had to catch up with my brother and sorted all his clothes out. There was three months of emergency measures, and we even had some prisoners to help to scrub the place.

We used to have milk coolers and separators. You put the milk in the container at the top, and you cranked the handle, and it spun round and by centrifugal force it separated the milk from the cream, and then we made butter. We had hurricane lamps because we had no electricity at Cringleford, only oil lamps. We only got a phone and electricity when we moved here to Little Melton. None of these cottages had it. Gradually it came in after the war.

In the '50s and '60s we didn't have a combine until 1966/67. At that time things were rather poor in the milking business, so we sold all the cattle off, which meant we didn't need a cowman. I'd been milking myself for years, but another chap then did it, but sadly he died suddenly outside the pub. Then we decided to get rid of cattle, so we were left with just one man, my brother and myself. We just had sugar beet and corn, and with the combine we could work it easily.

A lot of people got out of cows at that time. I'm not sure why it went bad, but if you've got a river and water, then you have a meadow and can keep it green, but here we hadn't, and if you had a dry season we were scratching around trying to find food for them to eat. And you were probably growing twice as much for the cows than was needed in a good year in case you got a bad year, because you never knew, you see, which is why we got out of cows.

With sugar beet and corn it was not too bad. We carried on reasonably well in the mid-60s. We did have pigs for quite a time in the 1970s. We bought them as weaners, 7 weeks old, and then sold them off as porkers. They did say that pigs went up and down in price so quickly, whereas with cattle you had three or four years before they came into production time. You got calves out of them. But with pigs if they're profitable, too many go into it, and it suffers again. They're either gold or nothing.

By the '80s we were getting two ton an acre of winter barley, which worked out at £313 an acre, and £150 a ton. This was in 1983. We used to get £120 a ton, so that was our peak period. But when I gave up in 1994, things had gone down again. Sugar beet was one of the main things. £354 an acre, £24 a ton you were paid. But as time went by, with the cost of seed and fertiliser, you weren't making that much from these crops, and then with taking away the overheads and labour, things got more difficult.

Things were going downhill. We were not making a lot of money so we sold off bits of land. Opposite the Post Office there was a pit, known as the Pound, which was filled in with rubble from Brunswick Hospital, knocked down to make

The Post Office, with' The Close' visible on the right. c1920

way for new buildings at the 'old' Norfolk and Norwich Hospital. The Council dumped other rubbish there, and village people started getting unhappy about it. Then it was filled in properly, and houses were built on that later on. So we sold that off.

We also sold land to our neighbour, Ken Smith, who lived at Colney. So we were selling off to keep going really, as the prices went up, not like when we sold the Manor House in about 1965 for £8,000 when father retired. You see, no local farmer was doing very well. The farms were getting bigger and bigger; that was the trend; to go to farming thousands of acres all around.

We kept ourselves viable through the 70s and 80s, and then I retired and my brother kept going on his own for a couple of years, paying me rent for my half. Then we decided to get rid of it, and invest the money. The village was still growing. It had been growing and growing ever since the 1940s. The Mill Road Council houses were built at the end of the war, about 1945-46, and the old 'Armes cottages on Burnthouse Lane were condemned and knocked down. We carted them into yards in the farmyard. There's been a lot of building recently, of course.

The big thing with farming is that it's a long-term process. I mean you know you're drilling the corn, but you're going to be twelve months before you get it in and get paid for it, and anything can happen during that time. We did fairly well out of the European Community with the cheap food policy, originally anyway, but it gradually petered out. There was a subsidy, and a lot of people couldn't have done without. But it was altogether wrong wasn't it? You'd get mountains of this and mountains of that, and it wasn't a good idea. Too much red tape and everything else.

In some ways I'm sad that my children didn't go into farming. I have tried to take my family history back, and I got to about 1800. They were farm labourers. My grandfather moved up to Yorkshire where he met my grandmother. He was working as a sort of general dogsbody and she was working in service I suppose. They were married at 19. They had their children and moved back here to a smallholding at Lakenham. That's how you started out, with one or two acres. You always had a few cows and pigs and poultry, but things have changed of course."

The late Noel 'Donny' Wilkins, formerly of Valley Farm, prepares straw for thatching the hayrick watched by his dog Candy. C.1960

Alice Plummer helping with the 'Steam' Threshing at Elm Farm c.1940

The Farmer will never be happy again;
He carries his heart in his boots;
For either the rain is destroying his grain
Or the drought is destroying his roots.
                                        A. P. Herbert

Did you know that ...

   ...Home Farm with its 9 acres, east of Braymeadow Lane, (a large house now known as 64 School Lane) **once played host to an abandoned baby?** Joseph Carter lived here for forty years from about 1872 till his burial in Little Melton churchyard in 1913. His wife was a Yorkshire woman named Eliza and together they raised a large family, their numerous sons obtaining eminent positions in the police force and legal profession. One day they were presented with yet another baby, found abandoned on their doorstep. His origins were unknown, (though his name was said to be Grey), and he had a definite gipsy cast of features. Whoever left him there had chosen well, knowing, perhaps instinctively, that these parents would not discard a baby. Joseph and Eliza decided that one more mouth to feed would not make much difference, and reared the lad as one of their own, until eventually, he too joined the police force.

   ...In 1538 King Henry VIII 'swapped' Little Melton for the manor of Codington near Cheam in Surrey, so that he could build a sumptuous palace there? Letters patent were issued to Sir Richard Codington enabling Henry to acquire Codington and achieve his dream of building a grand palace in Surrey to rival Fontainebleau in France, and show all the other great European monarchs of the time that he was in the same league as them. He engaged craftsmen who were familiar with Florentine-style architecture and furnishings, intending the palace to be the place where his sixth wife Katharine Parr could bring up Edward, his long-awaited son and heir, who had been made motherless by the death of Queen Jane Seymour. It was said to have everything to make the young prince happy and contented. The palace was called Nonsuch! Sadly, it was demolished in 1682, so we can have no idea just how it compared to the French château other than from surviving drawings.

...In the 1850s the Barn beside the road at Grey Cottage was also said to be used for worship? At this time it was whitewashed and had an altar installed. There has never been an 'official' Nonconformist Chapel in the village, but many farm workers were Freechurchmen, who would have welcomed the opportunity to worship locally. Chapels were built at both Bawburgh and Hethersett, but this entailed a long walk for families with young children.

Grey Cottage Barn (right) c2000

..The 4th (Queen's Own) Hussars held a Point-to-Point race at 3 pm on April 13th 1885 in the Meltons, 'to be ridden in Full Hunting Costume, over about four miles of fair hunting country'? The race started just north of High House, Great Melton, continuing in line with the Turnpike (today's B1108) before turning south at right angles, to follow the boundary between Great and Little Melton, then north past Wong Farm, ending up near the two churches at Great Melton. Seventeen horses were entered for the race, though three didn't run. The winner was 'Norwood' owned and ridden by Mr. Starkey, 'Chance' was in second place, owned by Mr Kincaid-Smith and ridden by Captain Follett, while 'Peter' was third, owned and ridden by Captain Wilson-Todd. Mr Dewhurst's 'Mickey' fell in Mr. Lack's meadow (at Church Farm, Little Melton) and a cup worth £50 was presented by Lieut. Colonel G. Philips to the winner, amidst great approbation.

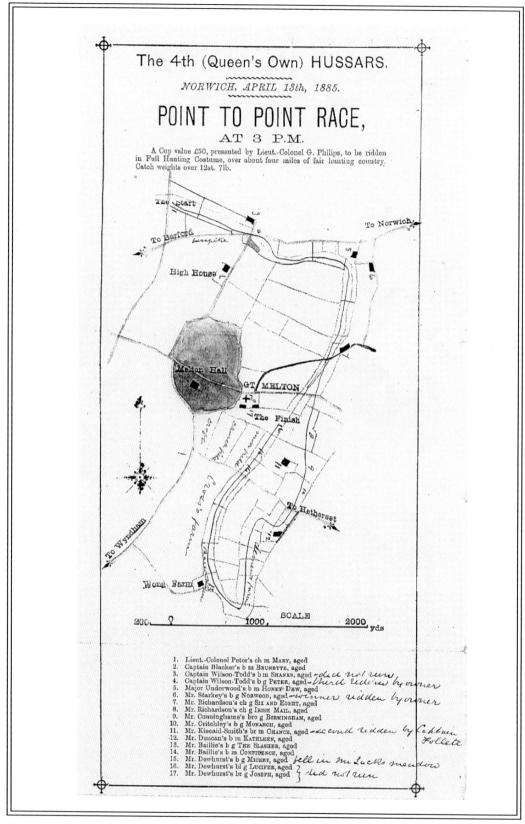

The 4th (Queen's Own) HUSSARS.

NORWICH, APRIL 13th, 1885.

POINT TO POINT RACE,

AT 3 P.M.

A Cup value £50, presented by Lieut.-Colonel G. Philips, to be ridden
in Full Hunting Costume, over about four miles of fair hunting country.
Catch weights over 12st. 7lb.

1. Lieut.-Colonel Peter's ch m MARY, aged
2. Captain Blacker's b m BRUNETTE, aged
3. Captain Wilson-Todd's b m SHANKS, aged *did not run*
4. Captain Wilson-Todd's b g PETER, aged *third ridden by owner*
5. Major Underwood's b m HONEY DEW, aged
6. Mr. Starkey's b g NORWOOD, aged *winner ridden by owner*
7. Mr. Richardson's ch g SIX AND EIGHT, aged
8. Mr. Richardson's ch g IRISH MAIL, aged
9. Mr. Cunninghame's bro g BIRMINGHAM, aged
10. Mr. Critchley's b g MONARCH, aged
11. Mr. Kincaid-Smith's br m CHANCE, aged *second ridden by Cahburn Follett*
12. Mr. Duncan's b m KATHLEEN, aged
13. Mr. Baillie's b g THE SLASHER, aged
14. Mr. Baillie's b m CONFIDENCE, aged
15. Mr. Dewhurst's b g MICKEY, aged *fell in Mr Lucks meadow*
16. Mr. Dewhurst's bl g LUCIFER, aged
17. Mr. Dewhurst's br g JOSEPH, aged *did not run*

Chapter Five

Schooling in Little Melton

Girls scream Boys shout;
Dogs bark School's out.
                    W. H. Davies

The important part Little Melton School plays in the life of our community today is very well recognised and appreciated, but what is not so well known is that it is following in a tradition that may well have started here nearly three hundred years ago, when the first teacher we know of was appointed for this village. For a long period, any person who wanted to take up either the profession of teaching, or of ministry in the Anglican Church, or of medicine, was required by law to declare his allegiance to the Church of England and to the sovereign, before being entrusted with the care of *'the mind, body and soul'* of pupils, parishioners or patients. This declaration of faith in the teaching of the Established Church and loyalty to the Crown was known as "subscribing', and a record of many who signed the appropriate documents can be found in the Subscription Books of the Diocese of Norwich which still survive for the years between 1637 and 1800. In return, all who signed, providing they were suitably qualified, were granted a licence to follow their profession. This system was finally abolished in 1869, but it is from these books that we find details of where these early professional people practised their skills.

There was no overall system of education in the 17th, 18th and early 19th centuries, but where schools existed, they were mainly of two types, 'Grammar' schools, based on the teaching of Latin and Greek, (essential for university entrance), and 'English' schools, where pupils were taught the 'Three Rs', reading, writing and arithmetic. Teaching was not necessarily given in school buildings, as we know them now, for classes were often held in the teacher's own home, or alternatively in the Parson's study in a Rectory or Vicarage, offering education to children whose family circumstances would probably not otherwise have permitted them the 'luxury' of schooling. Many leading figures, however, felt that education should be designed around a person's 'standing' in life, often holding the belief that 'too much learning' would make the poor dissatisfied and unfit for laborious employment – a feeling that persisted well into the 19th century. Examination of the Norwich Subscription Books shows a rather uneven distribution of towns and villages in Norfolk who had licensed teachers, but though illiteracy was the norm, many children living in the more heavily populated parts of Norfolk, whose families wished them to receive some form of schooling, probably had a teacher within reach, on foot or on horseback, even before 1700.

The first record of a teacher being appointed for Little Melton is in 1710, when a Mister Philip Low received a licence from the Bishop of Norwich to teach reading, writing and arithmetic. It is unlikely that Mr Low had a university degree or was conversant in Latin or Greek. He did not need to be to teach the 'Three Rs', but he would have had to produce references to prove his competency to teach, and his moral fitness to do so, before he could be recommended for a licence. Finally he would have had to declare, on oath, his belief in the tenets of the Church and his loyalty to Queen Anne, before he was granted a licence, his 'school' being very probably the cottage in which he lived.

By the early 19th century, however, the provision of education had begun to be regarded as an important priority by many individuals and groups, and not just for the better-off members of the population. Two societies, the British and Foreign Schools Society, founded in 1808 by the Nonconformists, and the National Schools Society, founded three years later by the Anglicans, had built more than 18,000 schools throughout the country by the middle of the century, their main aim being to instruct the young in the principles of religion. In Great Melton, for example, a National School for 66 boys and girls was erected in 1852, at the sole expense of the then lord of the manor, Mr. Charles Lombe.

Little Melton School, early 1900s

Unfortunately it has not been possible to find any more records that tell us about schooling in our village until the middle of the 19th century. We don't even know if schools continued in existence in the intervening hundred and forty years or so after Mr Low received his licence to teach. 'White's Directories of Norfolk' published in 1836 and 1845 make no mention of a school for a population that by then was over 300. However, the 1842 Tithe Award Map shows *'school house and gardens on Hethersett Lane'*, (now known as Burnthouse Lane), on land not built on at the time of the Enclosure of the village in 1817.

The 1851 Census includes details of a Miss Sophia Anna Jane Long, aged 22, daughter of James Long, a house and land proprietor of the village, and his wife Harriet, and describes her rather grandly as *'governess of a school'*. This may or may not have been a room in their house here. The next edition of 'White's Directory' in 1854 does mention a school in the village, with the information that it was *'a parochial school supported by subscription'* and that the teachers were Charles and Mary Child. We are reasonably certain that this school was again a 'dame school' with classes being held in the Childs' house in what is now called Burnthouse Lane.

The recent discovery of an earthenware inkwell on the site seems to add authenticity to the story, and older residents of Little Melton still remember a house, said to have been the old school, (demolished in the early 1960s), which contained a particularly large room. The 1861 Census reveals the presence of a teacher named Mary Goward, aged 20, living in the village with her parents John and Mary and brother James. Both men are described as agricultural labourers, but again we do not know if Mary taught in the village or elsewhere. By 1868 it was a Miss Robertson who was running *'a village school for boys and girls'* according to Harrod's Directory.

Two years later an Act of Parliament, Forster's Education Act, made provision for compulsory education for all children between the ages of 5 and 13, and schools and schooling started to assume the format with which we are familiar today. The act made large sums of money available for the building of school premises and set up boards of governors, elected from the local community, to run them. In 1874 a substantial brick-built school was constructed alongside the road connecting the two villages of Colney and Little Melton, on the parish boundary of the two, ever since known as 'School Lane'. It was built to accommodate eighty pupils from the two villages and built at the enormous cost, (in those days), of £750. It included living quarters for the schoolmistress and for *'a maid to wait on her'*. Many of the children who attended had fathers who worked as agricultural labourers on the Colney Hall estate, and had to walk the mile or so to and from school in all weathers.

'The Little Melton and Colney Board School', was officially opened on 6th September 1875, after Miss Alice Maud Mary Boughey was appointed first

18th century child's writing exercise sheet

mistress at a salary of £60 per annum, and Rev. John Hervey Payne, Rector of Colney, became Clerk to the Board of Governors. Miss Boughey's maid was to live rent-free and be subject to a quarter's notice to leave her position.

On the day of opening, twenty-two boys and twenty-seven girls were enrolled, and the following day nine more children attended. By 13th September there were sixty-eight pupils in all on the books, but the problem was getting them to class, and keeping them there, especially in the winter months. Sometimes the snow proved too deep for the children to get through, especially if their boots and coats were inadequate for the conditions, and there was a lot of sickness too. In, 1878, for instance, an outbreak of smallpox closed the school for three whole weeks. Epidemics of what are now considered to be minor diseases, but which were life-threatening then, before immunisation was introduced, regularly caused the school to close. Whooping cough caused numbers to fall so low from October 1888 onwards that the school had to be shut, and was only reopened after the Christmas holiday that year. Children were often kept away to help their parents, or in summertime to help with the harvest, or to take food out to the fields, where their fathers were working long hours. The few pence a week that children could earn by scaring birds in spring, gathering nuts for the pigs in autumn, or helping with harvest was an important supplement to the family income.

By March 1876 the number of children enrolled was 79, and the schools' inspector recommended that more staff should be employed. Fortunately a 16-year-old pupil teacher, a Miss A. Milk of Stanfield, was appointed in 1877, for soon afterwards Miss Boughey had 96 children on the register! Miss Boughey was to remain at the school for a further ten years, and to depart suddenly in February 1887, whereupon Miss Fryer was promptly appointed headteacher. 1887 also saw the arrival of new tenants at Colney Hall as Hugh Gurney Barclay (of the Norwich banking family), his wife Evelyn and children took up residence there. Like the Scott family before them, they took an immediate interest in the school where so many of the children of their labourers were being educated. The school flourished! HM Inspector of Schools Report of 1899 described the discipline as *'excellent'* and the instruction as *'careful and intelligent'*. By this time Miss Kate Hall was headmistress and the Punishment Books of her regime can still be seen at the school. The usual punishment, inflicted by Miss Hall herself, was either one or two strokes of the cane on the back of the hand, depending on the seriousness of the offence. The same names constantly recur. Little Eva Bowman, aged 9, was seemingly always in trouble in 1900, and received no fewer than five canings between September and Christmas for mistakes in her knitting, or for blotting her copybook, (yes, literally)! On another occasion Eva and her sister, Ada, also 9, (were they the *'Terrible Twins'*?) were punished for playing in the road and arriving in school a quarter of an hour late. And what did Miss Hall do, two years later, when another little Bowman girl, Winifred, appeared on the scene? She caned her for *"copying incorrectly'*. Miss Hall must have been very relieved when these children left the school for one in Norwich. Other punishable offences were playing with the ink, copying off other pupils, disobedience, kicking, fighting, climbing over the school wall in playtime and stealing turnips from the adjoining field. Very occasionally, indecent language was cited. Sometimes children arrived at school so hungry that the packed lunches brought by fellow pupils proved too much of a temptation, and were rifled. This led to canings on three occasions for one young pupil. By 1914 a rebellious young lady named Nellie Woods had become the bane of Miss Hall's life, on many occasions receiving as many as six strokes of the cane for such offences as spoiling her needlework, hitting her sister and playing with the ink. Nellie must have left before 1916 as in that year there were only three entries for the whole year, and none of them concerned Nellie! The admission register for the years 1884 to 1934 also survives and records the names of all the pupils, years of attending school and the date and reason for leaving. In the early years a very

Little Melton & Colney school outing to Colney Hall in the 1920s for Sports in the Park & Tea in the Coach house.
The adults standing to the rear, are thought to be, left to right; Miss Wilson, teacher; Miss Cobett, infant class teacher; Tom Crane, Mr. Barclay's chauffeur; The Rev. Priestland, Vicar of Colney; Rosamund Barclay, daughter of Mr. Barclay; tiny Miss Young; anon; Mrs. Kinch (part obscured by door) head teacher; and finally, Mr. Barclay

common reason was that they were wanted at home, but many children are recorded as leaving the district. This figure tends to be balanced by families coming into the area. In 1901 two children were withdrawn from school as their families were emigrating to Canada. Sadly, every so often, the death of a pupil is noted, a seven-year-old in 1895, an eight-year-old in 1896 and a ten-year-old in 1898.

By late 1877, 103 children were enrolled, (24 in the Infants Class and nearly 80 in the six standards covering the 7 to 13-year-olds). The school, originally built for children from Little Melton and Colney, was accepting pupils from Cringleford, Hethersett and Earlham by 1900. It was already bursting at the seams, and had been almost from opening. The need for expansion was obvious. Mr George Gleadhill, researching for an article he wrote on the early years of the school's existence, examined the parish registers of Little Melton for the years 1837 to 1875. These showed that, of the 85 couples who were married during that time, 39 men and 28 women were unable to sign their names in the register. Some families however found it impossible to pay the fee that was demanded by the new Board Schools for their children's education, or were unwilling to do so. The fees had been decided upon by the Board at its meeting on the 3rd September 1875, and were 4d. per week for the eldest child, and then 2d. for all the other children in the family, if the parents were rated at £10 per annum or more. If the parents were rated at less than £10, the charges were 2d. and 1d. respectively. No child under the age of four was admitted to the school. The attendance record was very important in the school's early years as it was used, together with the results of tests done by all the pupils, (except the under six-year-olds), to assess the level of the Norfolk County Council grant to the school. Failure by any child to pass the annual test in any one of the three basic subjects meant the loss of 2s. 8d. per year from the school's grant for that child! The maximum grant that could be obtained was 12s. per head per year for the older children and 6s. 6d. per head for the infants.

The curriculum also included geography, scripture, (regarded as very important), and needlework for the girls. Copying and dictation were also highly thought of. The infants wrote on slates that broke if dropped too often. Arithmetic consisted of addition, subtraction, division and multiplication, and it was arithmetic that the school inspectors reported as giving most trouble to the children. On the whole, however, the school got good reports in its early years. Learning was very much by rote with one qualified teacher, (sometimes a pupil teacher), and monitors, (older pupils considered bright enough to pass their acquired learning on to the younger children), doing the teaching. As state education established itself, the curriculum broadened, and so-called 'object lessons' and natural history were added. 'Object lessons' involved looking at everyday things in the home, the countryside and around the world, and included such different subjects as 'iron foundries' and 'monkeys'.

In 1902 School Boards ceased to exist, as Balfour's Education Act now gave local authorities the responsibility for running the education service in their own areas. In 1904 the newly created Norfolk Education Committee started to appoint its own school managers, who took over the running of the school, and in so doing, they abolished the old style grants, which had been, in effect, a system of 'payment by results'. The school curriculum noticeably broadened still further, and School Attendance Officers were appointed to check on absent pupils. Miss Hall would not accept any but genuine reasons for staying away, and the Attendance Man was promptly alerted about missing pupils. The children referred to him as 'The Kid-hunter', but no doubt the threat of his appearance was enough to scare the life out of them! Proposed teaching schemes had to be submitted in great detail for approval by the school inspectors. 'Object lessons' continued and again show great diversity! Between 1904 and 1907 they included, 'Public Baths and Washhouses', 'Flannelette', 'Tapioca', 'The Rainbow', 'Lighthouses and Lightships' and 'How to set a Tea-Table'. The Geography timetable included 'Latitude and Longitude', 'Cardinal Points', "Volcanoes', 'Arctic *animals'* and on 8th May 1906, *'The Earthquake of San Francisco.'* The natural environment was seldom used, but in June 1904 Miss Carpenter is reported as having taken the Lower Division into a hayfield to give them a lesson on *'Hay'*. It did seem to the children, though, that every odd unfilled moment had a scripture lesson inserted, Miss Hall being *'very religious'* and every school session, morning and afternoon, started and ended with prayers. A (non-corporal) punishment of this time was to be kept in at playtime, morning and afternoon, to write in their best longhand writing, *'Satan finds more mischief still for idle hands to do'*. However things seemed to relax a little on Friday afternoons, and as a welcome relief from the 'Three Rs' and scripture, the boys had drawing and modeling in Plasticine, and the girls had sewing or embroidery. Older girls were taken to Hethersett for cookery lessons, going by horse and cart and walking home afterwards, and by 1907 arrangements had been made for the older boys to be instructed in handicrafts at Bawburgh. In spite of the increasing range of subjects being taught, the Inspectors' Report of 1910 was critical of the teaching methods used for the older children, which left them seeming dull, compared to the bright infants who enjoyed *'learning by doing'*, and judged that the excessive use of *'learning by rote'* did not provide enough stimulus with which to fire their imaginations. Many pupils must have longed for the day when they could leave and start work, but the fixing of the school-leaving age at 14 in 1918 ensured that they could not leave before then. In 1921 Miss Hall's long reign as head teacher came to an end, and Mrs

10,656 The Schools, Little Melton.

Little Melton School 1930s

Gertrude Elizabeth Kinch was appointed head, and several of the more senior residents of Little Melton still recall her 21 years there. Mrs Kinch's husband was the village milkman, and her daughter Marie was one of her pupils. She remembered her mother as being very strict, with absolutely no relaxation of the rules towards her own daughter, (quite the reverse in fact!). No doubt the young lad who took mice into school and put them in Mrs Kinch's desk to get his own back was punished accordingly, but the cane was now only used when children were exceptionally naughty. By the 1920s there were two other teachers at the school beside Mrs Kinch. Miss Cobbett taught the infants and cycled out from Norwich in all weathers. Miss Wilson, who taught the next age group, lived at White Rails Farm at Great Melton. She also cycled, and one (now elderly) gentleman recalls how he used to run behind her bicycle when he went to see his grandparents on Great Melton Road. Mrs Kinch taught the senior children and also conducted the daily PT session in the gravel playground. An earlier generation had been instructed in 'drilling' on Army lines, as specified by the Board of Education, by a Sgt. Collins of Ketteringham, who had been paid 2s. 6d. per lesson by the School Board. All the teaching of the older children was done in one big room, while the infants had their own room. After assembly, with its prayers and calling of the register, a big curtain was drawn across the room and lessons commenced. As in the days of Philip Low, great emphasis was placed on reading, writing and arithmetic, but history and geography had now become equally important. Mrs Kinch took the English classes herself, and was very keen on getting her pupils to speak good English. There was very little emphasis on Science but Marie recalled the Education Committee running a *'Tree and Bird'* competition, perhaps to foster more interest in natural history. In cold weather a big coal fire with a huge black fireguard was lit by the school caretaker. There was no piped water, so water was drawn from the well, and the lavatories were outside and non-flush, of course. No doubt the children were glad to get back into the warm(er) classroom and did not dawdle too long outside in the winter months. The children sat in groups of three, on forms with desks attached, and with inkwells sunk in the top right hand corners of each section. At lunchtime, most of them went home for their meal, while the rest, who lived too far away, (at the far end of Little Melton or in Colney), had their sandwiches in the school. The children's health was monitored regularly by the school medical service, and the school dentist came for two days at a time in a mule-drawn caravan with Billy Briggs driving. Teeth were inspected on the first of the two days, and treatment, if required, was carried out on the second day with a parent present. The *'nit nurse'* also made regular inspections!

The Barclay family at Colney Hall continued to show their interest in the school, and every so often the children were invited to have a summer picnic in the grounds, and to walk down to the River Yare which flowed through water meadows there. The Hall itself was usually out-of-bounds. The children were also given treats at Harvest and Christmastime with tree presents for everyone, and *'plenty to eat'*, as recalled by one ex-pupil appreciatively. Mr. H. G. Barclay and his tenant farmers also offered jobs to all the school-leavers each year. At one time two lions had been kept at the Hall but a terrible accident had occurred in 1911. The eldest son of the family, Terence, (a lieutenant in the Scots Guards who had survived active service in the Boer War), was clawed in the neck and died of septicaemia. After this, the lions were sent away to a zoo in Dublin.

September 1939 was to see the start of the Second World War, and when school opened for the Autumn Term, there were 61 local children and 11 evacuees. One of the wartime pupils recalls that the evacuees were often late for school, but never seemed to get into trouble, which did not seem right to the rest of the class. The following April all the pupils were fitted with gas masks, and in January 1941 the first immunisations against diphtheria were given to the children.

Three years later in September 1942, the Managers' Minute Book of Little Melton Provided School, (as it was now called), records the sad death of Mrs Kinch and the appointment of her successor, Mrs Barbara Buckton of the School House at Baconsthorpe, who was to take up her new post in March 1943. Only just a little over two months later Mrs Buckton and her son, David, were returning to the Schoolhouse from the air raid shelter, at the end of a raid on Norwich, when the School received a direct hit from a stray German bomb. This damaged the whole building beyond repair. David was injured and carried by his mother to the nearest house to summon help. Fortunately his injuries were not too serious, and he and his mother were given temporary accommodation by Mrs Dorothy Broughton, and later by Rev. Frost, until they could be found a more permanent home. School, meanwhile, managed to continue, despite the difficult circumstances. Some pupils were taught in a room at the Rose and Crown Public House, (now the Village Inn), while others were sent to Bawburgh, Hethersett, Cringleford and Great Melton schools. Later, some months after the bombing, a temporary prefabricated school was erected on the site of the bombed school. This 'temporary' school lasted for over thirty years until the present school was officially opened in the mid-1970s.

It would probably have lasted a great deal longer, had it not been for the persistence of the then head, George Gleadhill! After combing through the Statute Books, he was able to find post-war legislation that provided for the rebuilding of all public buildings destroyed by enemy action, Little Melton School having the dubious honour of being the only school in Norfolk to be destroyed in this way. Very few children from Colney were now on the school roll, so a central site on a former orchard next to the Rose and Crown in Little Melton was chosen for the erection of the new building, and just under 100 years after the opening of the old Victorian

The 'Pre-fab' temporary School built on the site of the 'Bombed' school, demolished in the late 1970s

school, the new one came into use, again substantially built of brick. In March 1972 "The Eastern Daily Press" reported that Norfolk Education Committee had allocated £36,400 to build the school and work commenced in May 1973. The 'prefab' closed for half-term on 23rd May 1974, and school opened in the new premises on 3rd June 1974, with 81 pupils in four classrooms.

It was a great relief for teachers and children to get away from the privations of the prefab. school, where, initially, pupils ranging in age from 5 to 11 years had had to be crowded into two classrooms. Later, a mobile classroom had been added to make a third teaching area, but there had been no separate dining facilities, and every lunchtime all the desks had to be cleared of books and papers to double up as dining tables. The temporary school had tortoise stoves in the corners, and pupils any distance from them felt no benefit at all, and the tin roof made it a very noisy building in heavy rain! For a few years after the school moved out, this building enjoyed a new lease of life as Little Melton Village Hall, before a new building superseded it too, the present purpose-built one on Mill Road. In 1990 the prefabricated building was demolished and two houses built on the site, leaving little evidence of the century of dedicated teaching that had gone on there, nor of that terrible night when German bombs destroyed the old Victorian building.

At the time the present school was opened, the curriculum was very much the responsibility of the Head Teacher, though approval had to be obtained from the appropriate county council advisors in each subject, before teaching could be put into practice. Very high standards were achieved, and one year the school received the highest percentage pass rate for any school in Norfolk in the 11+ examination, which determined which pupils were selected for Grammar Schools. Every year, the school regularly sent eight or more pupils to Wymondham College, the local Grammar School. By now the staff had expanded to comprise the head, four teachers, the school secretary and welfare assistant, with help also coming from parents and other members of the local community. The school roll at times was approaching one hundred and twenty pupils aged from four to eleven. Talks from the local policeman, from farmers' wives and fire service personnel, and visits to farms were now used to introduce children to the life and work of their community. The reputation of the school attracted visiting groups of teachers from as far afield as Japan, Norway, Russia and Yugoslavia. By now the cane had been replaced by a fictitious slipper, which fortunately never actually needed to be used! At Christmas Santa arrived on a tractor belonging to the Chairman of Governors, and brought an individually wrapped and named present for every child. It was a far cry from the start of the century when the Barclay family had, in some years, given lace-up boots to every child in the school and, other years waterproofs, because their parents could not afford such necessities of life.

Little Melton First School c.2002

In the mid-1960s, the population of Little Melton began to rise rapidly, following the erection of much new housing, and the village seemed to be alive with children. The school had been designed for 75 pupils in 1973, but had 97 on the register by 1978! In line with changes that were taking place in the education system in Norfolk and elsewhere, a decision was made to take pupils only between the ages of 4 and 8, at which age they would transfer to the Hethersett County Middle School. In this way, in 1979, the Little Melton County First School came into existence, with Mr Geoffrey Hill as head. This change in the system was to lead to such a big drop in the number of pupils that by 1981 there were serious worries that the school might have to be closed, as there were only 48 children attending. House-building continued, however, bringing many families with young children into the village, so fortunately numbers began to rise steadily, putting an end to all talk of possible closure. In 1991 Mr Hill retired, and the present head, Mrs Anne Clements, was promoted from Acting Head to Head teacher.

****

Sadly, Mrs Barbara Buckton – Headmistress at Little Melton School 1943-1944 - died in the year 2000. Fortunately for us, however, she had previously reminisced about her time here, and this is a digest of what she said:

"I went for the interview in December 1942, and was asked some peculiar questions. They wanted to know why I was leaving, if I was as good as my testimonial, and if I was likely to marry again? I said I'd let the managers know before I put the banns up! Then they asked what my religious attitude was, and whether I would fit in with the villagers, as my accent was not Norfolk dialect. I was accepted, and began on March 1st 1943. There were two members of staff and I was stunned by the English that one of them spoke. She said "come you here, sit you down, bring you that book", and I had to find out what it was all about.

There was an outside toilet, and the water had to be pumped and brought in. The caretaker was very friendly, and the infant teacher had been here all her teaching life. I found the building solid, with nice oak windows. We had all the Colney children and the outlying country families. In those days the men were in the forces and the women were working on munitions. The older boys all seemed to have jobs, and there were no professional families here. I think Colney Estate people felt a little superior to our village people. There were no school meals. The children just sat around, so I used the picnic idea, pushed the desks together and put a cover on them.

On Friday afternoons I let the children have some freedom from playtime onwards. They could choose what they wanted to do, provided they brought the materials. It could be Snakes and Ladders, or a pack of cards, or a bit of knitting.

It also gave the teachers time to write up next week's scheme of work. We began to sort the school garden into plots for the boys. The needlework was for the girls, although to their great hilarity, I taught the boys to knit. They made squares for quilts for the sick and elderly and the troops. To everyone's surprise, I went round and asked permission for us to look at the farms and Braymeadow Gardens, which were producing cabbages and potatoes for the war effort. We went down there, and also got to Colney Woods where we collected samples, and started a Nature Table. We visited the Church too, and wrote up little bits of history of the village itself.

We had an Open Day at the end of term, so that the parents would know what newfangled ideas I was bringing in, and found that my North Country English was stunning them as much as their Norfolk was stunning me. The gas masks had to be checked daily. There was a drill whenever the siren sounded, and on May 4th 1943 a bomb hit the school and demolished both it and the house. By daylight, the Hethersett Headmaster and a Norfolk County Education Committee member were up on the premises to see what had happened, and what help could be given.

By mid-morning the HMI from County Office and the Architects and Mr Nash and the Managers were all here, and we had to make a list of the damage for the Education Office. By some miracle the beams from the big roof had fallen across the building, and not much of the furniture had been damaged. They protected a lot of the desks and chairs, though the school clock was demolished. Later, the Rector, the Rev. Thomas Frost, (who was very good at mechanics), collected the clock and took it away and mended it. Before this, neither the school nor house had any timepiece at all, so this was very useful.

Many of the children turned up at school the next day, because most of them didn't know a bomb had fallen, and with supervision we got a lot of the books out into the yard. Then parents came, and with their help we got the furniture out. Mr. Clarke, in the farm opposite, let us put it into the barn, with my house furniture as well, and later he let us use his field as a playground, and I'm sure he was never paid anything. It was a marvellous thing to do. We could use the Parish Room, and the Gospel Hall and the back rooms of the pub, which Mrs. Loomb let us have for the children, and in a very short space of time we got back into working order. The facilities were limited, but we managed somehow. We met together for lunch, but no extra stock was made available. I said "Thank God it was three o'clock in the morning, and not three o'clock in the afternoon when the bomb dropped" and this was misinterpreted, because one of the managers thought I was thinking "Thank God it had been bombed". But of course I wasn't, I simply meant that we might have had 72 children to carry out. The logbook and the registers and all the official documents were among the debris, but I packed them into a drawer and put them in the Church Vestry, and nobody interfered with them. The Church was brought more into the village by being used. The reconstruction of the school went on slowly, and as I'd had enough of the living conditions, I regretfully left after a year. I needed the security of a house for the future."

Miss Brant, Head teacher, Little Melton School, (1948-1966) and Miss Gallan, her Assistant, and Head teacher (1950 and 1966) were also kind enough to tell us about their time here:

"The school building itself was very primitive, but I had a classroom to myself for the first time in my career. The heating was an old tortoise stove, which more often than not had just been lit, and the room was full of smoke. There were no taps in the porch, so when we wanted water, we had to walk across the playground with buckets and do the old pump. The water laid on was cold, and the kitchen people had to use the pump before they could start their cooking. The playground itself was gravel, not tarmac, and we had outside toilets of course. The floors had lino, with holes in places, and the porch was very dusty. It was very damp in one corner, and the lino made things very noisy with the moving of desks and chairs. Miss Shaw (from County Office) provided us with tins of paint, and we ourselves painted the infant chairs, using different colours for different age groups.

The children and the parents were very friendly. The infant room had up to 33 pupils, and we usually had about 25 children. The first improvement we made was, of course, the floor. We had tarmac in the playground and then tiles in the hall. The cleaner, Mr. Bishop, used to say "I'll see you out Miss". He was 80, and he was still going strong when we left. He was a marvellous old man, and used to come down quite early, so the children always had good fires when they got there. And then one bad winter, ('53 was it?), Mr Buxton came along and said "I've been allocated 6 heaters – you've never moaned - you can have one of these." So we had heating in the porch. But everyone who came in would say the same, that this was a very happy school. We were our natural selves with the children. We didn't treat them in the infant room like babies, we talked ever so naturally to each other. There was a temperamentally difficult girl, but at her best she was great, and she used to put into practice what we learned in the Religious Instruction lessons. We'd been having the Good Samaritan, which was always popular with the children, and when they had their free activities, they used to chatter as they worked. She would say "Oh go on, do that for her – be a Good Samaritan". And the same girl did something I shall never forget.

Of course, we had no staff room, no secretarial help, and so on Mondays we had to do the dinner money and the saving stamps as well as registration, and

Little Melton School Photograph c.1953

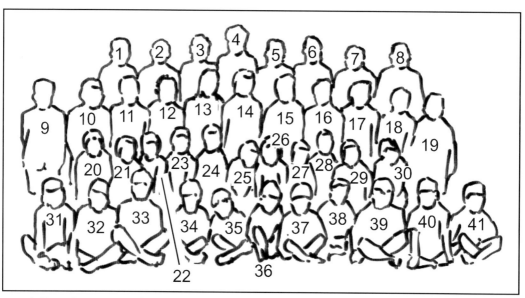

1, Peter Herwin; 2, Philip Broughton; 3, David Buck; 4, David Joy; 5, David Goulding;
6, Bernard Dack; 7, Victor 'Pip' Moore; 8, Trevor Jones; 9, Russell Norton;
10, Myrtle Harrison; 11, Diane Matthews; 12, Veronica Joy; 13, Penelope Eagle;
14, Caroline Mace ; 15, Christine Eastwick ; 16, Marion Denton; 17, Wendy Glister;
18, ?; 19, Barry Chamberlain; 20, ?; 21, M. Mallet ; 22, ?; 23, Jennifer Glister; 24, ?;
25, Eileen Dack; 26, ?; 27, ?; 28, ?; 29, ?; 30, Maggie Broughton; 31, Ray Goulding ; 32,
Dennis Moore; 33, ?; 34, ? Bailey ; 35, ? Daniels ; 36, ?; 37, Christopher Mace; 38, ?;
39, James Chamberlain ; 40, Eddie Dack ; 41, ?.

it was a little hectic. At lunchtime, one of the Juniors would go up to the Post Office for the stamps, and one Monday afternoon, Miss Brant came in to ask me something important, and I went back to the stamps I had been working on, and they'd gone. We looked everywhere. This same child said "Let's have a little prayer about it", and we did, and Miss Brant came in, and said "I'm sorry, when I picked up your book I must have picked up your stamps".

We used to have such fun at Christmas time, with concerts based on the work of the school year, singing, and a nativity play. We had no stage or curtains, and after the war we were still under the coupon business. We brought sheets from home, and all the mothers came and sat on the little tiny chairs, and we really did have a whale of a time, and they all loved it. One of the managers at Colney came along and said they loved it too.

We used to go on the road to practise for sports. We had a little whistle as soon as a car appeared, and the children would go to the side immediately. It was good fun. We were in a group of small schools that were all centred on Wymondham Secondary Modern. We used to go there for Music and Country Dance Festivals and for our sports. I remember when I first went into the infants room, my impression was of orderly rows of desks and I thought I must change this. I wanted the whole thing to be a little more matey, and I put the desks together in little groups, with four chairs facing each other. This created a much more friendly atmosphere.

As regards the actual teaching, we were free. Nothing was laid down, and in the afternoons I introduced a reading corner. Simple art and craft was going on, and there were games, so children could choose what they wanted to do and move from group to group. We made sure they did a mixture of things. There was powder paint and paper, and often we used to buy up kitchen paper from our own pockets so we could continue freely. The capital allowance didn't cover all the paint, so Bayliss and Wright found me a good customer! We had to cope with lots of different things, the medical inspection, for instance, was all in one room, with three to a desk, and on the day that the cheque came we had to go into the city to cash it. The library van came regularly, and we used to choose books for the little ones and the adults, before school for the children and after school for the grown-ups. We took over from Mr. Gibbs, Philip Broughton's grandad. He used to have the library on Saturdays.

The parents were mostly farm labourers, and a few commuters. We didn't obtain a high standard, the potential wasn't there, but it was a very happy school, and the children really enjoyed what we did. We weren't free as regards English or Arithmetic. We had music and movement, using the BBC pamphlets, and latterly we had school dinners, when the classroom became the lunch room. The tables were very heavy and we had oil cloth tablecloths. We had the wireless, of course, the radio lessons with the BBC, and we held the morning service in the infant room. We had our hymns and prayers and readings and played some music. The County Library gave us the records, often the children's own choice. We also had films, once a term, and this was a new thing. We used to black out the room in a very Heath Robinson way with large pieces of paper. Later on we had curtains and watched nature films.

Later on, the people in the catchment area began to change, and we started to have children of professors from the UEA too. When the weather was fit, we used to walk up to the village playing fields on Friday afternoons. Mr Nash mentioned about having a field, and a piece adjoining the school was promised as we got near retirement. Later it was occupied by an extra classroom. We had no Parent Teacher Association, but the atmosphere was very good.

We tried to instil into the children respect and thought for other people, and never "I want". If somebody said "I want", Miss Brant would say "I beg your pardon?" We look back on very happy memories."

The current Headmistress, Anne Clements brings us up to date;

There has been a school in Little Melton for over 100 years, but the changes have been significant. The school started as a 'Primary' school in the 19th century but became a 'First' school in the 1970s. The school punishment book which has existed since the school began is a real 'eye-opener' to the present students. Pupils were punished for poor handwriting, untidy sewing and for stealing potatoes. Corporal punishment was a common occurrence, but it is now illegal.

A really big change is that at Little Melton First School today, children take an important role in the running of the school. We have a schools council and the children deal with behaviour problems and make suggestions for improvement within the school, a little different to the idea that children should be seen and not heard.

The present school consists of 72 children ranging in age from 4 to 8 years. There are 3 classes, 4 teachers including the head and 3 learning support assistants. The school has been extended twice to include an administration area and to enlarge a classroom. The children enjoy excellent facilities, consisting of a school pond, a maze, playhouses and a willow tunnel, and the 'friends of the school' are always looking for new ideas to enhance the curriculum and experiences for the children.

Computers are used daily and eventually the hope is that every child will have their own computer in school. By 2004 the ratio will be at least 8:1 though we think Little Melton First School will be ahead of this target.

There are after school clubs, skipping, hockey and music. The school curriculum is very broad and the pupils have lessons in personal, social and health education as well as in numeracy, literacy, geography, history, PE, RE, art, technology etc., and although assemblies still take place, they consist of a much broader approach and often include stories from other religions. A great deal of emphasis is put on children working together and supporting each other.

The children come from Hethersett, Little Melton, Costessey and Norwich, as parents are no longer restricted to their local school. The school tries to link with the community and has an annual May Fair and various social events. Many people from Little Melton offer voluntary help in sharing books, playing numbers games etc.

Another big change over the years has been in the role of the governors. They have much more responsibility than formerly, covering for example, the budget, the buildings and the curriculum as well as staffing. This is all done on a voluntary basis.

In contrast to the school of 100 years ago, parents are always very welcome.

Little Melton First School c.1996

The opening of the School Play Equipment, 1992.
Masterminded by Heather Lenton and Rosie Stanley, fundraising
included proceeds from the Little Melton Light Railway.
The children are being watched over by village historian and long
serving churchwarden, Joe Day.

W'en you see a man in woe,
Walk right up and say 'hullo;
Say 'hullo and 'how d'ye do?
How's the world a usin' you?'

Sam Walter Foss

Did you know that ...

...in 1891 there were no less than nineteen Laundresses working here? This was a major industry in Hethersett too, with dirty linen by the cartload being brought from wealthy Norwich households to be washed, dried, starched and ironed here. What sheer drudgery it must have been, especially on rainy days, but it helped to pay the bills.

...Thomas Anguish, Lord of the Manor of Great Melton, founded Hospitals (or Schools) for poor children by his will of 1617? And that Hospital Farm, Little Melton, was bought with money given by Thomas Wisse in 1702 to support this charity? Thomas Anguish was a wealthy Freeman of the City of Norwich, being a grocer as well as a dealer in silks and textile fabrics, and lived at one time at what is now the Maid's Head Hotel. He was greatly distressed to see the ill-clad and ill-fed children of the poor sleeping at night in Norwich doorways, and left property in Fishergate to be used for *'the*

61 Fishergate Norwich, Thomas Anguish's hospital

keepinge and bringinge up of poore children'.

The boy residents rapidly became known as the Bluebottle Boys because of their distinctive uniform. They wore a short cutaway blue coat with bright brass buttons, adorned with the city coat of arms, a black speckled scarlet waistcoat and a blue cloth on the head, crowned by a flat, round red worsted cap with a blue band and blue woollen top-knot. Thirty years later girls were admitted, first to lodgings in the Blackfriars New Hall and later to a house in Golden Dog Lane, in the Great Garden of the Black Friars. They wore blue gowns, white cross-over stomachers, long gloves, low shoes and black poke bonnets. The schools are no longer in existence, but the charity is still going strong, known today as Anguish's Educational Foundation, and continues to make grants for all sorts of different projects. Children who are residents of Norwich, Costessey, Hellesdon, Catton, Sprowston, Thorpe and Corpusty still benefit from this charity which had its beginnings in the early seventeenth century.

...Ferrets and Pullets don't mix? In the 1950s two families lived in adjoining cottages near the crossways, each with their own orchard. One family bred ferrets for the extermination of rabbits, while the other reared hens for egg laying. Alas! One night the ferrets escaped and had a high old time decapitating all the birds in the chicken run. For many years afterwards the neighbours never spoke a word to each other.

...Little Melton Windmill was erected in 1832, built by Robert Lovett, a miller of Besthorpe? Only its stump now remains. By 1904 it was worked by wind and steam power, but by 1940, in the second world war, its cast iron top works were torn off to help make munitions.

...the payment of Tithe (a tenth of all produce) to rector or vicar, (commuted to a rent-charge in 1836, and finally abolished a hundred years later) **was much resented by local people?** In 1932 the owner of Elm Farm had refused to pay, so an order was obtained for the sale of both implements and livestock. The police were there to keep the peace, but there was no disorder, all playing a canny game. The auctioneer took the bids but little money, he like everyone else, hating the farce. Cows and implements were sold for a few coppers each and left on the farm. All that the Church Commissioners received was a bill from the auctioneer, the final comment being *'Here endeth the first lesson'.*

...that All Saints church in Little Melton belongs to everyone in the parish, and that ever since the church was built in the middle ages all kinds of fund-raising activities have taken place to keep it in good repair? For example, on December 14th 2002, no less than seventy-five teddy bears paid a pound each to descend by parachute from the top of the church tower, all landing safely, and with a signed certificate to prove it. Inside and outside the building were stalls selling soup and hot dogs to their owners, as well as mulled wine and mince pies and all sorts of other goodies, making the church into a real hub of activity, the centre of village life, just as it would have been in early times. This was a fitting celebration of all the hard work that has gone into the recent re-decoration and re-heating of the building, which has made its interior strikingly beautiful.

Amongst the Little Melton archives is a dog-eared seventy-year-old brochure from Advent 1933, when Canon Paine, the vicar, was thanking 'all who have helped so generously' in the renovation of the church. This was the period when the medieval wall paintings were discovered, and the present day pews installed, and the vicar wrote 'Now that we have good pews to use, cannot we see that they are filled on Sunday with reverent worshippers'? Today's vicar and church council would surely say "hear hear!" to this.

All Saints church, Little Melton c.2000

Chapter Six

Church and people.

Church and people

> *DIARY OF A CHURCH MOUSE*
> *Here among long-discarded cassocks,*
> *Damp Stools, and half-split open hassocks,*
> *Here where the Vicar never looks*
> *I nibble through old service books.*
> *Lean and alone I spend my days*
> *Behind this Church of England baize,*
> *I share my dark forgotten room*
> *With two oil-lamps and half a broom.*
>
> *John Betjeman.*

Our parish church, All Saints, lies at the far end of Mill Road, just before you reach the big lime tree on Rectory Lane, planted to commemorate Queen Victoria's jubilee. It is a good half mile from the centre of the village, and many people ask why this is, thinking perhaps that the fourteenth century Black Death caused people to move away from their plague infected huts and to set up home at a distance. This seems to be most unlikely, as field walking in the area has uncovered pieces of medieval pottery and other artifacts dating from Saxon times to the eleventh century, but very little of a later date. This must mean that originally people did live in the area round the church, but moved soon after the Norman conquest, with the expansion of farming.

Manorial records show that the *'Church Field'* (some 90 acres round the church) had been what is known as *'Common Field'* for many hundreds of years before the 1817 enclosure. It was divided into a large number of small arable strips, each tenant of the manor holding a few of these, varying in size from about an eighth of an acre upwards, held by copy of court roll, and there were also a number of enclosures, known as *'closes'*. The remains of an old well in the lower field has sometimes given rise to the belief that there must have been human habitation here at one time, but this was probably for agricultural use only, early maps showing no buildings at all in the locality.

One important building which did stand near the church, however, was Melton-Hall, at the far end of Great Melton road, Little Melton, on the site of the Grange of today, with its adjacent moat. (This is not to be confused with Great Melton Hall, whose ruins lie near the two churches in our adjoining parish of Great Melton). The lords of the Manor of Melton-Hall lived in the village many years ago,

Ladbroke engraving 1843, All Saints Church Little Melton

and it surely must have been they who built the original church near to their home. At one time, the early lords of this manor and of the separate but larger manor of Little Melton were linked by kinship, both being members of the great Norman baronial family of de Montchensy.

Although there is no mention of a church in Little Melton in the Domesday Survey of 1086, we know that there was a church here as early as 1030 A.D., because that was about the time when Edwin, (the Anglo-Saxon lord of the manor) wrote his will, leaving 10 acres of land *'to the church at Little Melton'*. The land was wrested from Edwin by William the Conqueror, so his wish was never fulfilled, but astonishingly the will itself survives! In 1121 Ralf de Montchensy gave the patronage of the parish church of Little Melton to Gilbert, the Prior of the House of Augustinian Canons at Ixworth, Suffolk. At this time the church would have been small and probably made of wood, apparently being rebuilt in about 1180 by the same family, who continued to hold the manor here. The undercroft of the Priory, with its splendid thirteenth century vaulting, may still be seen today; it was visited by the Hethersett Guild a few years ago, and is apparently well worth seeing, but the property is now in private ownership.

At the period when the vaulting was being erected at Ixworth, the people of Little Melton were felling and removing trees from the churchyard here, without permission from the Priory. This caused such a furore that in the years 1278/79 a case was heard in the Court of the Bishop of Norwich between

Church interior c.2000

the Prior and Convent of Ixworth and the parishioners. Unfortunately, we don't know the outcome, but a very fragile document held by Emmanuel College outlines part of the case.

It was not until 1300 or thereabouts that our present stone church of All Saints came into being, constructed on the same site as the earlier two churches. In use today we still have a huge stone slab, a 'Mensa' or altar top made of Purbeck marble, and a large octagonal font of the same material, which both came from the second church.

There were no architects in the early fourteenth century, everything being hand crafted under the eagle eye of a master builder. What experts he and his masons were, with their beautiful stone carving, and their delicate leafy capitals, arches and arcades. The single Early English lancets and 'Y' shaped traceries of the chancel windows date the church to 1300, as does the double 'Piscina' near the altar. The left hand basin has a four leaf design and was used for washing the Communion vessels, while the drain on the right has a plain circular basin and was used by the priest to wash his hands. This arrangement was only fashionable at the end of the 13th and the very beginning of the 14th centuries. Beside them is a double sedilia, or carved stone seat for the priest and deacon. To the right of this is a low window, through which a hand bell may well have been rung at the elevation of the Host (the body of Christ), so that workers in the fields might pause, cross themselves, and share in the celebration of the Mass.

The early fourteenth century paintings are of great interest too, some of them having been badly damaged by past work to the church. They were only discovered in 1933 when limewash was removed from the walls, and today the Friends of Little Melton Church have raised money to conserve them. There is a scene of the Annunciation in the chancel, with the Virgin Mary depicted to the right of the altar, and the Angel Gabriel to the left. The remains of a frieze can be seen in the Lady Chapel, and one half of St. Christopher, the patron saint of travellers, survives above the north door.

The most original painting is known as 'The Scandalmongers' or 'The Gossips' and lies in the nave for all to see. On close inspection it shows two women seated on a bench, chatting away with their heads close together. No, they are not

The Scandalmongers

making daisy chains, as one visitor suggested, but are telling their rosary beads! Behind to the right, and only just distinguishable, is the head of the devil, presumably noting everything down for the dreadful day of judgment. There should be another devil on the left, according to the experts, and with a little imagination one can just make him out. In medieval times church pictures were sometimes used as teaching aids, and took the form of awful warnings against particular bad habits, such as the over-valuation of rank and riches, the sins of blasphemy and swearing, Sabbath-breaking and (as here) idle gossip. This picture is a rare survival, and is well worth preserving. Our nearby parish of Colton has a similar wall painting, (though very faded) as has Peakirk in Northamptonshire; a fine example has recently been found at St. Andrew's Church, Eaton, Norwich.

At the rear of the church of today hangs an attractive oak board listing the vicars who have served the parish. The first named priest we know of was Sir Rowland, but he was probably not a knight, many a cleric being given 'Sir' as an honorary title. He is followed by William in 1275, who may well have had a hand in encouraging the rebuild of the church, this time in durable flint with Barnack stone for the quoins (the outside corner stones). It was the Prior of Ixworth's duty to present the priests to *'serve the cure of souls'* in Little Melton, and this was done until the dissolution of the monasteries in the mid-sixteenth century.

In the battlemented square tower hang three bells, two of them made in Norwich about 1380, being some of the oldest in Norfolk, and one re-cast in 1607.

The 'Marsham' Bell c.1984

Both medieval bells bear Latin inscriptions, the small treble bell tuned to C sharp, weighing four cwt, reads in translation, *'All men sacred'*, while the seven cwt, middle bell, tuned to B flat, reads *'Free us, save us, justify us'*. The lettering of their maker's name says 'William of Norwich' which is identical to that on the bells of Barford and Hellesdon, known to have been made by William Brend in 1380. Thomas Marsham is remembered by the largest of the three bells, the tenor, weighing half a ton, which bears his name and date, *'Thomas Marsham 1605'*, his family being lords of the manor here, and a junior branch of the Marshams of Stratton Strawless. Unfortunately, these bells are too fragile to be rung today, though they are chimed before service. Wouldn't it be wonderful if All Saints were to have a full peal of bells again one day, their splendid sound resounding over the village for all to enjoy?

The great Norfolk historian, Francis Blomefield, says that in medieval times there was a rectory house and 24 acres of glebe (land belonging to the church) in Little Melton, and that the great tithes (ten per cent of corn, hay and farm animals) were assigned to Ixworth, the vicar here holding the small tithes (ten per cent of minor farming enterprises, such as hens, eggs, honey etc). Later, the rectory and all that belonged to it was granted to the vicar and his successors, paying the prior a perpetual pension of 46s. 8d a year. When this happened is unclear, but it shows that Little Melton was never a rich living, and that the priests were far from free agents, required to do much as their masters the Priors wished.

Little Melton, like everywhere else, was ravaged with plague in 1349, at the time of the Black Death, when flea-carrying black rats caused the death of between a third and a half of the villagers. No less than three priests serving our parish died here in that one year, their names being Thomas Cosse, Walter Bate and John Gilbert. They tended the sick and buried the dead, and so became victims of the pestilence themselves. Although this was of course a terrible tragedy, the parishioners who were left did benefit in the long run. Before the sickness there had been an enormous increase in population, so men and women were quite literally starving. Due to the consequent shortage of labour, the survivors were able to demand higher wages from the manorial lords, while a fair day's pay was just beginning to be paid for a fair day's work. This was certainly an improvement on back breaking services in kind.

As you enter All Saints today, there are inside the porch, on either side of the door, two weather beaten stone corbels, believed to represent the heads of King Edward I (1272-1307) who was reigning when the church was built, and of Queen Eleanor. The tale is told that when he was only fifteen years old, Edward went to Las Huelgas in Spain to marry Eleanor, the daughter of the King of Castile and Leon. This of course was a political arrangement, but the couple fell in love and became inseparable. When Edward set out to join the Crusades in 1270 there

Corbels of Edward I (left) and his Queen, Eleanor (right). c.2002

is the romantic (but probably untrue) tale of Eleanor sucking the poison from his wounded arm after he had been struck with a poisoned dagger. On Eleanor's death in 1290, Edward was devastated, and escorted her body from near Lincoln to London, erecting a cross at every stopping place. A replica of the last of these can be seen in the forecourt of Charing Cross station in London.

Most porches were added to the main church buildings some years after they were built, and this is the case at Little Melton, where late 15th century bricks may be found embedded in the outer stonework. Inside the porch there is also a small sundial carved into the stone just under King Edward's head, which must mean that this was once an outside wall. In the days before the invention of clocks or watches, a stick (or gnomon) was placed in the central hole, in such a way that its shadow would fall on the time of day at which Mass was to be held. This worked well (at least when the sun was shining) and two more of these scratch dials are to be found on the south east corner of the nave, as you walk down the church path.

Porches were important, for it was here that Marriage Banns were read, here that the bridegroom placed the ring on his bride's finger, that the baptism service started, where notices were published and legacies paid. In a 1615 will, for example, Jeremy Rose, Yeoman, asks his wife to pay a legacy to his daughter Marie, *'when she shall come to the age of 18 years, at or in the Church Porch at Little Melton'*. Nearly thirty years later, the 1643 will of John Rose, another Yeoman, requires his brother Isaack to pay his several legacies *'in the South Porch of the parish church of Little Melton'*, and in the Manor Court Books, for a court held on 18th October 1659, George Hadnam was to pay £40 to Richard Barker of Great Melton, Husbandman, in the Little Melton porch, on a conveyance of a piece of land. Financial dealings were then, as now, fraught with difficulties and mistrust, and were felt to be more secure if carried out in a public place and on holy ground.

Like the porch, the big west window in the church, is a later addition, probably replacing a smaller one of earlier date. This perpendicular window was inserted in 1454 when Richard Manger gave five marks (£1. 13s. 4d) in his will *'to a new glass window in the tower'*. Do the few coloured glass fragments at the very top remain from this period, one wonders?

In the late fifteenth century the beautiful screen dividing the chancel and nave was erected. This has richly ornamented ogee or flowing 'S' shaped arches and a great deal of tracery colour, though the panels are blank. Above the screen, until after the break with Rome in 1538, the Rood Loft would have had a huge crucifix in the centre with figures of St Mary and St John on either side. Part of the steps up to the rood are still visible in the Lady Chapel, which contains the unmarked graves of the onetime lord of the manor of Melton-Hall, Thomas Batchcroft and his first wife Margaret, she dying in 1489 and he in 1501. As well as giving money for the rebuilding of Earlham bridge, Mr Batchcroft left £400 in his will for the construction of a Rood Loft in the Chapel in the Fields Norwich, where the Assembly House now stands. During his lifetime, had Mr. Batchcroft also paid for the building of our screen, as was suggested by Mr Joe Day of Little Melton? Joe died in 1998, having loved and cared for this church over many years. He spent hours researching its history and felt it was very probable that Mr Batchcroft had been the donor, as he would surely have wanted a screen in his own church. Fitted into the nave pillar just north of the screen is an endearing little piscina, which was almost certainly carved there to serve the Lady Chapel at the time the screen was erected. Normally the piscina is on a wall immediately to the south of the altar it serves, and this would probably have been its original position before the stairs to the Rood were built.

In 1508 money was found for the replacement of most of the windows in the main body of the church, the masons using a two light design under a flattened arch. At the same time, the roof of the Lady Chapel was raised, being re-timbered and re-thatched in the process. The internal beams, now silvered with age, are still there to be enjoyed today. Until Henry VIII's break with Rome, two religious guilds used to meet in this chapel, one dedicated to St Mary and the other to St John the Baptist. These were voluntary associations of local people who tried to put into practice the command *'to love thy neighbour as thyself'*. They gave time, energy, support and money with which to help each other in time of need, and women were welcomed as full members alongside their menfolk – a very forward looking arrangement in a most unfeminist age.

Today, it is very fitting that this chapel, dedicated to Mary the mother of Jesus and linked with Walsingham Abbey, is used by our local branch of the Mothers' Union, a world wide movement which tries to encourage Christian family values.

Another of the victims of the dissolution of the monasteries in 1538 was the Priory of Ixworth, which was now disbanded. This enabled Henry VIII to grant the patronage (or advowson) of Little Melton church to whomsoever he liked, or, more precisely, to the person who would pay him the most money for it. Eventually, it went to Richard Codington of Codington, Surrey, and six years later to Francis Chamberlain of Great Melton, who conveyed it to Emmanuel College, Cambridge, in 1577, together with the glebe and tithes *'thereto belonging'*. The Master and Fellows of Emmanuel hold it to this day, more than four hundred years later, and have a wonderful archive of material in their possession, relating to both the Meltons. This can be seen in their library by special request.

In the same year of 1538, Thomas Cromwell instructed each parish in the country to purchase a *'sure coffer'*, the parson to have one key and a churchwarden the other. Each marriage, christening and burial was to be registered weekly by the priest with the churchwarden acting as witness, and the papers were to be kept in this chest. The huge old wooden coffer in All Saints was used for just this purpose, and sixty years later, an order signed by Queen Elizabeth herself required that all the loose-leaf registers be written up into parchment books and kept here under lock and key. Her commands were carried out in Little Melton, and it is a great disappointment that our early church registers have long since disappeared, and only start from the year 1734. Just a few of the Archdeacons' and Bishops' transcripts of the earlier lost registers remain in the Norfolk Record Office as proof of their original existence.

Coffer c.2000

A strange story relating to this coffer is told by two men of the parish who were asked, in the mid 1990s, to carry it from the west end of the church to the east end of St. Francis' chapel, by the children's corner. It was a fine day without a cloud in the sky, but as soon as they started to struggle under its enormous weight, huge claps of thunder began to erupt, continuing only until the chest was in its final position, when the noise stopped as abruptly as it had started. It was a scary experience.

But to return to the church in days gone by. In the mid 16th century the Latin Mass was forbidden, and services started to be conducted in our native tongue, the first English Prayer Book dating from 1549. The next year an order was issued to remove all stone altars and to replace them with wooden tables. The huge Mensa slab of Purbeck marble was too heavy to carry, so it was just buried in the floor nearby, and lay there, undisturbed for years, before being returned to its original position. The stone pillars which supported it were sadly too broken to use again, so the ancient altar slab lies today on a wooden frame.

We only know of two events that occurred in Little Melton during the church's brief return to Roman Catholicism during Queen Mary's reign (1553 to 1558). From the Inventory of Church Goods of 1552 we find that *'Thurston Browne vicare of the parysshe of lytle melton'*, was deprived of the living two years later, which must have meant that he was a married man, just one of many non-celibate clergy ousted by Rome for this reason. Then on 25th March 1556 there was a dispute between Francis Chamberlain of Great Melton (who held the patronage of All Saints, Little Melton) and three parishioners of Little Melton, John Austen and Christopher Wrightsonne, husbandmen, and Robert Hammond senior, ploughwright, concerning the parsonage of Little Melton; these are some of the earliest names we have, preserved amongst the archives of Emmanuel College, Cambridge.

In 1636, Bishop Matthew Wren of Norwich, (uncle of Sir Christopher Wren who built St Paul's), ordered that *'a rayle be made before the Communion Table reaching crosse from the North wall to the South wall, neer one yarde in height, so thick with pillars that dogges may not gett in'*, and his successor Bishop Richard Montague in 1638 asked his parish clergy whether this had been done. There is no record of Little Melton's reply, but here, as at Taverham, the Communion rails were made from old screens, as 17th century churchwardens in poor country parishes were not going to be put to too great an expense. Our rail, pulpit and chancel pews, are believed to have been made from the screen that once divided the Lady Chapel from the nave. However the rail itself, made of open linked arches from the top of the screen, would have been of no use at all in keeping out dogs! At that period, the churchwardens' staves were used to round up any strays that had found their way into church, and these poles now stand at the end of two pews in the nave. Perhaps, after all, Little Melton did manage to keep to the spirit if not exactly to the letter of the law.

'A rayle .... that dogges may not gette in'? c.2000

In 1641/42 a petition was sent to Emmanuel College by the inhabitants of Little Melton asking either that the vicar's stipend be increased, or that he be allowed to lease the tithes, but these appeals seem to have been unsuccessful. Twenty years later, the parishioners wrote a further, heart-rending letter to their patrons at Emmanuel, pleading for a small stipend or salary to be paid to the clergyman looking after the parish, Mr. Alexander Burnett of Colney. One or two signed their names, but most could only make a cross or were able to write an initial letter, R. for Robert for instance, or J. for John. They said that from time immemorial the college had been pleased to give £8 per annum to successive ministers for their maintenance, but that Mr. Burnett had received nothing *'and that he will leave us if the former benevolence be witheld and we have then to be as sheepe without a sheppard and like to perish for want of vision.'* The parishioners were at least partially successful, for from this time, the College authorities agreed to pay £5 to the priest annually.

At much the same time, June 9th 1661, a strange entry appears in the service register of the parish of Pinchbeck, Lincolnshire. This reads *'Collected for Little Melton in the County of Norfolke the full sum of one pound one shilling and five pence. Signed Nico East, Vicar, Edmund Calthorp and George Carr, Churchwardens.'* What was this for? Why should this faraway parish be interested in Little Melton? It seems, on enquiry, that Emmanuel College also owned land in Pinchbeck, and that 17th and 18th century parish registers often show lists of 'briefs' for collections towards some supposedly deserving object, being almost as common as are charitable appeals today. We don't really know whether Little Melton had suffered a terrible fire or pestilence, because the church registers of this date do not survive, but as nothing startling is mentioned in the Little Melton manorial books, it seems unlikely. In all probability, our parish, desperate for money to support the priest it shared with Colney, was simply widening its request for funds.

Someone who tried to alleviate individual poverty in the village was a lady named Sarah Johnson, daughter of Robert Johnson of Little Melton, who died in 1680. A fine marble monument to his son Thomas, who died in 1714, is on the south wall of our chancel, with Sarah's ledger stone lying on the floor nearby. The family probably lived at Grey Cottage, Green Lane, for nearly forty years from about 1678 to 1716, when Sarah moved to Colney. When she died in 1741 she left forty shillings a year in her will, to be shared between two poor widows of our village, but sadly after some years this ceased to be paid, and a later incumbent took up the matter with the Charity Commissioners. He was informed that the bequest was chargeable on property Sarah had owned in Brooke, but the new owners were resisting payment, and this could not be enforced as 'gifts to charitable uses were void under the Mortmain Act of 1736'. Such bureaucracy must have made Sarah turn in her grave, as two pounds was worth a lot of money then, and would have made all the difference to elderly widows without much in the way of support.

There are also some fine monuments to the Skottowes in the chancel of All Saints, many members of this family having lived and held court here as lords of the manor. Several gave bequests to the poor of the parish, Katherine Skottowe, for example, leaving £3 for this purpose in her will of 1769, a stone in her memory being found on the chancel floor. Another ledger stone, this time in the nave, reads 'Elizabeth wife of Robert Buck died Aug 18 1727, aged 65'. From time immemorial the Manor Court for Little Melton took place on or around St. Luke's Day, 18th October, each year, and the tenants were summoned to attend by 'the Cryer' who for years was Robert Buck.

Not far from this memorial, lying close to the pulpit, is our only brass, dated 1604, depicting the arms of the Anguish and the Marsham families. In 1534 Elizabeth Marsham, widow of John, a former Mayor of Norwich, had bought the manor of Little Melton, the lordship remaining with her descendants until about 1620 when it was sold. Elizabeth's grandson, Robert Marsham, had a daughter Dorothie who married Edmund Anguish, son of Thomas Anguish of Great Melton Hall, lord of the manor there. The young couple had a son, another Robert, who died as a baby in June 1604, his mother Dorothie following him to the grave only seventeen days later. The brass is to their memory. The baby's paternal grandfather, Thomas Anguish, by his will of 1617, set up 'hospitals' or schools for poor children in Norwich, founding a body now known as the Anguish Educational Foundation. The land at 'Hospital Farm', Little Melton is still owned by this trust today.

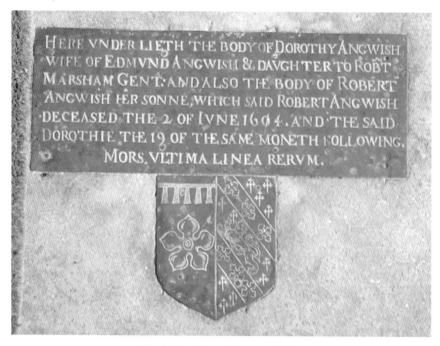

HERE VNDER LIETH THE BODY OF DOROTHY ANGWISH
WIFE OF EDMVND ANGWISH & DAVGHTER TO ROBT
MARSHAM GENT: AND ALSO THE BODY OF ROBERT
ANGWISH HER SONNE, WHICH SAID ROBERT ANGWISH
DECEASED THE 2 OF IVNE 1604. AND THE SAID
DOROTHIE THE 19 OF THE SAME MONETH FOLLOWING.
MORS. VLTIMA LINEA RERVM.

The 'Marsham Brass' c.2000

Another ledger stone just to the north of the altar in the chancel, dated 1691, is in memory of the baby son of John Brandon, who had just become vicar here that very same year. He continued to serve the parish for more than half a century. He had succeeded Gawen Nash, a Minor Canon of Norwich Cathedral, whose tenure was much more short-lived. Nash had been ordained as a priest in 1674, so would probably have been about forty years old when King William and Queen Mary came to the throne in 1689. He had taken his solemn vows of priesthood in the time of the Stuarts, and like many another courageous clergyman at that difficult period, felt he could not go back on these. He therefore refused to take the oath of allegiance to the new monarchs, although he knew that this would probably mean the loss of his livelihood, as indeed it did. In technical terms he had become a 'Non-Juror' and was deprived of his living as a result.

Many of the vicars whose names feature on the clergy board hanging inside the church were Emmanuel men, the college as patron understandably giving preference to its own graduates. Thomas Bulbek of 1640 and John Brandon of 1691 were both of Emmanuel, and from the time of Robert Potter in 1746, all but two of the next eleven priests listed held Masters' degrees from the college. Many were scholars or had other interests outside the parish, and often appointed curates to carry out their daily duties for them, as shown by the surviving registers. These men were often poorly paid, most of them hoping and striving for future livings of their own. A clergy list is given in appendix B.

Repairs to the church fabric were continually being carried out when needed, just as they are today, and the parish Faculty Books now stored in the Norfolk Record Office give evidence of this. For example, restoration work took place in 1823, by order of Mr. John Girling, the churchwarden who lived at Manor Farm. It was he who paid £18. 6s. 8d to Mr Charles Cook for 'laying lead to steeple'. Work must also have been done prior to this date, as a sheet of lead was later found to bear the date 1754, complete with the plumber's mark and initials. In 1868 the windows of the entire building were restored and re-glazed, so giving rise to one of the glories of this little church. Nowadays, when the sun shines, light pours in on all sides through the clear glass, and when the wind blows, the different shades of the green of the trees can be seen dancing away in the leafy churchyard.

In 1885 the church acquired a site on Mill Road on which to build a Church Hall. The Rev. Henry Evans-Lombe gave the land, and the Rev. John Soden, vicar of Little Melton, and his two churchwardens were signatories, with him, to the Indenture dated 8th August of that year. It was to be 'a School for the education of poor persons in religious knowledge and for no other purpose'. A flourishing Sunday School was duly set up and continued for very many years. By 1936 the room was also being used as a Social Club, meeting on no less than three evenings each week, and the Women's Institute and local Football Club met there too. In 1999, after some years of disuse following the building of the modern village hall, and with the permission of Sir Edward Evans-Lombe, it was sold for private housing, the proceeds being used to start a church building trust.

Back in the 1880s the thatched roof of All Saints was beginning to let in water, and in February 1892 Emmanuel College paid for re-roofing. All thatch was removed, and best Hull Tiles (French pattern) were put in its place. Tiling of the nave and side aisles (or chapels) cost £222. 8s. 11d, while that of the chancel cost £174. 14s. 0d. This was a large sum over a hundred years ago, but seems ridiculously small compared with costs today. There was not enough ready money with which to buy new seats until June 28th 1895, when some of the old deal benches in the nave and south aisle were replaced with chairs at an estimated cost of £41.

In 1912 our present organ was installed. It came from Old Costessey Church and was built by the Rev. George Buck, Rector of Belaugh for 36 years, son of Dr. Zachariah Buck, who was organist of Norwich Cathedral from 1819 to 1877. The Rev. George used to beg for organ parts discarded by Norman Bros.,

Norwich, from which he assembled his organs. It has an attractive, mellow tone, and the organists of today, Mrs Judy Aslin and Mrs Lavinia Ganley, who play it with such verve, give much musical pleasure to a growing congregation.

War Memorial c.2000

Near the organ is the 1921 War Memorial to the men of Little Melton who died in the First World War. Their names are also inscribed on the Lych-gate, together with the names of those who fell in World War Two. The gate was made in 1946 and dedicated two years later. 'Lych' is Latin for corpse, and the Lych-gate is where the coffin rests before being brought into the church for the burial service. For some unknown reason there are many more such gates in country places than in towns, and Norwich has only one, at St. Andrew's.

In the 1920s, the Little Melton Church Plate was stolen, consisting of a Chalice (used for the consecrated wine) and Paten (for the consecrated bread). The Chalice was marked 'Melton Parva, All Saints, Anno Domini 1715' with a Britannia and Lion's head erased, and the Court hand 't' for 1714. The maker was John Eastt. The Paten was of a later date, bearing the Leopard's head, lion passant, queen's head, and 'O' for 1849, Charles T. Fox and George Fox of London being the makers. Had these been given, perhaps, by two faithful long-serving vicars of the parish, John Brandon, (1691-1743), and John Charles Barkley, (1839-1883)?

By great good fortune, the plate was soon to be replaced by a totally unexpected present from the Society for the Promotion of Christian Knowledge. In 1925 a letter from an anonymous donor was sent by S.P.C.K. to our vicar, saying *'It has come to my knowledge that Little Melton is in need of Communion Plate after theirs was stolen one or two years ago, the parish being too poor to replace it from its own resources.'* The gift is in use today.

1933 was a year of great upheaval. Canon Nigel Wood Paine of Great Melton, who was also vicar here, set about raising money locally to put the Lady Chapel to rights. It was almost totally derelict, the walls were filthy, and there was little seating. In the process, the old limewash was removed, and to everyone's amazement, the medieval wall paintings were discovered. These pictures caused something of an uproar. After all, they had lain hidden ever since the mid sixteenth century break with Rome, their original purpose being as 'teaching aids' in an age when few besides clergy and lawyers could read or write. Canon Paine was a good P.R. man, who 'seized the moment'. He sent a photograph of 'the Scandalmongers' to the Eastern Daily Press, asking whether another like it had been found elsewhere. He wrote that the church restoration was costing £300, that another £80 was still needed, adding *'If any of your readers are kind enough to help a small agricultural parish to put its church in good order, we shall be very grateful to the donors'*. Today these murals are treated with great respect, only trained conservators being allowed to touch them.

That very same year of 1933, enough money was raised with which to install the oak pews that are now in use. Many local families paid for and adopted one pew each, inscribed with 'I. M.' (in memory of), followed by a name. There is one, for instance, for the Rev. John Charles Barkley and Mary his wife, who had done much for the poor and sick of the parish during their many years here. Another is for Samuel Barrell, our long-time miller, and Mary Ann his wife, while a third is for Mary Diaper of Manor Farm, to name but a few.

The only stained glass window in the church was given by Mrs Mildred Pratt in 1968. She and her husband were some of the very first tenants of the council houses in Braymeadow Lane, constructed in the early 1930s, locals (who watched them being built) nicknaming the properties 'The Tintacks'. The Pratts, who were great supporters of the church, grew a special variety of daffodil in their garden and kept goats, making cream cheese and draining it in muslin bags from their linen line. Sadly, their two infant sons died young, and Mrs. Pratt, as a widow, decided to give this window in their memory. What a beautiful and unusual creation it is, tucked away in the children's corner, and what a task it must have been to fit the design of the glass into the Y-shaped stone tracery of nearly seven hundred years earlier. Mrs. Pratt, (born Milly Mapes), died just before the window was installed, but she saw its final design and was delighted with it. She wanted it to be a 'teaching window' like the murals of old.

Mildred Pratt's gift to Little Melton Church c.2000

Milly knew exactly what she wanted and put the work into the hands of George King & Sons, Paul Jefferies being the young designer. It shows St. Francis, with a hare peeping out behind his cloak, surrounded by birds and flowers often seen in Norfolk, including a jaunty cock pheasant and a lively robin, as well as lovely daffodils of course. There is also a rose tree. Why? Because one of the many legends surrounding the saint says that at a time of great trial, to avoid giving in to temptation, he threw himself into a tangle of thorns, which immediately blossomed into a rose bush. The three knots in the cord round his waist remind us of his Order's vows of poverty, chastity and obedience. The Stigmata are shown, the marks (corresponding to those of Christ's wounds on his crucifixion) were said to have been impressed on the bodies of St. Francis and other saints, and are attributed to divine favour.

This window symbolises everything that the church stands for, the people of Christ as well as the building in which they worship. In this confused, frenetic and violent century, church going may be temporarily out of fashion, but the number of worshippers at All Saints continues to creep slowly but steadily upwards. Could this have something to do with the constancy of the wonderful old building at the centre of it all, which many find a place not only of worship and spiritual peace, but also of real companionship and fellowship?

. In the millennium year, a most beautiful banner embroidered by ladies of the village, was presented to the church (depicted on the rear cover of this book). This shows the dove of peace hovering over the church and mill, with parishioners in Victorian, Edwardian and modern dress walking together up the path. One young fellow who wears the green and yellow of the Norwich Canaries, is pointing heavenwards, perhaps echoing some of the words of today's Communion service, as though to say 'Though we are many, we are one body'.

This feeling of community and continuity has been strengthened, since 1984, through the setting up of 'the united benefice of Hethersett with Great and Little Melton' served by one minister, known as the rector (for Hethersett and Great Melton) or vicar (for Little Melton), wholeheartedly supported by a team of workers, consisting of the curate, retired clergy and readers. The benefice lies within the Rural Deanery of Humbleyard, the Archdeaconry of Norfolk and the Diocese of Norwich, and has been served since 1995 by our first woman priest, the Rev. Di Lammas, who is also the Rural Dean. The wheel has certainly come full circle since medieval days.

In 2003 the first major phase of church restoration has been completed, at a cost of many thousands of pounds, all paid for by the parish. The twelfth century font has now been moved to its rightful position near the south porch, the interior has been totally re-painted, original stone work on the arches exposed, new electrical heating installed in each pew, and three medieval paintings conserved with money raised by the Friends of the Church. During this work, fragments of several further paintings were discovered, indicating that the building was originally full of colour. In addition, three shadowy horned devils can now just be made out above and to both sides of the ladies in the aisle painting 'The Scandalmongers'. They seem to be having a great time pushing both heads together, to encourage the dreadful sin of gossip!

> *In the drinking well*
> *Which the plumber built her,*
> *Aunt Eliza fell –*
> *We must buy a filter.*
> Harry Graham

Did you know that ...

...a pair of cottages on the West corner of Braymeadow Lane were once occupied by a well sinker, who plied his trade until the 1940's?
Digging a well then was a skilled operation, carried out entirely by hand. Once a hole was dug to the depth of a few feet, a circular, bottomless wooden structure was lowered into it, onto which a wall of bricks was laid. As digging progressed below the box, the whole apparatus would sink, and another layer of bricks would be laid at the top, the process continuing until a good spring of water was reached.

Standing above the new well was the well sinker's tripod, three wooden poles fastened at the top, on which a wooden roller was fixed, with a long rope and a hand crank. In this way a man could be winched to the bottom and back, and soil removed by the bucket load.

Way back in time our Little Melton well sinker, Arthur Baxter, was not the easiest person to work with, and on one occasion, when deepening a well, he is said to have abused his helper at the top; possibly some soil or bricks having descended into it by mistake. The result was that, after exchanging a few choice words, the labourer went home and left his master to his own devices at the bottom of the well. He was discovered a few hours later in a very unpleasant state of both mind and body.

...on 31st March 1851 the one and only census ever taken of people attending worship on Sunday was carried out? This followed the rapid expansion of Nonconformism, the appearance of new sects such as the Mormons, and the creation just the year before of 32 English Sees in the Roman Catholic Church. The census showed that:
Little Melton (population 379) had 38 people at Church of England morning worship, and 74 at the afternoon service. The vicar the Rev. John Charles Barkley reported *'In consequence of adverse circumstances the Sunday School has been discontinued during the past year. It will be re-established during the coming summer – but in the winter the Church is too cold for the*

*children, and the Incumbent is unable to build or purchase a School House –
having no-one to share with him in the expense.'* [There was no 'dissenting
chapel'].

Great Melton (population 393) had 17 people at Church of England morning
worship and 121 at the afternoon service. The rector was the Rev. Robert
Dodd. [Again there was no 'dissenting chapel'].

Hethersett (population 1209) had 133 people at Church of England morning
worship and 258 at the afternoon service. Jeremy Day, Minister of Hethersett,
commented *'In the summer the attendants are considerably more in number
but the average cannot be stated'.*

The Hethersett Wesleyan Methodist Chapel, erected about 1817, had 105
people at afternoon service and 111 in the evening. Sunday Scholars were
51. Isaac Richardson signed as Chapel Steward.

The Hethersett Primitive Methodist Chapel had an attendance of 15 in the
morning and 17 in the afternoon. William Morter was the signatory.

Total population figures for England and Wales in 1851 were 17,927,609. The
proportion of people who attended a religious service on Census Sunday was
60.8%, of whom 29.5% were C. of E, 27.2% nonconformist, and 2.1% Roman
Catholic.

In Norfolk 65.3% in all attended some form of worship, 52.3% at an Anglican
church, 44.7% at a Nonconformist chapel and 0.7% at a Roman Catholic
church. Contemporary society was shocked and surprised by one particular
finding of the census, notably that the number of people who failed to attend
any service on census day proved to be far higher than anyone had expected.

**...on August Bank Holiday Monday, 3rd August 1942, the village was
organising a whole day of activities during War Charities Week?** A utility
poster, made of brown paper and emblazoned with a Union Flag and a church
tower, informs us that at 2.30 pm an Open Air Whist Drive was to be held at 'The
Grange' by kind permission of Mr and Mrs H. Eagle, and that at 6.00 pm sports
and competitions for children would take place on Jubilee Meadow, Little Melton
cross-roads, by kind permission of Mr. E. A. Clarke. There was also a vegetable
and flower show, a dress-making event for women, and a rabbit show for
children. *'Bring the rabbits in a box with wire front'* say the instructions. Later, at
8.30 pm in the Club Room at the Rose and Crown Public House, everyone was
invited to a dance, admission one shilling. The Victory Swing Trio provided the
music, and a hairdressing competition was just one item on the programme, to
be judged by Mr A. Martin Phob at 10.00 pm. All proceeds went to the Red Cross.

...that there used to be a flourishing Girl Guide Company in Little Melton? Miss Crabbe, who taught at our school here, was the first Guide Captain well before 1918. She lived at Pond Piece on School Lane, and meetings were held in the scullery or outhouse there. Ivy Humphrys of Colney restarted the unit in the late 1920s, and then Violet Mace took over, and kept things going right up till the end of the second world war. The children met in the Church Room, and in summer went hiking and camping, making almost inedible 'dampers' (dough twisted round sticks), cooking them over smoky camp fires, and declaring them to be delicious. Marie Kinch was Brownie leader until the start of W.W. II., when she left the village to join the forces. By the late 1970s there were Brownie, Guide and Ranger units in the Village affiliated with Swainsthorpe, Cringleford and Hethersett groups, one leader being Ranger Guider Mrs. Pamela Rudd formerly of Manor Farm. Sadly, interest has waned in our village and those wishing to take part do so in other units in neighbouring villages such as Hethersett.

Little Melton Guides at Sandringham in the 1930s.
Marie Kinch standing right, with Kathleen Reynolds (left) and Olive Warnes (right)
seated in front of her.

Chapter Seven

Little Melton in 1842 and 1924

*"The Monday afore Micklemas day someone asked Granfar where Mrs. W--- lived, he
say Go you down to yin ind o' this rud, till yow git nearly down to the tarnpike. On yar
rite you'll see a double dweller cottage wi' tew lots a warshen a hangen out. Hars'll be
the warshen wot look as if that want doin agin."*

Sidney Grapes. *The Boy John Letters.*

      Little Melton lived up to its name in the early nineteenth century, being very rural and very little! Two invaluable maps of 1817 and 1842, now housed in the Norfolk Record Office, give us some idea of how the village looked then, with wide open spaces and only a few scattered farms and cottages dotted about, with a small nucleus round Manor Farm. An interesting point to notice is that today's road layout is almost the same as it has always been, except that School Lane, which once was the main route to Norwich, is now blocked to wheeled traffic where it comes to a dead end at the bypass, and that Braymeadow Lane was little more than a track in those days, while Gibbs Close and Ringwood Close are, of course, much later twentieth century additions.

      Let's now walk round the parish as it would have been in 1842, starting from the western or Great Melton end of the village, and following the numbers on the accompanying sketch map. House location is taken from the 1842 map, (but total accuracy cannot be guaranteed), while family details are from the 1841 census, (where ages are only approximate) and from notes made by Rev. John Barkley to the Poor Law Commissioners in 1841/42.

      In case anyone is interested in further research into their own home at the Norfolk Record Office, the numbers given in brackets, at the end of each entry, refer to those in the 1842 Tithe Apportionment and Map which may be consulted there on microfilm, and also give the amount of land that went with the property. For more detailed histories of the houses built before 1800, please see the chapter called 'House Histories'. All measurements used to be in Acres, Roods and Perches, abbreviated here, as in old documents as A. R. P., (and nothing whatever to do with Air Raid Precautions or with parrots for that matter!) Today, measurements are in hectares, with 2 ½ acres to the hectare. In times gone by an acre consisted of 4 roods, while a rood was made up of 40 perches, a perch being some 5 ½ yards in length.

      There were just 44 houses in the village in 1842, compared with 400 in 2003.

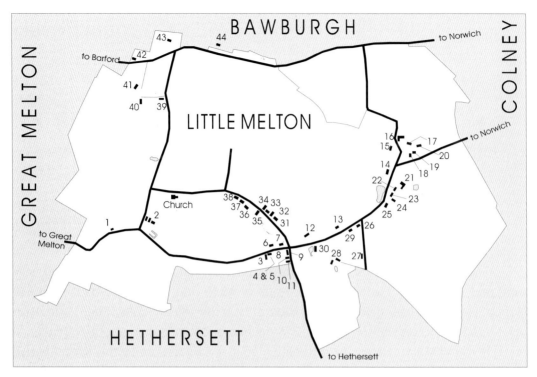

Village Map 1842

1. Steward's House, Great Melton Road, which served Church Farm (or Melton-Hall as it was originally called). This attractive cottage with 1739 and the initials I.W.M. on its gable end has been altered over the years and may have once belonged to the Marshams who were lords of the manor here. It was owned by Edward Lombe Esq in 1842 and occupied by John Gaff, who farmed just under 18 acres. There were 4 in his family altogether, John and his wife Barbara, both aged 30, his mother Ann and 3 year old Robert. (No.29 on tithe map, with 17A. 2R. 29P.)

2. The old Church Farm with its outbuildings. The Grange of today was built some years after 1842 on the site of the old farmhouse, known originally as Melton-Hall, and then as Church Farm. Church Farm had been owned and occupied in 1817 by Edward Heath, who later sold it to Edward Lombe Esq. In 1842 the Great Melton estate owned it, (as it still does today), when it was occupied by Mr Thomas Dove Aldred. There were 9 in the Aldred household, Thomas aged 35, his wife Mary aged 40, three children, Thomas (12), Joseph (10) and Eliza (8), and 4 living-in servants. (Today's Church Farm House was built in 1963 by Mr Bob Richardson). (No. 26 on tithe map, with 215A. 0R. 11P.)

1. Steward's House c.2000

3. 1 – 3 Great Melton Road, being cottages & gardens owned and built in about 1821 by Thomas Hubbard and occupied by Edward Bacon & others in 1842. Edward was a farm labourer, aged 60, living here with his wife Mary. The 'others' were probably James Woods, a 50 year old farm worker, his wife Mary, and three children Elizabeth (15), Matthew (14) and William (13). Matthew and William were both agricultural labourers. (No 107 on tithe map, with 1R. 2P.)

4. Su Cottage, Great Melton Road, and
5. Stone Cottage, both built by Thomas Hubbard in about 1821 and still owned by him in 1842, when they were occupied by Charles Woodbine and Robert Bailey. Charles was a shoemaker aged 20, recently married to his wife Hannah, also 20. Robert was a 25 year old farm labourer with a wife Hannah, and three children, James (5), William (3) and Jonathan (5 months). Robert's was a terrible story of misery and impoverishment, as noted by the Rev. Barkley, and told in the chapter called 'Social Welfare and the Poor'. (No 106 on tithe map).

6. Crossways Cottages, (8 & 10 Great Melton Road). In 1817 these had belonged to Edward Heath. In 1842 they were owned by the Great Melton Estate, (as they are today) and occupied by Charles Bishop and William Robberts, who worked on the estate farm. Charles and his wife Mary were both 35. They had four children in 1841, George (12), Mary (10), Charles (5) and William (3), but one had died earlier, in January that year. The Rev. Barkley noted that the baby had been ill for 3 weeks before medical relief was applied for, when the Relieving Officer had visited. It was too late, however, as the child died next day. Charles was buried in Little Melton aged 78 in 1881, having been Parish Clerk for some years, and his wife was buried here in 1893, aged 89 (ages are often inaccurate in the 1841 census). William Robberts and his wife Sarah were both 50, and had Elizabeth Goward, aged 10, living with them. (No. 101 on tithe map, with 1R. 2P.)

7. Rambler Cottage, near the crossways, with half an acre. This was originally the Town House, a double cottage built in 1792 to house the sick and infirm poor. After 1836 it was let to parishioners by the year and sold by the Parish Council for private housing in 1962. No named occupants are given in 1842, but it may have been occupied by George Brand and his family then. He had been brought from Wymondham to Little Melton in October 1830 under a Removal Order, with his wife Susanna and their children Mary Ann aged 7, John aged 4 and Sarah aged 18 months. The 1841 census also gives his family details. George (aged 40) was an out-of-work weaver, now employed as an agricultural labourer, with a wife Susan and four children, Sarah (12), Robert (7), Harriett (5) and William (2), making six children in all. In 1842 the Rev. Barkley noted his great concern about this family. George had fallen off a wagon at hay time, and had been ill for 4 weeks with an order for medical relief, the Medical Officer visiting twice. The previous March his child aged nearly 6 had become ill, and he had applied for help three times before the doctor visited. A week later the medical officer visited again, but the child (presumably Harriett) died the next day. Earlier, a month before harvest, his child of 9 months had whooping cough, and he urgently requested a doctor's visit. Next day 'a young gentleman' came to visit, (George believing he was the doctor's son), but the child was already dead. (No. 103 on tithe map, with 2R.)

8. Crossways. Two acres of un-built land. There is a problem here, as the apportionment (or description of rent charge of 1842) shows Samuel Bailey living here on Great Melton Road, in a house and garden belonging to Thomas Hubbard, but the accompanying map shows no building of any sort. The archivist's advice at the Norfolk Record Office was that the map was probably the more reliable document of the two. (No. 105 on tithe map, with 2A)

9. A double cottage, originally one room up and one down, now extended and part of Crossways and the former Crossways Stores. This was almost certainly built by Thomas Hubbard in the 1820's but by 1842 was owned by Edward Lombe Esq., and occupied by William Allen and William Cook. William Allen was a 45 year old manservant with a wife Alicia. William Cook was a 45 year old carpenter with a wife Jemima, a son Thomas (15) and a lodger Joseph Bunn (25) an agricultural labourer. (No 104 on tithe map with 1R. 16P.)

9. 'Crossways' c.1975

10. Terraced cottages which were end on to the road, owned by Ann Davey and occupied by James Symonds and others. James was a farm worker of 45, with a wife Susan of the same age. They had four children, James (20) and John (15) who both worked on the land, Henry (11) and Betsy (7). James features in the Rev. Barkley's notes, when his ten year old son was ill, and the doctor only visited twice in six weeks. Eventually James took the boy to another medical practitioner *'and in three weeks the boy was well'*. These buildings, later known as 'the Armes Cottages' (after their owner of 1924), were condemned and demolished in the 1960's, the boundary wall having been bought by Mr and Mrs Swann of Crossways Stores, marking the boundary of their premises. (No. 108 on tithe map, with 14P.)

11. A Cottage, School House and garden owned by James Long in 1842, and occupied by himself and Mary Sheen. James was 45 and a farm worker. His wife was Harriett and they had a 12 year old daughter Alma. Mary Sheen was a widow of 70. (In the 1841 census Mary is listed as living on her own, so she must have only just moved in with the family. Single-occupancy households were very rare in the early 19th century, quite unlike today, Mary's being the only household of one person shown). The School used to stand where the chalet 'Eastwinds' is now, (built in the late 20th century by John Lofty). The 'Dame School' did not serve all the children of the parish, for only the better-off parents were able to afford the fees of a penny or so per week. (No. 110 on tithe map, with 13P.)

12. Willow Cottage (or farm) c.2000

12. Willow Farm, standing back on the corner of School Lane. This was owned in 1817 by the Rev. Edward Frank, lord of the manor, and occupied by John Childs. In 1842 it was still owned by the manor, the lord now being Frank Bacon Esq., and occupied by William Childs. The Childs family lived in the village for seventy years in the 19th century, starting as farm labourers and becoming market gardeners. Later Willow Farm became the property of the Woodgetts, who delivered milk to many surrounding parishes. In 1841 Childs was a farm worker of 30 with a wife Maria and two children, Sarah Ann (7) and Mary (2). (No. 117 on tithe map, with 6A. 2R. 30P.)

13. The Village Inn. This was a house belonging to William Allen in 1817, which by 1842 had become 'The Rose & Crown' known as *'The Cold Blow'*. According to a map of 1698 (which sadly has long since disappeared), this was even then a place of refreshment with a 'Brew House' behind it, while about 20-25 yards away, a circle was shown on what is now the car park. Was this the well and the source of its water supply? Mention of the village 'Ale House' is also made in 1707 in the Manor Court books. Originally *'The Cold Blow'* was only an off-licence, and drinks were taken outside. In 1842 it was owned by Mary Barker and occupied by William Burcham. William was 25 and styled 'Inn Keeper'. He had a wife Mary Ann and three children, Ann (4), John (3) and Esther (1). Also living with them were Matilda Child (14) and Mary Mitchell (15). (No. 136 on tithe map, with 3A. 2R. 8P.)

14. Dormer Cottage (formerly known as 'Dowes'), and at one time two separate cottages. This is an early 17th century brick house with an interesting history. In 1817 it was owned by William Copeman, who left it by will to his two nephews, William and Edmund Fox who were owner/occupiers in 1842. William Copeman was a local benefactor, having lent £120 to parish officials in 1810 to repay a bond on the Town House. William Fox was a gardener aged 65, with a wife Elizabeth aged 62, and a lodger called Jane Emms of 25. Edmund was 30, a painter, with a wife Mary. They had four children, Edmund (9), Thomas (6), William (2) and Elizabeth (8 months). (No. 160 on tithe map, with 3R. 30P.)

15. Laburnum Cottage, Green Lane, at one time two cottages. This belonged to the lord of the manor in both 1817 and 1842, and on the latter date was occupied by John Bacon and Thomas Childs, both farm labourers. Today it has been turned into a very attractive house, overlooking a large pond, and is owned by Mr and Mrs Norman Nash. John Bacon was 25 in 1841, with a wife Maria of the same age, and a one year old daughter called Fanny. (No. 157 on tithe map, with 2R. 8P.)

16. Grey Cottage with outbuildings and a very fine barn standing alongside Green Lane. It is one of the oldest houses in the village, dating from the 16th century. In 1817 it belonged to Mrs Elizabeth Girling of Manor Farm, and by 1842 was the property of her son John. In 1841 Mrs Mary Girling was living there, (John's sister), with her daughters Elizabeth (25) and Hannah (20), who between them kept the village shop. James Webster lived in the other part of the property, and tenanted land. He is described as a 'Gardener' aged 50, with a wife Elizabeth, and a lodger, 25 year old Hannah Bacon. (No. 156 on tithe map, with 14A. 1R. 16P.)

17. White Lodge, standing well back from School Lane after its junction with Green Lane. In essence, it is a 17th century house, previously known by the strange name of **Noggs,** when it was divided into three separate dwellings. James Tompson owned the property and lived there in 1842. He was a 'Gardener' aged 30, living with Alan Tompson (25) and Sarah Tompson (55). (No. 174 on tithe map, with 2A. 1R. 14P.)

18. A cottage belonging in 1842 to William Davey, occupied by William Culham, who was a farm labourer of 40 with a wife Elizabeth and 7 children, William (16), John (13), Richard (11) and Samuel (9) all of whom were called 'agricultural labourers' in the census, and Henry (6), Hannah (4) and Mary Ann (1). (No 175 on tithe map, with 30P.)

19. A double cottage belonging in 1842 to Henry Copeman, one part he occupied and the other was let to Thomas Middleton. Henry Copeman was a carpenter of 55 with a wife Sophia. Thomas Middleton was 25 and a farm worker, with a wife Melinda, and a lodger, Susan Wiseman aged 12. (These are number 176 with 1R. 6P. and number 177 with 1R. 15P. on tithe map).

19. 'A double cottage' - 22 & 23 School Lane. C.1930

20. House, garden and orchard with 11 ½ acres belonging to Joseph Wilkinson and occupied by Edmund Eden in 1842. Edmund was said to be 60 in 1841, with a wife Mary of the same age. He was a farmer and gardener, and had a son George aged 30 and a lodger (or servant?) named Eliza Wild aged 30. (No. 179 on tithe map with 11A. 1R. 25P.)

21. Manor House and Farm with 145 ½ acres, belonging to Frank Bacon Esq. and let to John Girling in 1842, one of the oldest houses in the village. John's widowed mother, Mrs. Elizabeth Girling was living here in 1841, with her granddaughter Juliana Girling aged 20 as housekeeper, and Ann Baldry aged 20 as a family servant. John himself lived in Earlham. (No. 172 on tithe map with 145A. 1R. 32P.)

22. Pond Piece and **Hospital Farm** belonged in both 1817 and 1842 to the Trustees of the Boys and Girls Hospitals in Norwich, who purchased the land in 1705. It still belongs to the same charity today, and is farmed by Mr Philip Eagle. Its farm house, known from old manorial records as 'Moores' once stood on the site of today's 'Pond Piece', the latter probably built in the mid 19th century. William Forster was farming its 40 ¾ acres in 1842, and was said to be 70 in 1841, as was his wife Sarah. He is described as a farmer, with a resident lodger Sarah Clarke aged 20. There were two living-in servants, Mariann Brand (16) and John Long (60). (No. 198 on tithe map, with 40A. 2R. 32P).

23. The pair of cottages next door, known today as **Resthaven** and **Old Post Office Cottage**, (which at one time belonged to Manor Farm) are shown on both the Enclosure and Tithe maps. In 1817 they were freehold property, owned by Ann Davey (wife of William Davey, sister of Sarah Forster, and daughter of the late Thomas Palmer), and in 1842 to William Davey, in the occupation of Charles Bishop and others. Charles was a farm labourer of 60 with a wife Mary of 50, and four youngsters (possibly grandchildren), Jemima (20), Jeremiah (13, and a farm labourer), Mary (age 6 months) and 20 year old Robert Rayner. (No. 170 on tithe map, with 30P.)

24. An elongated cottage, shown on both the enclosure and tithe maps as end on to the road, and standing well back from it, which must be the flint and brick cottages of **'The Close'.** This was copyhold and owned in 1817 by Sarah Forster, (wife of William Forster, sister of Ann Davey and daughter of Thomas Palmer deceased). This belonged to Mr William Forster of Hospital Farm in 1842, and was then occupied by Thomas Forster and Jonathan Smith. Thomas was a 45 year old farm worker, living with his wife Elizabeth and daughter Mary, aged 5 years. Jonathan was a 60 year old farm worker, living with his wife Ann and Maria Smith, aged 10, perhaps a granddaughter. (No. 169 on tithe map, with 3R. 14P.)

25. The Homestead and Home Farm Cottage, with 16 acres in 1817. By 1842 the Home Farm and 25 ½ acres was owned and occupied by William Cooper, (45), together with his wife Esther, two children, William (2) and Robert (1 month) and three living in servants, Emily Mitchell (15), Miles Mace (15) and Elizabeth Parker (60). These are described more fully in chapter eight - House Histories. (No 162 on tithe map, with 25A. 2R. 14P.)

26. A double cottage owned by John Saint and occupied by John Elliot and Robert Auger in 1842. Robert was a farm labourer aged 50, with a wife Charlotte and three children, Susan (10), Sarah (13) and Charlotte (11). John Elliot was also an agricultural labourer aged 55, with a wife Mary and a daughter Maria aged 20. James Pettett lived with them, a farm worker aged 25. (No. 130 on tithe map with 3R. 8P.)

27. A cottage owned by Samuel Bailey and occupied by Mary Barnes and others in 1842. Mary was a 45 year old shopkeeper in 1841, with 5 children, Harriett (15), James (15 - an agricultural labourer), Mary Ann (10), Rebecca (8), and Robert (5). Living with them were Ann Larkman (75), Samuel Bunn (20) and William Mitchell (15) both farm labourers. (No. 128 on tithe map, with 1A. OR. 26P.)

28. Elm Farm c.1950

28. Elm Farm, (a late 18th century property) with about 40 acres, owned by Rev. Thomas Starling Buckle in 1842 and occupied by Thomas Forster. The Rev. Buckle lived in Hethersett, but was a member of Little Melton Vestry for many years and Curate for a period, being much involved with the administration of the Town House (or Poor House) of the village. Thomas Forster was a 65 year old farmer in 1841, living with Elizabeth Forster aged 40, (perhaps his daughter?) and a 25 year old manservant. He served the village in many capacities, for example as Parish Clerk in 1835 and as Churchwarden in 1836 and 1837. (No. 122 on tithe map, with 38A.1R.36P.)

29. A house owned by Samuel Hipperson and occupied by William Larkman in 1842. In 1841 William Larkman was listed as a 25 year old farmer living here, with a wife Martha of the same age. This is **Rose Villa,** built by Samuel Hipperson in 1833, extended and owned today by Dr. Christopher Aslin and family. (No. 131 on tithe map, with 2A. 1R. 7P.)

29. Rose Villa c.1995

30. A cottage owned by Ann Davey and occupied by William Joy, a rat and mole catcher. The Rev. Barkley said that William (30) had a wife Sophia and 3 children, though the census lists only Martha (2) and Thomas (4 months). William had been ill in 1841, and had obtained a medical order but the doctor did not visit, and he was obliged to obtain the services of another practitioner. The cottage had originally been owned by the parish and sold to Mary Hempstead in 1816. (No. 112 on tithe map, with 1R.21P.)

31. The Blacksmith's Shop, house and yard, owned by William Howard in 1817 and later sold to Thomas Hubbard, and occupied in 1842 by William Hubbard. William was 25 in 1841 with a wife Rosella, and was styled 'Farmer'. (No. 95 on tithe map, with 15A.3R.17P.) Could this be '1 The Farmhouse' and '2 The Farmhouse' today?

32. A double cottage (each half being 'one up and one down') owned by the Executors of Edmund Copeman in 1842, with one part occupied by William Gould. He was a farm labourer of 35 with a wife Rebecca and 7 children, John (14 - an agricultural labourer), and Caroline (12), William (10), Charles (8), James (6), Elizabeth (4) and Mary Ann (2). (William Gould's family gave grave concern to the Rev. William Barkley and features in the chapter 'Social Welfare and the Poor'.) The other half was occupied by John Oaks, a 65 year old agricultural labourer, with family members listed as Mary (20), Charlotte (15), Betsy (25) and Sarah (5). The Rev. Barkley noted that John was receiving outdoor relief. His daughter of 14 was ill for 7 weeks, during which time his wife was taken ill and died after eleven days. Another daughter was 'ill of the fever' for seven weeks. In all, the doctor visited three times. (No. 94 on tithe map, with 10P.)

33. A cottage owned by the Executors of Edmund Copeman in 1842, and occupied by John Kemp. John was 50 years old and styled 'Gardener' in 1841, living with his wife Lucy and daughters Mary (2) and Charlotte (15). (No. 93 on tithe map, with 3A.3R.24P.)

34. A double cottage owned by the Executors of Edmund Copeman in 1842, and occupied by Thomas Mitchells and William Symonds. Thomas was a 65 year old agricultural labourer, with a wife Mary Ann, and five children, Thomas (20) and Henry (17), both farm workers, and Caroline (12), Lewis (10) and Eliza (5). William Symonds was a 20 year old agricultural labourer with a wife Sarah. The Rev. Barkley noted that Thomas Mitchells had been ill, had received medical visits and had recovered. William Symonds's wife *'was suddenly taken with fits'*. He sent for the doctor who came without an order being issued. Symonds paid him 7 shillings for the visit, which included *'pills and a mixture'*. (No. 92 on tithe map, with 34P.)

35. The Mill, House and Gardens built in 1832 by Robert Lovett and still owned by him, occupied by Thomas Ringer. Thomas was said to be 20 years old, living there with a 15 year old assistant Daniel, and two other members of the family, Susanne (20) and Tabitha Ringer (15). (No. 71 on tithe map with 32P). William Russell, the miller, lodged at Hatherley Farmhouse nearby.

36. A Cottage owned by Ann Duckett in 1817 and in 1842, when it was occupied by John Pearse. In 1841 John Pearse was 35, a farm worker, with a wife Charlotte and five children. The older two, William (15) and Stephen (14) were both agricultural labourers, while the younger three were Hannah (1), James (8) and John (5). (No. 70 on tithe map with 3R.27P.) This was 'The Gardens', recently demolished, a new house of the same name having been built on the site in 2001.

37. Rosecolm c.1963

37. Cottages owned by James Long and occupied by Samuel Briggs and William Goward. Samuel was 25, a farm worker, living there with his wife Lucy, and three children, Sarah Ann (5), John (3) and George (1). William Goward was also an agricultural labourer, aged 30, with wife Mary Ann, and three children, James (8), Godfrey (3) and Mary Ann (9 months). (No. 69 on tithe map, with 1R.19P). This is now the house named **'Rosecolm'.**

38. A House, yard and buildings with 6 ½ acres, owned by James Long and occupied by Samuel Todd in 1842. This is **Hatherley Farmhouse**. Samuel was a 45 year old farmer, living with his wife Sarah and his son David aged 5. Lodging with them was Richard Hovell (15) and William Russell aged 45, who was the local miller. (No. 68 on the tithe award, with 6A.1R.35P.)

39. Valley Cottage owned by John Reynolds and occupied by Edward Bacon and John Smith. Edward Bacon was an agricultural labour of 30 with a wife Charlotte aged 25, and three children, Edward (7), Thomas (5) and Philip (3). By 1845 when he was in the Swainsthorpe workhouse, (as described in the chapter on 'Social Welfare and the Poor'), he said he was 42 years old and had another two recently born children, David (3) and Solomon (1). Eventually, the whole family was bodily *'removed to Hempnall'*. (No 11 on tithe map with 1R. 16P.).

40. Another cottage owned by John Reynolds and occupied by Robert Woolsey and others. (No. 12 on tithe map, with 2R.6P.)

41. Valley Farm c.1955

41. Valley Farm owned by John Reynolds in 1817 and by Edward Lombe Esq. in 1842, when it was farmed by Samuel Hipperson. Farming was a side-line for Samuel (41) who had by now set himself up as a builder. He had a wife Ann and nine children. The eldest William (15) helped his father as a bricklayer, and the others were Mary Ann and Elizabeth (both 15), Eliza (14), Hannah (11), Sarah (9), Samuel (7), Henry (2) and Charles (10 months). (No. 9 on the tithe map with 20A.1R.2P.)

42. Cottages owned by John Saint and occupied by John Blake and John Frank. John Blake was a 45 year old farm worker, with a wife Lucy and four children, Robert (20) an agricultural labourer, and Sarah (20), William (9) and Edward (6). John Frank was a 55 year old farm worker, with a wife Sarah and a daughter Anne aged 15. They had a lodger John Ruby (25) also an agricultural labourer. (No. 5 on the tithe map with 1R.27P.)

43. The Vicarage with a 5 acre garden. The land had been owned by the church in 1817, but the house was built after this date. It was occupied in 1842 by the Rev. John Barkley, vicar of the parish, who was 40 years old with a wife Mary and five children. They were George (14), Edward (12), Frances (6), Henry (4) and Robert (2). There were also two living-in servants, Ann Vince aged 35, and Mary Ann Canham, aged 20. (No. 7 on the tithe map with 12A.1R.16P.)

43. The Vicarage c.1920

44. A house and orchard belonging to Thomas Webb and occupied by George Roper. (probably Babur Cottage). (No 55 on the tithe map, with 1R.19P.)

The 1841 Census for Little Melton shows that there were 330 people living in Little Melton then, divided into 77 households, often in shared accommodation. Nearly half the population was under twenty years old, while only 28 were 60 or over. The workers were:

Agricultural labourers	73
Servants	15
Farmers	7
Market Gardeners	5
Millers	3
Carpenters	2
Bricklayers	2
Shopkeepers	2
Innkeeper	1
Painter	1
Builder	1
Shoemaker	1
Gamekeeper	1
Drover	1
Rat & Mole Catcher	1
Blacksmith	1
Clerk in Holy Orders	1

Nearly everybody was engaged in agriculture and its supportive trades, and there were very few 'tied cottages'. In estate or 'closed' villages, like Colney or Great Melton, most labourers lived in houses owned by the farmers who employed them, but this was not the case here, cottages being owned by a large variety of different people. It is quite surprising how few cottages, in fact, belonged to either Church Farm (owned by the Lombe family), Manor Farm (owned by the Bacon Frank family), or the Colney Estate (owned by the Barclay family). The census for 1841 and the Tithe documents of 1842 are not totally consistent, some people having come into the village during these two years, and some having left, as people moved about in this period far more than we used to think.

Eighty years later the village does not seem to have changed all that much. **The Little Melton Rate Book for 1924** shows that there were now 49 houses, (an increase of only 5 properties), many with multiple occupancy. These were, including the pub and two shops:

1.   Joseph James Aldous at Rose Villa   Owned by J. J. Aldous
2.   William Bailey at Home Farm   Owned by Ernest H. Bailey

3.	Charles Bilham at Vine Cottage	Owned by Charles Bilham
4.	Herbert G. Beeston at Grey Cottage	Owned by H. G. Beeston
5.	Edwin Alfred Clarke at Elm Farm	Owned by Edwin A. Clarke
6.	James Daniels by the Mill	Owned by James Daniels
7.	William S. Diaper at Manor Farm	Owned by Bacon Franks Ex'ors.
8.	William S. Diaper at Hospital Farm	Owned by Hospital Trustees
9.	George W. Denny at the Shrubbery	Owned by George W. Denny
10.	Arthur S.H. Dicker at Hill House	Owned by Arthur S. H. Dicker
11.	William H. Davy on Hethersett Rd	Owned by William H. Davy
12.	Henry G. Denny at The Brambles	Owned by Rosina Smith
13.	James Bird by Hingham Road	Owned by H. G. Barclay Esq
14.	Cecil Hipperson at Valley Farm	Owned by Evans-Lombe Esq
15.	Richard Hill at Garden House by Mill	Owned by Mrs Murton
16.	Gertrude E. Kinch at School House	Owned by Norfolk Educ'on C'tee
17.	William Lack at Church Farm	Owned by Evans-Lombe Esq.
18.	Charles Lofty by the Mill	Owned by H. G. Barclay Esq.
19.	Thomas H Loomb at Rose & Crown	Owned by Bullard & Son

Little Melton Windmill c.1900

20.	Thomas. R. Robertson at Mill House	Owned by Thos. R. Robertson
21.	Sparkes Executors by the Green	Owned by Sparkes Ex'ors
22.	Charles S. Simpson at Vicarage	Owned by Rev N.W. Paine
23.	Arthur W. Symonds by the Green	Owned by Thomas Fox
24.	George Woodgett at Willow Farm	Owned by Bacon Franks Ex'ors

Cottages

1.	Donald C. Duncan at Rose Dale	Owned by Robert J. Aldred
2.	Rbt. J. Aldred at The Rookery	Owned by Robert J. Aldred
3.	John Joy by Crossways	Owned by Frederick Armes
	Wm E. Mallett by Crossways	Owned by Frederick Armes
4.	Wm Goward by the Mill	Owned by H. G. Barclay Esq
	Arthur Bishop on Mill Road	Owned by H. G. Barclay Esq.
	Charles Lofty on Mill Road	Owned by H. G. Barclay Esq.
	James Ringwood on Mill Road	Owned by H. G. Barclay Esq.
5.	Bailey Walker - Shop by P.O.	Owned by Mary Barham
6.	Azalear Jeckells by The Green	Owned by Mary Barham
7.	Thomas Harvey by The Green	Owned by Mary Barham
8.	George Symonds by Crossways	Owned by Eva Bailey
9.	Wm J. Childs House & Shop by Crossways	Owned by Eva Bailey
10.	Alfred Harvey by Rose & Crown	Not marked

Mill Road, between the two world wars

	John A. Burcham by Rose & Crown	Not marked
11.	George Mace by The Green	Owned by Ernest H. Bailey
	William Mitchell by The Green	Owned by Ernest H. Bailey
	George Dunton by The Green	Owned by Ernest H. Bailey
12.	Frederick Mace by Norwich Rd	Owned by William H. Davy
	Herbert Rudd by Norwich Rd	Owned by William H. Davy
	John Child by Norwich Rd	Owned by William H. Davy
	Eliza Joy by Norwich Rd	Owned by William H. Davy
13.	Edward Mayes by The Green	Owned by Bacon Franks Ex'ors
	Ernest Bunn by The Green	Owned by Bacon Franks Ex'ors
	Thomas Arthurton by The Green	Owned by Bacon Franks Ex'ors
14.	Russell Lofty by Mill	Owned by Mary Ann Hill
	Amelia Etheridge by Mill	Owned by Mary Ann Hill
	Archibald Bailey by Mill	Owned by Mary Ann Hill
	Gilbert A. Herwin by Mill	Owned by Mary Ann Hill
15.	Wesley Hill by Mill	Owned by Miss Knights
	Fanny Bailey by Mill	Owned by Miss Knights
	John Palmer by Mill	Owned by Miss Knights
	Elizabeth Hill by Mill	Owned by Miss Knights
16.	Alfred Ottaway by Crossways	Owned by Miss Knights
	George Bunn senior by Crossways	Owned by Miss Knights
17.	Mary Fox by Crossways	Owned by Francis Leeds
	George Bunn junior by Crossways	Owned by Francis Leeds
18.	John Lynn by Norwich Road (Greycottage)	Owned by Herbert G. Beeston
19.	Thos Carman by Gt Melton Rd	Owned by Evans-Lombe Esq
	Chas Doubleday by Gt Melton Rd	Owned by Evans-Lombe Esq
20.	Ellen Davey by Hingham Rd	Owned by Evans-Lombe Esq
	Edwd Harrison by Hingham Rd	Owned by Evans-Lombe Esq
	Bertie Cullum by Hingham Rd	Owned by Evans-Lombe Esq
	Wm Parselow by Hingham Rd	Owned by Evans-Lombe Esq
	George Bishop by Hingham Rd	Owned by Evans-Lombe Esq
21.	Joseph Symonds Parish Cottage by Crossways	
		Owned by Parish Council
	James Symonds Parish Cottage by Crossways	
		Owned by Parish Council
22.	Samuel Hill by Gt. Melton Rd	Owned by Walter Sheldrake
	Alfred Eden by Gt. Melton Rd	Owned by Walter Sheldrake
23.	Robert Allcock by Gt. Melton Rd	Owned by William Sheldrake
	Matilda Nichols by Gt. Melton Rd	Owned by William Sheldrake

	Albert J Eden by Gt Melton Rd	Owned by William Sheldrake
24.	Percy Reyner by School	Owned by Eva Lewis
	Arthur W Symonds by School	Owned by Eva Lewis
	George Blake by School	Owned by Eva Lewis
	Charles Sparke by School	Owned by Eva Lewis
25.	Robert Carr by Hethersett Road	Owned by Uttings Executors
	Henry Denmark by Hethersett Road	Owned by Uttings Executors
	Elizabeth Denmark by Hethersett Road	Owned by Uttings Executors
	Lydia Howes by Hethersett Road	Owned by Uttings Executors

Some six years later, in the 1930s, building plots began to be sold for £50 apiece, while in the 1960s, development began in earnest and has continued ever since. Now in 2003 Little Melton has some 400 houses.

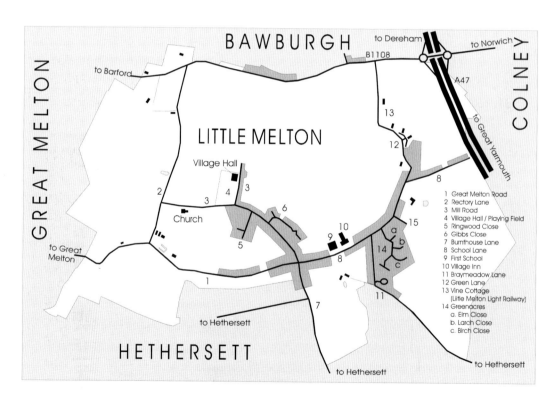

Little Melton 2003 (shading indicates developed areas)

There is nothing which has yet been contrived by man, by which so much happiness is produced as by a good tavern or inn.

Samuel Johnson

Did you know that...

...the Rose and Crown (the predecessor of the Village Inn), **was known locally as The Cold Blow?**

There seems to have been an ale house in the village since at least 1698, probably on the same site as today. By the 1830s and until World War I, the 'Cold Blow' seems to have held an off licence only, with the serving hatch set to the side of an outside door. For years, the roadside bank opposite had a form or seat for the use of customers, while others imbibed while sitting in their gigs or wagons, hence its facetious name.

In 1841 William Burcham was the licensee, but he had left by 1851. Later, Mary Ann Reynolds held sway for at least twenty years from 1861 to 1881, followed by Mr. and Mrs. Joshua Reynolds in 1885. Later, it seems to

The Rose & Crown c.1896

have been owned by the Lofty family for a time, with Samuel Crome Drake as licence-holder. Emma Reynolds, widow, was here in 1891, with a large family of 8 children, while Dick Reynolds (who was also the postman) and his sister were the licensees from about 1900, until Bullards bought the property in 1911 or '12, when it ceased to be a Free House.

When he came to Little Melton at the turn of the century, Dick Reynolds built the clubroom, originally for the use of the Ancient Order of Foresters, who held their regular meetings there, as well as their Annual Dinner. It was a one-storey building, lying behind and at right angles to the main house, being made mainly of wood with a corrugated iron roof, and was much used as a centre of village life for the next seventy-five years. Well-attended dances, socials and whist-drives were held there, and during the war, it acted in many capacities, not only as a temporary classroom, after the school was bombed, but also as a cinema, and even for a short time as a barracks for soldiers, when an army unit was billeted there. There was also a large pond where the rear carpark is today.

From 1914 Mr and Mrs Thomas (Happy) Loomb were mine hosts until September 1940, when their son Herbert and his wife Mollie took over from them, and Mollie's amusing anecdotes appear elsewhere in this book. Amongst other things, she describes being David Niven's batman when he stayed at the pub in the war, while serving in the army, but she remembers things very differently from what follows! The famous actor wrote a letter to Mr Joe Day of Little Melton in 1979 in which he says '*I do remember being billeted for a week or so in the Rose and Crown. I was in a very secret reconnaissance unit*

Herbert and Mollie Loomb outside the 'Rose & Crown' in the 1940s

called *"Phantom" and I slept on the floor in an upstairs room between a mad major who was commanding my squadron and his great dane. I don't know which smelled the worst! One morning at breakfast a junior officer, who had been blown up at Dunkirk, decided that he was even madder than the major, so he broke two eggs on his head and was dismissed. I wish I had had the sense to pretend to be mad too, because this fellow became a bank manager and very rich, and I was scared to death in Normandy, Belgium, Holland and Germany, and came out of the war very, very poor. P.S Mistake by secretary. I said SNORED THE WORST! He did not smell too bad.'* The other officers were Major Tony Warre, and the Hon. Michael Astor, each of the three occupying a private bedroom, with no great danes around, according to 'mine host' Mollie Loomb!

Also in wartime, the vicar, the Rev. Frost, used to give film shows in the clubroom at the back of the pub, much enjoyed by both troops and parishioners, and senior residents can still remember Monday nights as much enjoyed 'picture nights'.

By 1958 Mr Joe Hambling and his wife Edie were the proprietors. At this period the Little Melton Football Club boasted two teams, and met regularly at the pub, getting as far as the quarter finals of the Norfolk Mercury Cup on one occasion. When Mr "Curly" Potter was treasurer, he used to keep the club funds in a biscuit tin under the stairs, until Mr. Harcourt, the Vice-President, and

Joe Hambling at the 'Rose & Crown' in the 1960s

144

A gathering in 'The Cold Blow' - 14th October 1966
1, Fred Defew; 2, Joe Hambling; 3, Edith Hambling; 4, Jack Reynolds;
5, Archie Harmer; 6, Bob Hart; 7, Harry Chamberlain;
8, Arthur Easter; 9, Albert Loader.

a builder by trade, put a stop to this, insisting on a bank account. The football club ended in about 1974 to '75, through lack of members, but a strong darts team continued to flourish.

Mrs Edith Hambling only retired in 1975 after 17 years service, ably assisted by her son Rex. The Rose and Crown closed after they left, and from 19th October 1975 there followed a time of great uncertainty as to its future, many fearing it was the end of an era, with plans to build residential properties on the site. David and Helen Bales eventually bought the place, pulled down the club room, (now in a dilapidated state, with a rat run in its roof), and refurbished the main building, opening it as 'The Village Inn' on 14th December 1976. It was a cold, foggy

Joe Hambling

night, but the place was completely packed out. The building was extended in 1978 and now does a roaring trade under the ownership of Whitbread Chiltern Inns.

...it was the end of an era when Mr. William Spenser Diaper died in 1939 after tenanting Manor Farm for well over half a century?

He would ride round the farm on his horse, or stride along with a walking stick and a dog, giving instructions over his shoulder to his farm steward, (Symonds by name), who would walk decorously a number of paces behind him, armed with a tall pole like a shepherd's crook. The instructions and Symonds' 'Yes sir' could be heard all over the parish.

Mr. Diaper farmed the land from the 1880s, after training in management as a pupil, and employed no less than ten men, also paying two girls one penny apiece for each day's work guarding his sheep. Why his leading horse should have been considered similar to a leading sail is a little inexplicable, but it was apparently for this reason that he was always known locally as 'Spinnaker'.

His wife, Mrs. Mary Diaper was a character too. She would don her hunting outfit and ride round the village on her horse. If goods were required of the shop, a rattle on the door with her hunting crop would soon bring attention, whatever the hour. She died some years before her husband, who then hired a housekeeper, Miss Savage, to care for him.

...market gardening increasingly flourished here from the late 19th century? In 1891 as many as fifteen men were employed in this business, and numbers grew as time progressed. John Watson Sparkes cultivated two acres near Grey Cottage as a Violet Nursery for nearly fifty years from the 1880s, employing many local people, and the Little Melton Light Railway was built where there was once intensive market gardening. Glass houses stood here until the 1960s growing grapes and other exotic fruits, while earlier, in the late 19th century, the little known 'love apples' were a special delicacy. This is the old word for tomatoes, which now line our supermarket shelves in abundance. The sixty houses on the Greenacres estate, erected in the year 2000, were built on land once used for market gardening.

...there are Ghost Stories from the Meltons as told by Percy Garrod and W.H. Barrett in their book 'East Anglian Folklore' (1976)?

In 1875 in a yearly periodical known as The East Anglian Handbook, the following story was told,

'There was formerly a curious legend told amongst Melton folk, how a bridal party, driving along what was known as the old Norwich Road, were accidentally upset into a very deep pit, so deep that it was reputed to be bottomless. The unfortunate people were never seen again, at least, not in the flesh. Nevertheless every midnight and every noon a carriage drawn by four horses, driven by a headless coachman and footman and containing four headless ladies in bridal dresses, rises, all dripping wet from the pool. This outfit careers silently around an adjoining field then just as quietly sinks again into the pit.

Little Melton lane (the one now known as 'Rectory Lane' fits the story) is also reputed to be haunted by a tall man in black. He springs from the adjoining marl pit upon belated travellers. Perhaps this is a local equivalent for the Erl King (or Oak King) of Danish mythology, who dwelt in the innermost recesses of the forest and thence lured unsuspecting travellers to their destruction.'

The devastated garage with the remains of an acetylene cylinder.

...that a major fire destroyed Little Melton Garage on Saturday 19th June 1993?

Neighbouring residents feared for their premises as the inferno raged in the early hours of the morning. Sixteen firemen attended the fire during which a gas cylinder exploded and fears grew as more were inside.

The owners of the neighbouring Post Office, Beryl and Ken Hillsdon were awoken by their dog barking at 2am and thought their property was next to be engulfed by the flames. Another neighbour, Rosemary Warnes, believed the situation could have been much worse with the spread of the fire, had there not been torrential rain the evening before.

The garage was re-built and now operates on the same site next to the shop, once the Post Office, on School Lane.

Chapter Eight

ouse Histories

If I ever become a rich man,
Or if ever I grow to be old,
I will build a house with deep thatch
To shelter me from the cold.
Hilaire Belloc.

Little Melton is not a picture postcard village, with thatched cottages rubbing shoulders with each other, but older buildings do still exist, if one looks for them. With its proximity to Norwich, development has been inevitable, as gradually, ever since the 1930s, comfortable up-to-date houses have largely replaced the older properties, though it's sad that none of the original clay lump or wattle and daub cottages remain.   The preface to a small book of printed Little Melton Parish Registers (1732-1837) says *'Although once a plague village, hardly anything remains of its antiquity; it is now mainly a few rambling streets of modern bungalows'.*

However, if one cares to look a bit deeper.....

The Manor House, School Lane.

The Manor House in Little Melton is hidden away behind trees just past the Post Office Stores and garage, and one could formerly get a glimpse of a donkey or two grazing in the field alongside its drive. It is believed to be sixteenth century in origin, being an *'L-shaped manor house with stepped gables, two of them with polygonal single shafts, a three-bay front, and a later one storey porch. It was the seat of a branch of the Marshams 1534-circa 1620 and of the Skottowes, circa 1630 to circa 1720.'* (This is an extract from Burke and Saville's Guide to English Country Houses, Volume III, East Anglia).

Nikolaus Pevsner and Bill Wilson in their book on the buildings of England for North-West and South Norfolk have this to say about it: *'Brick is still English bond, which for Norfolk means only earlier than c.1700, but the stepped end gables and polygonal angle-shafts suggest about 1600. So too do the sunk-quadrant mouldings of the ground floor tie-beam to the lower rooms. Early nineteenth century stick-baluster staircase.'*

Mr and Mrs Tony Rudd, who after 30 years residence sold the property in late 2002 to Mr. & Mrs. Hazell, still possess a photo-copy of some very old, dilapidated deeds, dating from 1588 (though the last number is very indistinct), and so believe the house was built shortly before the Spanish Armada took place. Certainly, these dates fit well with those suggested by the experts.

Elizabeth Marsham, widow of John of Norwich, (a member of the younger branch of the well known Marsham family of Stratton Strawless), purchased the manor of Little Melton from Giles & Mary Alyngton in 1534, and the family held the lordship until about 1620, when it was sold. Elizabeth's grandson Robert Marsham had a daughter Dorothie, who married Edmund Anguish of Great Melton. This young couple feature on Little Melton's only church brass, together with their baby son, Robert Anguish, whose death in 1604 was closely followed by that of his mother. It was probably the baby's grandfather, Robert Marsham, (or even Robert's father Ralph), who built the original Manor House.

Robert Marsham wrote his will on 2nd June 1614 when he is described as *'of Little Melton, Norfolk, Gentleman, sick in body but of good and perfect memory'*. He died the following year, when his will was proved in the important Prerogative Court of Canterbury, leaving a wife Elizabeth and three sons, John, Edward and Thomas. He had already assigned part of his property in Melton to Elizabeth, and part to his son Edward, and now requested his wife to allow John to occupy her portion, provided he paid £10 to her *'at Little Melton Church Porch'* each quarter. Robert also left houses and grounds in St Peter Mancroft and St John Maddermarket, Norwich, to this same son John, as well as lands *'of the Manor of Cossey, Norfolk'*.

The Norfolk historian Francis Blomefield wrote that at the time of the sale in 1620, the Little Melton manor was let at £125 per annum, and contained above 320 acres. He said that it had been 'manumised' by the Marshams, meaning that they had agreed to receive money payments from most of their tenants, instead of demanding actual physical labour from them. As we have seen, the family obviously had a great affinity with the village, and in addition, Thomas Marsham gave a tenor bell to the church in 1605. This weighs half a ton, and still hangs in the tower today, being chimed before Sunday service.

Thomas Sayer and Will Barker held the manor for a year or two after the Marshams, and settled it on Laurence Sotherton, Gent, in 1623. He was grandson of Nicholas Sotherton of Norwich, who had bought Melton-Hall in 1574, and son of Henry Sotherton, who died intestate in Little Melton in 1618. Henry's inventory shows his house had five main rooms, almost certainly Melton-Hall, Little Melton, on whose site 'the Grange' stands today.

Later, some time before 1636, Augustine Skottowe, Alderman and Sheriff of Norwich, purchased the manor of Little Melton, (the Sotherton and Skottowe families being intermarried), though it seems unlikely that he lived here. He died in 1637 and was succeeded by his eldest son Richard who died in 1656. Richard's brother, another Augustine succeeded him, and probably lived at Melton-Hall, dying in 1683.

From the Little Melton Hearth Tax returns of 1664, we find that Thomas Rackham was living in a house with nine hearths or fireplaces, far and away the biggest property in the village, the next largest having only five hearths. Was he perhaps tenanting the Manor House? From his will of 1678 we find he was a man of considerable substance, holding both freehold and copyhold lands and houses in Little Melton, Colney, Fritton and Morningthorpe, which he left to his sons. The Rackhams continued to play a prominent part in village life here for many years, and it may well be that other members of the family also tenanted the property.

The Ledger Stone to Thomas Skottowe's wife and children in Little Melton Church

It was Thomas Skottowe, (Augustine the younger's son), who seems to have really cared about the village and its inhabitants. He lived at the Manor House from about 1696 to 1720, and presided over many of the manor courts himself, together with his steward, taking an enormous interest in local happenings. From the court rentals we know that the tenants met *'under the Walnutt tree on the Lower Green'* (very near the Manor House) before adjourning elsewhere for the actual proceedings to take place. From 1698 to 1704 Thomas himself noted that the court was *'Kept at my Howse'*. In 1705 and 1706 it was held at *'Henry Bucke's house'*, and in 1707 at the *'Ale House'*, but from 1708 to 1710, and again from 1712 to 1715, Thomas headed each court entry with the succinct words *'Adjourned to Manor House'*. No locations are given after this date. He loved Little Melton so much that though he had left the parish by 1725, when he retired to the Cathedral Close in Norwich, he still wanted to be buried here many years later, as did his daughter Katherine who lived with him. Memorials in the chancel of All Saints and wills proved in the Prerogative Court of Canterbury record that his burial here was in 1766 and Katharine's was just three years later.

The Skottowe monument in Little Melton Church chancel

Sir Benjamin Wrench, a famous Norwich physician, was lord from 1724 to 1747. For at least part of this time, it seems he lived in the village, presumably at the Manor House, but we have no details. On one occasion when a patient had been bitten by a dog, the good doctor prescribed sea bathing, which apparently worked!

Edward Bacon Esq. bought the manor from Sir Benjamin's executors and held his first court at Little Melton on 18 Oct 1749. Members of the Bacon Frank family of Campsall, near Doncaster, (and also of nearby Earlham), had the lordship for nearly 200 years, until 1939 when it was bought by the Colney estate. During this whole period, the Manor House was let to long-term sitting tenants.

An interesting paper on the history of Little Melton was written some 25 years ago by Mr Frank Marston Gibbs, who had lived in the village for many years. He wrote about the Manor House having *'great solid oak roof rafters, seen before oak became scarce in the later part of the sixteenth century,'* and said that *'the house was originally fitted with oak mullioned and transomed windows with a great central chimney with an open roasting fireplace. All that remains of this is a half submerged cellar, used for storage and frost free in winter, where bricks of an earlier date than those of the present house can be seen.'* He also noted that *'the height of the gables, crow-stepped with original trefoil shaped ornamental bricks, above the roof, implies that this roof was pantiled on erection. There were 4 polygonal corner towers but one was removed when the present wing was added about 1830. At that time new farm buildings were also erected, replacing the old, but without a corn barn, indicating that mechanical threshers had now arrived. A new westerly domestic wing was then built, and an Elizabethan type porch was added. The great central chimney was removed, making ample room for the present hall, staircase, landing and bedroom. The windows were replaced by the*

The Manor House c.2000

present country style pinewood frames with inside shutters. Curiously these windows were topped with wooden hood moulds in imitation of 15th century masonry hoods. The attic was refloored for use as maids' bedrooms, complete with jangling wire pulled bells.'

The Manor dovecote used to stand on the site of the nineteenth century farm buildings, and apparently had foundations similar to those of the Manor house itself. Mr. Gibbs said that *'It was circular with 500 holes in the brickwork, where the birds lived and nested. At the peak was an extended louvred inlet and outlet above the coned roof. Like most circular lofts it had a centrally pivoted wooden tree with a ladder mortised into the central pole, upon which the owner would climb after dark, and propel himself around to collect eggs and birds for the cooking pot as required.'*

Free-standing dovecotes of this type were only permitted to be built by the aristocracy, and the damage done by the birds was greatly resented by the villagers, who had no redress at all when their crops and vegetables were decimated. The National Trust property of Felbrigg Hall still has a fine dovecote of this type, and, with permission, one can also visit a similar one at Great Melton, near the remains of the Hall there, which was itself built about the year 1611.

Over the centuries, then,

Little Melton Manor House was owned by:

The Manorial Lords , the **Marsham, Sotherton** and **Scottowe** families, from the late sixteenth century to 1723.

Sir Benjamin Wrench from 1724 until his death in 1747.

The **Bacon** (later Bacon Frank) families from 1749 to 1939.

The Colney Estate owned by the Barclay family from 1939 to 1957.

Mr James Nash and sons from 1957 to 1967.

Professor Lasko, Professor of Fine Arts at the University of East Anglia, who embarked upon an ambitious restoration project, removing several fireplaces from the dining room. He lived here from 1967 to '69, and then sold the house to

Mr & Mrs Willmott, who removed both chimneys and installed central heating, living here from 1968 to '69, who then sold to

Mr and Mrs Anthony Rudd in 1970. Mr Rudd replaced the chimney on the new wing in 1988.

Mr and Mrs Hazell in 2002.

Little Melton Manor House was tenanted by:

William Girling from about 1790 to his death in 1805, and his widow Elizabeth from 1805-42. Their grave is a chest tomb in Great Melton churchyard.

(The farm was run by their son John from 1805 to about 1850, when he moved to Baconsthorpe. Though farming at Little Melton, John lived at Earlham).

Francis Gray Rudd from 1851 to the late 1860s. (No relation to the previous 'Rudd' owners of the Manor House!)

John Utting from about 1870 to 1883.

William Spencer Diaper from about 1885 to 1939

James Nash & Sons from 1939 until purchase in 1957

The Grange, Great Melton Road,
(built on the site of Melton-Hall).

If you walk to the far end of Great Melton Road, just before the turning onto Rectory Lane, you will see a driveway on your right leading up to a fine, large mid-nineteenth century building, called the Grange. This was built sometime after 1842 (when the Tithe Redemption Map was published) on the foundations of 'The Old Hall Farm', which were incorporated into the new building. To the right of the drive is a horseshoe-shaped moat, which may well be medieval in origin.

'The Old Hall Farm', as it came to be called in the early eighteenth centry, was all that remained of Melton-Hall, a small manor within Little Melton, (originally quite separate from the main, and larger, manor of Little Melton), which had existed from at least the twelfth century, according to the Norfolk historian Blomefield. It is highly probable that the lords of Melton-Hall were the builders of our parish church of 1300, which lies close by, just across the fields.

Thomas Batchcroft was lord of Melton-Hall in the fifteenth century. We know from his will of 1501 that he was living at the hall before his death, when he asked to be buried *'in the Chapel of our Lady on the north side of the Church of All Halowes in Litell Mealton'*, as his first wife Margaret had been in 1489. Thomas left the manor to his second wife 'Crystine' with all its lands, meadows, pastures, rents, profits and appurtenances, in both Little and Great Melton, within the Hundred of Humbleyard.

You may remember that the Marsham family held Little Melton Manor for eighty years from 1534 till about 1620. They probably built and lived at the Manor House, but there is also believed to be some connection with **The Steward's House**, just beyond today's Grange. There are distinct signs in the brickwork here that this may well be a rebuild of an older house, now marked by the date 1739 and the initials I.W.M. in bold letters on the far gable. Some think that this most attractive cottage may well have been Marsham property once, the home of their steward or farm bailiff, who would have served them in the big house, but this is only conjecture.

In 1574, Nicholas Sotherton of Norwich, Gentleman, bought Melton-Hall, and the small manor that went with it. Nicholas's son Henry seems to have lived at Melton-Hall, and to have died there in 1618, leaving an inventory showing that his house contained just 5 main rooms. The Skottowe family followed as manorial lords of Little Melton from the 1630s to the 1720s.

In 1665 the estate known as 'The Old Hall Farm', with some 200 acres belonging to it, was settled by the Lombe family on Augustine Skottowe, lord of the Manor of Little Melton, on his marriage with his bride-to-be, Susan Wells. It was to be *'to the use of Augustine Skottowe and his sons lawfully begotten'* for the term of 39 years. (Norfolk Record Office document EVL 251/1 No.2 457X6) Augustine died in 1683 when his son Thomas came into the inheritance. A further document in the same series (EVL 251/1 No.3 457X6) shows that in 1705 Thomas Skottowe duly released the estate to Mr John Lombe, worsted weaver of Norwich. There is no doubt about the location of the farm which is described as *'All that messuage called The Old Hall Farm wherein Thomas Buck now dwell, (before him Thomas Smyth and before him Robert Baxter), and lands etc. adjoining, containing 20 acres, between a lane leading from Little Melton to Great Melton, the south part of the Churchyard of Little Melton in part, and the Queen's Highway called the Towne Street in part on the north part, and abuts upon the same Towne Street towards the west, and a Close called Middlecroft next after mentioned towards the east'.* The lengthy document goes on to give the abuttals of the whole estate, which is,

The Grange - viewed across the moat c.1950

in essence, very much the same both in extent and in lay-out as that owned by the Evans-Lombe family within the parish today.

'The Old Hall' was sometimes referred to as *'The Capital Messuage'* (or big house) of this estate, and immediately on possession, Augustine leased it to others for a year, when it is described as *'the Capitall Messuage where Augustine Skottowe doth sometimes inhabite'*. This must imply that Augustine had been living at 'The Old Hall' himself from time to time, and this is further borne out by the 1664 Hearth Tax returns. These show him as having a house with 5 hearths in Little Melton, (meaning five rooms with fireplaces), the same number as was listed in the inventory of Henry Sotherton's house, after his death in 1618.

In the seventeenth, eighteenth and nineteenth centuries property was constantly being mortgaged and re-mortgaged, assigned and re-assigned and divided into many different parts to be sold or leased etc., and the Evans-Lombe documents bear witness to this in good measure, as they are extremely complex and difficult to understand. One document of 1826, for example, contains no less than 87 pages listing hundreds of indentures, mortgages and land allocations, with a further 6 pages of Counsel's opinion on disputed rights!

But let's go back to 1775 when records show that Elizabeth Dade had been in occupation of 'The Old Hall' for some years; she was the widow of Robert Dade who had farmed the estate of over 200 acres earlier, dying in 1764. Their attractive angel-headed tombstones lie side by side near the porch of All Saints, Great Melton. They had a son Henry, who played a large part in village life, serving as a member of the jury every year from 1765 to 1776 and taking his turn as constable. He leased the property before buying it for £4,200 in 1797 from Thomas Lane of Bressingham. Immediately after this purchase, Henry himself died, leaving everything by will to his widow Esther (née Howlett) requesting her to sell. After her death proceeds were to go to his nephew William Dade who was living with him. Even here, Chancery proceedings had to be entered into in 1799 to sort out the rightful ownership. Eventually Henry's executors agreed that Edward Heath should have occupation, as from 10th October 1801.

Edward Heath came from Panxworth, his wife being Elizabeth Howlett, Esther Dade's niece, and for ten years they lived happily at 'The Old Hall', (now called the 'Church Farm' of 215 acres), where nine children were born to them, all being baptised at Little Melton. They were Harriot, John Howlett, Ann Howlett, Robert, Susannah, Jane, John, Maria and Caroline Howlett, and all seem to have survived infancy. Their mother, Elizabeth, worn out by bearing 9 children in 10 years, died in 1811 aged 37, and is buried in a brick tomb in Earlham St Mary's churchyard. Their father stayed at the farm for a further six years, and was allotted 210 acres in the Enclosure Award of 1817. Shortly afterwards he sold his estate to the Lombe family, in whose hands it remains today.

Benjamin Norton was the next farmer to live there, shortly followed by Mr. Thomas Dove Aldred in about 1830. In 1841 he is shown as aged 35, living with his wife Mary aged 40, three children and four resident servants, one of whom was Miss Martha Gates aged 30. Mary died soon after this, and on 29th January 1843 Thomas Aldred and Martha Gates were married by licence at Little Melton Church, and one can just imagine the tittle-tattle that went on in the village. A son John was born to them a year later. In 1841 Mr Aldred was farming 215 acres, but in ten years time this had increased to 282 acres, when he was employing 15 men and 4 boys. He had died by 1870, and his son Joseph Miller Aldred took over, farming the same amount of land as before, with 6 men, 5 boys and 2 women working for him. Joseph died in 1875, and both father and son are buried in our churchyard. Thomas, in particular, played a substantial part in village affairs, as churchwarden and overseer of the poor, while Joseph served as surveyor of the highways. It must have been during the Aldreds' tenancy that The Grange was built, incorporating the old building.

Mr Henry Lack followed the Aldreds, with his wife Emily and son William. He, too, was a prominent figure in Little Melton, serving as churchwarden when the Church Room was erected, and doing much to support the community as a whole. He died in 1897, and his son William carried on farming here until his death in 1938. It was William who did a lot to help the local mens' club, by providing them with a level field on which to play football and cricket. Minutes of the club show that as a Vice-President he was widely admired and respected, club members standing in silence to remember his passing.

Church Farm Barns adjacent to the Grange c.2001

Several of the Evans-Lombe family, who own the Grange, lived here for a time in the latter part of the 20th century, including the late Vice-Admiral Sir Edward Malcolm Evans-Lombe, C. B. who was Chief of the British Pacific Fleet from 1944 to '46, and Commander in Chief of the Allied Naval Forces of Northern Europe from 1953 to 1955. Today the Grange is home to Mr and Mrs David Bolton and their children.

The Grange in the time of Mr. Lack c.1920's

In 1963 Mr Bob Richardson built today's Church Farm House close by. His autobiography 'Some Fell on Stony Ground' published in 1978 is a wonderful evocation of the rural way of life we have lost for ever. Mrs Patricia Batty Shaw, President of the National Federation of Women's Institutes, wrote the foreword, in which she said *'the last 70 years have witnessed what some have called the greatest convulsions in the history of mankind.'* Bob was a lay-reader, travelling miles to take chapel services all round the district, a musician, and a true countryman.

Grey Cottage, Green Lane.
(This house has only been 'Greycot' since 1949, but is referred to by this name in what follows.)

This, together with the Manor House, is one of the two oldest houses in the village, and a splendid, illustrated history about it was written recently by Simon Rowe, when he was 12 years old, as a school project. He knows the house well, having lived there with his younger brother and parents, Larry and Carole Rowe, the present owners, for his whole life.

Pevsner describes the house as: *'A 16th century timber-framed hall house, floored in the seventeenth century and altered in the 19th.'* The Rowe family has also altered it recently, doing much both to modernise the interior and to preserve the older portions of the building. The 19th century alterations were demolished by them in 1998, when a substantial extension was built onto the north side of the house.

'Greycot' 2000

Mr Frank Marston Gibbs wrote of it as being early 15th century in origin, which is probably a century too early, but his comments are most interesting. He noted that *'Greycot itself was timber built, thatched cottage fashion over the gables. Two open roasting fireplaces with their great pyramid like chimneys once supporting the timber structure are still in use. It is much altered, with most of the clay lump and wattle and daub being replaced by bricks of all ages. The roof was renewed during the last century, using much of the old wood, from its former thatch pitch. This is indicated by the marks on the chimneys whereby a lower pitched, pantiled and slated roof was formed. Its cellar has bricks that were imported, laid in a very curious random bond, suggesting that the present chimneys were rebuilt a century or more later than the timbered house.'*

It is just possible that Greycot was built by a member of the well-to-do Rose family of Little Melton who lived here from the fifteenth to the mid seventeenth centuries. The 1555 will of Robert Rose, proved in the Norwich Consistory (or Bishop's) Court, is an interesting document. He asked to be buried in Little Melton Churchyard, and gave 6s 8d to the 'reparacion' of the church, *2 pence to the altar there*, and *'one ewe to every godchild that I have'*. He left *'houses and land both free and bond'* to his wife Margaret, for her lifetime, on condition that she makes no waste, and brings up *'honestlie my childer'*. These are two daughters named Cristane Rose and Alis, and another child is expected shortly, whom Robert hoped would be a boy. His actual words were that *'if the Childe that my wiffe is now grete with fortune to be a man child'* he is to have the property after Margaret's death, otherwise it is to go to his daughters.

If only the early church registers had survived, we might have known more! Was Thomas Rose, Yeoman, who died in 1613, the longed for son of Robert? Thomas left 5s to the 'reparacion' of the church, and 6s 8d to the poor of the village. He lived in a large house, leaving *'the parlour and parlour chamber with the two little chambers thereunto adjoining'* to his wife Alice for life, and the use of *'backhowse and oven for her necessary brewing and baking'* as well as liberty to take water from the well. The rest of the house was to go to Thomas his son *'with the homestalles hereto adjoining, except such as are bequeathed to Alice my wife, and except the east end of the barn belonging to my tenement'* which was for the use of Jeremy, another of his sons. Thomas was to have *'the middlestead of the said barn for the bringing in, threshinge and carrying away of all such corne, haye, strawe and other fodder as Jeremy shall lay in the east end'*. Thomas Rose, senior, left his three sons no less than 87 ½ acres of land in all *'both freehold and charterhold'*, giving Thomas 29 acres in 18 pieces; John 26 ¼ acres in 19 pieces and Jeremy 28 ¼ acres in 18 pieces. Jeremy died just two years later. His copyhold house named 'Priestes' was to go to Marie his wife for life, and then to Marie his daughter, and the east end of his late father's barn was to revert to his brother Thomas. He left freehold as well as copyhold lands and houses in both Little Melton and Bawburgh.

Thomas Rose the younger had died by 1643 when the remaining brother John wrote his will, leaving everything to Merrye his wife for life, and then to Isaac Rose his brother. From the court books it seems that Isaac inherited John's copyhold property called 'Wiltons'. No will for Thomas has been found, so once again we are left in the dark.

What happened to Greycot next? We are now on surer ground, as by linking information from the manorial court books and from deeds kindly lent to the writer by Mr Larry Rowe and by his next door neighbour Mr David Buck, (whose twentieth century property 'Fuchsia House' was built on land that used to belong to Greycot), it has been possible to trace its ownership from the mid seventeenth century.

Aerial view of Grey Cottage and gardens 1971

By 1659 it had been owned for some years by Joseph Rackham, a member of a large and prosperous family. His mother Elizabeth died in 1661, leaving no less than £286, (a very large sum in those days), to be shared between her nine children, Joseph and his brother Thomas being the two executors of her will. Joseph himself served on the court jury nearly every year from 1659 to 1682, during which time he was elected constable twice, and hayward once. His wife was Diana, (could she have been born a Rose?), and together they had two children, Robert and Elizabeth. Though Joseph died in 1706, without having made a will, his Administration Bond shows that his daughter Elizabeth and Francis Betts of Stratton Strawless, a worsted weaver, were ordered to make and display an inventory of all his goods. Unfortunately, Norfolk Archdeaconry inventories of this date do not survive, so we can only surmise that he was probably a worsted weaver himself, as it was normal for at least one of the assessors to be of the same trade as the deceased, so that a knowledgeable valuation could be made. Weaving was in fashion in Little Melton then, and at least one other member of the family, his nephew Nicholas Rackham, was a weaver, (son of his brother Nicholas).

The hearth tax returns for 1664 show that Joseph's home had three fireplaces, while his brother John and his sister Margaret (married to Martin Bucke) each had two, and his brother Thomas no less than nine hearths, the largest in the village. House owners did not necessarily live in their own property, and it seems strange that Greycot should only have three hearths when we know it had two enormous chimneys, capable presumably of heating at least eight rooms, if there were first floor chambers in existence as seems probable. Was Thomas Rackham perhaps living in Greycot then, or was he leasing the Manor House as has been suggested earlier? Above all, was Joseph living elsewhere? We shall probably never know for certain, but the latter does seem very likely, particularly as Joseph served as the 'Hayward' for the village in 1685. This was a very important post, only held by tenants of copyhold houses, and 'Greycot' was freehold. This does seem to point to the fact that Joseph, a weaver, may well have set up his looms in a copyhold house on the manor, and was now letting 'Greycot' and getting a lucrative rent into the bargain.

The Rev. Jeremy Revens of East Tuddenham purchased the property after Joseph's death, and owned it from 1696 to 1705, before selling to Charles Wenn, a yeoman of Norwich, who had it for nearly forty years from 1726 to 1764. Richard Rust, a Norwich milliner, bought Greycot in 1765, dying in 1792 when his wife Frances was the owner. She sold it to William Girling of Little Melton, farmer, in February 1795, whose will, proved in 1805, devised *all his freehold and copyhold messuages, lands, tenements and hereditaments situate in Little Melton or elsewhere* to his wife Elizabeth for her lifetime, and then to his only son John. We have now come full circle, as Elizabeth Girling was allotted Greycot in the 1817 Enclosure Award.

During the many years that the house must have been tenanted, it would be interesting to know a little about its occupants, as they probably played a leading part in village life. There were only three large houses in the village then, the Manor, Melton-Hall and Greycot, and we already know the probable occupants of the first two at this period. However, there was one family of some importance living in Little Melton during the years 1678 to 1716, consisting of Mr Robert Johnson, his wife Mary and their three children, Thomas, Mary and Sarah. They were of Stoke Holy Cross at the time of the 1664 Visitation of Norfolk by the College of Heralds, and bore arms which are mounted on a fine marble monument in the chancel of All Saints. These are described as *'On a saltire 5 crosses moline pierced, with a crest of a Wolf's head erased, per pale, frenellés, argent and gules'.* By 1678 'Robert Johnson, Gent' is paying homage at Little Melton manor court, only to die a couple of years later. His son Thomas also paid homage in 1689, dying in 1714, and Mrs. Mary Johnson followed him to the grave two years later. Sometime after this, the youngest daughter Sarah moved to Colney, and left 40 shillings in her will of 1741 to two poor widows of Little Melton. The church monument is dated 1718 and is to Thomas Johnson and his sister Mary, but it seems that the whole family is buried here, as there are ledger stones to each of them, Robert's in the floor of the nave, and the other four in the floor of the chancel. Did they all, perhaps, live at Greycot?

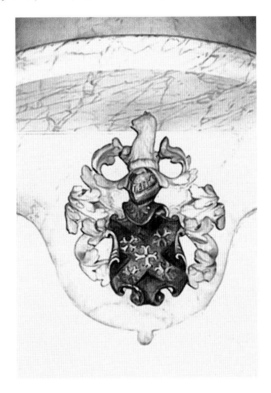

The arms on the Johnson monument in Little Melton Church chancel

Almost certainly Mr John Mills was the next tenant. He was a wealthy Woolcomber who employed many men in his 'Shiftning Room' where he also stored large amounts of wool. One hundred and twenty pounds worth of 'Fleece Wool' and one hundred and sixty one pounds worth of 'Wool already at Spinning' were listed in his Inventory of 1729, and the huge barn would have been a perfect venue for this. (To 'Shiften' is an archaic term meaning *'to change linen'* or *'to shift stitches from one pin to another in knitting'*, but quite what it means here is unclear). Mills was a wealthy man leaving goods worth over £365. His rooms, (and they may not all have been listed), included a kitchen, dairy, parlour, cellar, parlour chamber, kitchen chamber, shiftning room and combing shop. He employed at least two resident servants, and farming was a sideline; as he had two cows and calves, a horse, saddle and bridle and a small cart. The rooms must have been large, as the parlour alone contained: *'An old stove and an oval table; six leather chairs a couch and five cane chairs, two little tables and a stool, a tea-table and corner cupboard, a chest of drawers and dressing-box and a cabinet, a clock and case, a bed as it stands, small pictures and sconces, and a pair of bellows and brush.'* (It was quite normal to sleep in the hall and parlour at that time, indeed these were usually the main bedrooms of the house). The parlour chamber contained a further *'bed as it stands'*, another bed and a chest and nursing cradle, and there were two cradle quilts listed amongst the household linen. He left a silver tankard, 2 pots and 3 spoons, valued at £7, *'given by the deceased on his dying bed to his children'*. We don't know whether John Mills was buried in Little Melton or not, as the registers do not survive before 1734. His widow Letitia was left to take out his Administration Bond, as he died intestate.

Mrs Elizabeth Girling was allotted 'Greycot' in the 1817 Enclosure Award, as mentioned earlier, when the house was divided into three parts, in the occupation of Elizabeth Wince, George Goward and Samuel Baily. Mrs Girling was the widow of William Girling, (who had died in 1805), and lived in the Manor House, their son John, living at Earlham but farming at Little Melton. He played a prominent part in village life and leased the church lands belonging to Emmanuel College, Cambridge, as well as the manorial lands belonging to the Bacon Franks family.

In 1828, Mrs Elizabeth Girling sold her life interest in Greycot, and the estate of just under 34 acres that went with it, to her son John. The house was divided into two separate dwellings at that time, then in the occupation of Mrs. Mary Girling and James Webster. Mary had a year by year tenancy, and occupied the *'easternmost end'* of the house, with the garden in front, and James held a 14-year lease dating from 1818 and had *'the westernmost end,'* with the barn outbuildings, yard, garden orchard, and a considerable quantity of land.

Mary Girling was John's eldest sister. She had married William Girling of Cawston in 1807, had four children, Edmund, Hannah, Mary Elizabeth and Juliana, and had been shopkeeper at Little Melton since 1813. In 1841 the census shows Juliana housekeeping for her grandmother Mrs. Elizabeth Girling at the Manor House, and Mary living with her other two daughters Elizabeth and Hannah, (presumably at Greycot). Mrs. Girling senior died the following year, and is buried beside her husband William in Great Melton churchyard. Ten years later in 1851, Mary now aged 64 was still shopkeeping and was still living in the same place, assisted by Elizabeth (aged 38 and unmarried) and Juliana (aged 34 also unmarried). Mrs Mary Girling was buried at Little Melton on 17th July 1852, and the two 'girls' continued to run the shop and to live at Greycot, which now became theirs. The Reconveyance of that date shows that the property now contained 1 acre 1 rood and 26 perches of yard and garden ground. Juliana died in February 1870, and was buried at Little Melton in the same grave as her brother Edmund, who was to die in America two years later. The house was now vested in Elizabeth, who by 1851 had decided to retire at the age of 60. She continued to live at Greycot, with a resident servant, for the next twenty years or so until 1883, when she apparently moved to Hethersett. In all, the Girlings had been shopkeepers here for an uninterrupted period of nearly 60 years, and when Elizabeth retired, it must have been the end of an era.

By November 1883 Miss Mary Elizabeth Girling had sold Greycot to Robert Jay, for the sum of £375, who in 1899 sold it to John Lynn. Robert Jay may have let the property, as in 1899 he is described as *'a Florist of the City of Norwich,'* but John Lynn was a market gardener, who certainly lived here, using the gardens, house and barn for his business. In 1913 he sold to Mr Herbert John Beeston of Norwich, gentleman, who conveyed the property to his wife Mrs Violet Maggie Beeston four years later.

The Beestons lived in one part of the house and John Lynn lived in the other, and both were on very friendly terms, as their gravestones in Little Melton

Grey Cottage viewed across the pond at Laburnum Cottage. 1999

churchyard testify. John Lynn died in 1932 aged 77 and Mr Beeston in 1936, his wife remaining in Little Melton until 1949. She lived until 1980 when she was 97 years old, and is buried with her husband. The front pew on the south side of the nave of All Saints was the family pew, and Violet had the church installed with electric light in her husband's memory. After John Lynn's death, the Goulding family lived in one part of the house, and David Goulding now of The Bungalow, School Lane, was born there. As a small boy he remembers Mrs. Beeston as being dressed entirely in black, tending her flower garden and keeping chickens!

In 1949 Mr Albert Brown bought the property from Mrs Beeston, for the sum of £2,200, and it was in the conveyance of 12th August of that year, that the name 'Greycot' is first mentioned. Was it so called because it was roofed with grey slates at that time? In 1950 he sold to Thomas Daniel Lee of 15 Earlham Road, Norwich, a Mobile Cinema Proprietor, who seems also to have had a business with the amazing name of 'the Washing Machine Hire Service'. Perhaps, unsurprisingly, Lee's business got into financial difficulties, and two Norwich solicitors, Mr. W. D. Price and Mr. J. T. Price took over his mortgage.

From 1958 to 1987 the property belonged to Colonel Alexander Turnbull of the Royal Norfolk Regiment. The house was let as two separate dwellings for some years when Col. Turnbull was serving away, but later he lived there with his wife, and turned it back into one. Mr and Mrs. D. G. Vargeson bought the house in 1987 and sold part of the garden to Mr and Mrs Luraschi who built a bungalow on it, to the north of Greycot. Mr and Mrs Rowe, the present owners, bought in 1988.

One of Greycot's great features is its barn which lies alongside Green Lane between the road and the house. It is timber-framed and some ten metres in length, old maps indicating that it was almost twice as long in earlier days. Mr. Gibbs wrote about the barn in 1975 as follows: *'Standing on the edge of the lane is a small 17th century adzed timber barn with a lower extension on the north end. Once it was thatched and infilled between the upright timber with clay lump. During the 1850s it was clad with power sawn weather boarding, much new timber was added to the roof, the thatch was removed and pantiles fitted. This all dates with the house restoration and its new or lower roof. A perusal of the deeds might well indicate that Greycot had a new owner, also that this person was of strong nonconformist opinions. For a period this barn was used as a Chapel, (perhaps for this purpose the barn was restored and suitably whitewashed). An Altar was erected in the extension that quite recently collapsed'.*

The use of the barn as a chapel has also been mentioned by other people in the locality, but no one, as yet, can find further written evidence of its existence. In the 1850s the property belonged to Mrs Mary Girling and her two daughters, and it may well be that it was their wish to use the barn as a place of worship, for nearly everyone in Little Melton at that time was involved in agriculture, and farmers and labourers alike were inclined to be chapel folk. In addition, the Girling ladies would probably have had little use for the barn for other purposes, as they were not running a business at home. Matters would have changed, however, when Robert Jay bought the place, as he was starting a market garden, and needed a store.

The loss of the chapel must have meant a lot to many people, because it was in the very next year of 1884, that Mr Jay was to sell a piece of land adjoining Greycot to a group of local men, on which to build a place of religious worship. He was obviously in sympathy with their aims, as the agreed asking price was only £15. According to the official documents for the sale, everything had been settled beforehand with the Rev. John Hammond of Queens Road, Norwich, the Superintendent and Preacher of the Circuit or Station *'in the primitive Methodist Connexion'* on which the piece of ground to be sold was situated. The trustees were William Bailey, butcher, George Bloomfield Sowter, hawker, John Bacon, labourer, George Hill, grocer, all of Little Melton, John Harvey, labourer, of Colney, William Morter of Ber Street, Norwich, bootmaker and Charles Meale of Alexandra Road, Heigham, Police Sergeant. The conveyance was duly enrolled in the High Court of Justice (Chancery Division) on 31st July 1884. Stranger still is the fact that less than two years later, on 15th May 1886, the same piece of land was sold back to Robert Jay from the same trustees for the same sum of money, with the full authority of the General Committee of the Primitive Methodist Connexion.

One possible reason for this change of heart was that nonconformist worship had just started in another building in School Lane, Little Melton, and the village was certainly not large enough to support two chapels as well as the village church, for 1883 was the year when a small Mission Hall was first opened here.

Dormer Cottage, School Lane,
(then known as Dowes).

Mr Frank Marston Gibbs, writing about the village in 1975, noted that *'This is one of Little Melton's earliest brick built cottages, confronting the Manor House. In 1817 a small common separated them, with three gates to open and shut each time a traveller used the village street. Judging by the Flemish brick bond used, it was built about but not earlier than 1650, with two stepped gables and a roof of thatch.'* This was a copyhold property whose history can be traced through the Little Melton Court books. Henry Dowe was a manorial tenant for twenty years from 1650, who probably gave his name to the house and to Dowes Hill, a field nearby.

In 1665 William Denny surrendered Dowes and 17 ½ acres to Thomas Smyth, when it was described as '*a house late built near Nethergreene*' (This was the village green near Manor Farm, which was not enclosed until 1817, and Mr Gibbs was spot on in dating the property).

'Dowes' or 'Dormer Cottage' c.1988

In 1666 it was reported at court that Thomas Smyth had died, leaving his three daughters as co-heiresses. They were Anna, wife of John Burgis; Maria wife of Matthew Mitchells and Diana wife of Joseph Rackham, (the last two couples living in Little Melton). The property then went to Jehosophat Davy.

In 1667 Davy surrendered it to Thomas and Anne Rackham. Thomas Rackham died in 1679, and the property went to his youngest son, Nicholas.

By 1701 Nicholas Rackham had moved to Great Melton and sold to Thomas Fox of Hethersett.

In 1711 Gilbert Carter purchased the property on the surrender of Thomas Fox. Gilbert was one of the sons of John Carter, Yeoman of Little Melton, who was prominent in village life. John died in 1725, being given the title 'Mr' (meaning Master) in the Bishop's Transcript of our lost parish register. John and his wife Anne lived in a house called 'Priestes' which was burnt down shortly before the 1817 Enclosure Award, so we don't know where it stood.

In 1719 Dowes and 5 acres of land seems to have been occupied by Peter Harrold. By 1729 Peter Harrold had died, his son, another Peter, being admitted in his place. By 1732 Peter Harrold junior had died, his son Charles Harrold being admitted under age. (Charles' mother Philadelphia Harrold was Guardian).

In 1743 the death was reported at court of Gilbert Carter, the copyhold owner, his first wife Mary *'having died many years since'*. He left 3 daughters and co-heiresses. They were Elizabeth, wife of William Chesson of Ashill, husbandman, Mary, wife of Edward Smith of West Walton, tailor, and Anne, wife of Christopher Morton of Little Cressingham, husbandman.

These three at first surrendered the property to William Pue of Norwich, Gent, but the same year sold it to John Freezer of Norwich, baker.

In 1766 John Freezer of Little Melton, baker, surrendered Dowes to John Mayes of Colney, farmer, with 9 acres of land. Mayes also purchased The Grove and 4 acres, and in 1767 and 1771 was in trouble at the Leet Court, as described in the chapter on 'Village Government'.

In 1787 John Mayes had died, leaving a will in which he left the property to be divided between John Chapman, farmer, the son of his wife Elizabeth by her first husband, and William Thompson, his nephew, of Great Holland, Essex. The property was described as *'3 acres land, with messuage thereupon built called Dowes, and 2 acres at Dowes Hill called Rogers Close, 2 acres in Coulsey Field, and 2 acres in Church Field, and a further small estate called 'The Grove'.'*

In 1788 William Thompson sold it to John Chapman, farmer, of Bixley. It seems to have been quite soon after this, in about 1790, that Mr Chapman extended the property by building on another cottage (with a tiled roof) on the northern end of the seventeenth century house, the old part remaining thatched and gabled at both ends.

FIRST PHASE BRICKWORK
SECOND PHASE BRICKWORK
FIRST PHASE TIMBER FRAME - REBUILT
SECOND PHASE   "   "
BLOCKING

Sketch of the phases of building since 1650

In 1805 John and Susanna Chapman, now of Stoke Holy Cross, surrendered Dowes (now divided into two tenements) with gardens and 1 acre to William Copeman, farmer, of Little Melton.

In 1810 it was presented at court that William Copeman had died, and his son William was admitted to Dowes and 1 acre, under the terms of his father's will. The two cottages which William (senior) had bought from Mr. John Chapman were then in the occupation of Frances Dunnell and Elizabeth Fox.

In 1818 William Copeman (the son) was admitted under the Little Melton Enclosure Award to just under an acre, on which a messuage (Dowes) was standing. (It was this William who was generous enough to lend money to repay a bond due on the parish 'Townhouse' or 'Poorhouse')

In 1835 it was presented at court that William Copeman had died, and the report read as follows: *'to the court came Edmund Fox, plumber and glazier of Little Melton, bringing the will of his late uncle William Copeman, in which William bequeathed the cottages to his two nephews, Edmund and William Fox. The brick cottage late in the occupation of James Cook but now of Edmund Fox was bounded on the south by the thatched cottage of William Fox.'*

From the 1891 census we read that Edmund Fox still lived here then, with his wife Harriet, and was by now a market gardener. They had eight children, Edward, Thomas, William, Elizabeth, John, George, and the twins Mary Ann and Sarah Ann. All three daughters died young, being buried in Little Melton churchyard, as were their parents later.

Amongst papers belonging to the Fox family are two intriguing documents, one, just three lines in length, gives an undated address in Ontario, Canada, for Mr. G. Fox, and the other is a note from Miss Barkley of Little Melton Vicarage, dated April 2nd 1872. The recipient was obviously Edmund Fox and the writer Miss Frances Barkley, the unmarried 37 year-old daughter of the Rev. John Barkley, Vicar of the parish. It reads as follows: *'Miss Barkley sends Mr Fox the change out of his 10£. His son will find his r'lway ticket at Wymondham Station tomorrow morning – and his ticket for the sea voyage with Mr Pease at Liverpool. He will have to spend about 10/s on things for the voyage at Liverpool.'* Edmund's youngest son George was just 25 years old at the time, and it seems that he must have been emigrating to Canada, with practical assistance from the Vicarage. Did George have any descendants and are they still over there? It would be most interesting to find out.

Edmund himself died on 30th January 1897, and 'Dowes' went to his eldest surviving son, Thomas Fox, a farmer of Elsing, near Dereham, under the will of William Copeman, Edmund's uncle. There is a small sketch attached to the family papers which is reproduced here, showing a central gable, which was moved to the north end in about 1897, when the whole double cottage was tiled.

This re-roofing must have been the work of Thomas, the new owner, who was now in his early fifties. We know little of Thomas' life, but another Thomas Fox, (almost certainly Edmund's grandson and probably Thomas' son), inherited in due course, and died in 1947, his executors later selling 'Dowes' to Mrs. Rose Sewter, his daughter, who had made her home there for many years. Her

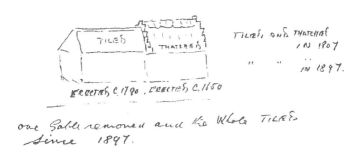

1974 sketch of roofing before complete tiling.

husband, Mr Carlos Sewter, was killed, tragically, in a Norwich air raid in 1940, the couple having tenanted the property previously, together with their three children. Their son, Mr Kenneth Sewter and his wife built next door, on land formerly belonging to Dormer Cottage, and still live here today, so tracing their lineage back over six generations to the first William Copeman of 1805.

The present owners of Dormer Cottage are Mr and Mrs Keith Alcock, who bought from Mrs Rose Sewter, and who have updated the property.

White Lodge, School Lane,
(formerly known as Noggs).

Noggs seems such an odd name for a house, but do you remember 'Newman Noggs' in Dickens' Nicholas Nickleby? He was described as a tall middle-aged man with a very worn ill-fitting suit which was *'placed upon such a short allowance of buttons that it was marvellous how he contrived to keep them on'*. Perhaps, long ago, there was a similar Mr. Noggs living in Little Melton, who gave his name to this property! Who knows?

This is another house whose origins can be traced back through the court books. So here goes:

In 1652 the messuage Noggs with barns, stables etc. near the Common Pound (lately belonging to Henry Alexander) was surrendered by Thomas Smyth to the use of Henrie Dawkins of Norwich and Anne his wife, who purchased it for £140.

In 1656 Henrie Dawkins (a master worsted weaver) surrendered Noggs to the use of his son-in-law Nicholas Rackham, who had married his daughter Bridget.

By 1678 Nicholas Rackham had died, leaving a will. He was then a yeoman of Bawburgh, and left his house and lands to his wife Bridget. The will stated that Henrie Dawkins was then living at Noggs.

In 1712 Bridget Rackham died. She was Nicholas' widow, and left a will in which she bequeathed everything to her son Nicholas, a worsted weaver.

In 1729 it was stated at court that Nicholas Rackham, worsted weaver, had died, and by his will he left all his property to his wife Elizabeth.

In 1739 it was reported that Elizabeth had mortgaged Noggs to Francis Lawes. (This was the normal way by which to borrow money at this period). Elizabeth remained in the property.

By 1745 Elizabeth Rackham had died. By her will she bequeathed Noggs to her son Charles Rackham, and to John Howlett of Great Melton, (probably her son-in-law).

In 1746 Charles Rackham and John Howlett sold Noggs to John Machin, the elder, Susanna his wife and John Machin, the younger. This was an outright purchase, the copyhold tenancy being made for the term of their three lives. Noggs was described as *'a messuage, with 1 pightle abutting on Parke Lane, near the Common Parke'*. (A pightle is a small field or enclosure, a close or croft. *'The Common Parke'* was another name for the village green near Manor Farm.)

In 1776 it was reported that the three members of the Machin family had died, John Machin the younger since the last court. The relatives of John Machin,

White Lodge or 'Noggs' 2002

the elder, then came to court. The first was Ellen Baley, wife of Peter Baley, who produced her father's will, which said that after his son John Machin the younger's death, *'Ellen is to have the new built end of my house in Little Melton, with the orchard and pightle containing two acres, abutting on Norwich Road.'* The second was Elizabeth Baker, daughter and heir of Elizabeth Baker, deceased, who was another daughter of John Machin the elder. She produced her grandfather's will, which read *'Elizabeth is to have the parlor and parlor chamber where I now dwell'.* The third was Priscilla Thompson, another daughter of John Machin the elder, wife of Edward Thompson. Her father's will stated *'I give the west end of my house consisting of a kitchen and 2 butteries and 2 chambers over them and the orchard at the west end of the house, and 2 pightles on the back side of my house to Priscilla'.*

In 1777 Elizabeth Baker sold *'the parlor and parlor chamber'* to Thomas Palmer, farmer, of Little Melton.

In 1802 Edward Thompson was admitted to the west end of the house, kitchen, 2 butteries, 2 chambers above, and an orchard at the west end, as heir of Priscilla Thompson.

Also in 1802 James Copeman was admitted on the surrender of Samuel Downes of Costessey, gardener and Elizabeth his wife, John Baley of Costessey, husbandman, Edward Baley of Moulton, husbandman, and Benjamin Howlett of Norwich, carpenter, to *'a new built end of a house'.* This had come down to them from Ellen Baley. James Copeman and Rebecca his wife surrendered their property to the lord of the manor and were then re-admitted *'for their lives and the life of the longer liver of them and their heirs for ever.'*

In 1816 it was reported that Thomas Palmer, farmer, had died, leaving two daughters, Ann, wife of William Davy of Hethersett, farmer, and Sarah, wife of William Forster of Little Melton, farmer.

In 1818, under the Little Melton Enclosure Award, Elizabeth Thompson, wife of Edward who had the house in 1802, was admitted to 2 acres 1 rood and 14 perches, cottage and outbuildings. (This was described as *'the west end of a house, consisting of a kitchen and 2 butteries and 2 chambers over them, and to an orchard at the west end of said house and to 2 pightles on back side of said house of Little Melton manor'*). (This was No. 8 on the Enclosure Map.) Also under the same award, Ann Davy, daughter of Thomas Palmer deceased, was admitted to 32 perches of land. (No. 7 on Enclosure Map). She and her sister Sarah Forster had other property belonging to their late father, much of it freehold, with dwelling houses in which to live.

In 1818, under the same award, James Copeman was admitted to 8 perches of land *'on which a cottage is now standing, called a new built end of house'* and 1 rood 19 perches of land, *'on which a carpenter's shop is now standing'*. (These are numbers 4 & 5 on the Enclosure Map).

In 1829 James Thompson of Little Melton, yeoman, youngest son of Edward Thompson of Little Melton, yeoman and his wife Elizabeth, was admitted to a cottage and outbuildings, 2 acres 1 rood and 14 perches of land. The property was described as being *'the end of a house, with 2 butteries and 2 chambers, and an orchard at the west end, with 2 pightles.'*

In 1834 James Thompson, only son of James Thompson of Little Melton, yeoman, deceased, was admitted to the above, under his father's willl.

In 1842 the Tithe Map shows James Thompson as still living there, with a house, yards, garden and pightle, his land totalling 2 acres, 1 rood, 14 perches.

In 1882 John Watson Sparkes lived in the property. He had a market garden for many years.

Today, White Lodge is owned by Mr and Mrs Mark McDonnell, who bought it from Mr and Mrs Gorton in December 2001.

The Grove.
(64 School Lane)

This is another copyhold house, whose history can be traced in the court books from the mid seventeenth century. From its earliest days until the late 1800s it was always called 'The Grove', but later it became known as 'Home Farm', a name recalled by a few senior residents of Little Melton today. It is now the home of Dr and Mrs Beeby.

64 School Lane was the original farmhouse, (the doctor's home) while 62 School Lane, (Bill and Rosemary Warnes' home), was built on at a later date. By the 1817 Enclosure Award, they are named as 'The Homestead' and 'Home Farm Cottage' with 16 acres of land. By the time of the Tithe Redemption Act of 1842 they were together called 'Home Farm' with 25 ½ acres. Both properties have been much altered over the years, but parts are very old, and there are still splendidly spacious outbuildings, though part of the barn has been demolished.

The original house must have been built a short time before 1649, because at the court for the Feast of St Luke (18th October) that year, Andrew Tanner (the occupier) had defaulted over payment, and Henry Alexander had been admitted as copyholder. By March 1654 Andrew and his wife Frances had settled their debts, being re-admitted as tenants by Henry Alexander, to what was then called *'a tenement late built called The Grove and 4 acres'*. Some seven years later, on 11th December 1661, they surrendered their tenement called 'Le Grove Close' and 4 acres to John Rackham, a member of a well-known local farming family. John paid homage at court in the early 1660s, and was appointed Messor (or Field

Master, a responsible post), on 18th October 1664. The location of The Grove was given, showing that it *'abuts on the Green of Melton on the west, and Cowsell Field on the east, and Slead Lane on the north.'*

By 1667 John Rackham had surrendered the property to Matthew Chambers, and in 1682 Susanna Chambers, (daughter of Matthew Chambers, deceased, and Margaret his wife, now Susanna Pittman, wife of Robert Pittman) gave the house and 4 acres to the use of Alice Wilcox of Norwich, widow, and Marie Wilcox, her daughter. Henry Alexander died in 1694, when his property was inherited by his brother Jacob Alexander.

The Grove c.2002

Jacob does not seem to have bothered much about maintenance, and in 1697 is found guilty at court of having damaged his property 'Moores' by fire, (then in the occupation of Martin Buck), and of *'having laid waste'* his other house (presumably 'The Grove', then in the occupation of Thomas Davy). He was ordered to carry out repairs, but probably did the minimum amount of work, because just three years later, in 1700, he surrendered his two properties in Little Melton '*into the hands of Thomas Skottowe, lord of the manor.*'

By 1705 Christopher Bloom (gentleman) and Mary his wife had been admitted, he dying in 1731 when Felix Bloom of Wicklewood, yeoman, his brother, inherited it by virtue of Christopher's will. (This will referred to '*all my estate in Little Melton in occupation of Marey Buck, widow,*' and is named as '*Le Grove and 4 acres adjacent*'). In 1740, Felix's son, Christopher Bloom, carpenter of Norwich, came into possession as youngest son and heir of Felix, who had died. Two years later John Freezer of Norwich, baker, was admitted on surrender of Christopher Bloom to '*The Grove, orchard and lands, in occupation of Edward Smith*'. John Freezer later also held Dowes, now Dormer Cottage, School Lane, and though we know that he worked in the village, we don't know exactly where he carried on his bakery business. He didn't surrender The Grove and Dowes to John Mayes, a farmer, until 1766.

On 10 Nov 1767 there is an interesting entry. This states that John Mayes was fined '*for stopping up a driftway out of and through his yard leading from thence to Coulsey Field*', and 'driftway', according to the Oxford English Dictionary, means '*a lane or road along which cattle are driven; a drove-way*'. Today, behind the house at 64 School Lane, there is still a fine grassy track, under which are rounded flint cobbles, carefully laid, leading from the outbuildings north for a considerable distance, so Coulsey Field must have been on or near the market gardens which provided the site for the building of the Greenacres estate in the late 1990s. There is another longer track next door, leading from Hospital Farm up to Braymeadow. Could this be the old 'Slead Lane'?

On 28th Nov 1787 it was reported that John Mayes had died since the last court, and John Chapman (his wife's son by her previous marriage) was admitted to half the property, his nephew William Thompson having the other half. William lived at Great Holland, Essex, and the following year surrendered his share to John, who was a farmer of Stoke Holy Cross. The final entry in the Manor Court books shows that on 2nd July 1810 William Cooper was admitted to The Grove and to Dowes. From the 1842 tithe papers we find that William Cooper, (aged 45), his wife Esther and their two children, William (2) and Robert (1 month) lived at The Homestead and Home Farm Cottage with three living in servants, Emily Mitchell (15), Miles Mace (15) and Elizabeth Parker (60). According to the census, William Cooper was still there in 1861, a farmer of 16 acres, now aged 70, together with his wife Esther (60) (both born in Hethersett). Their two sons William (21) and Robert James (19) were born in Little Melton and still lived with them.

By 1871 Joseph Carter (33, born Hethersett) and his wife Eliza (32, born Yorkshire) were living at Home Farm, with three small children, and were farming

7 acres. By 1881 they had six children, Joseph (11), Emily (9), Edith (5), Alice M. (3), Herbert (2) and Oscar (1), all but the eldest having been born in Little Melton. By 1891, Joseph and Eliza were still here with their two youngest children. Both parents are buried in All Saints Churchyard, Eliza dying in 1894 aged 55 and Joseph in 1913 aged 78.

Little Melton Post Office 1920/30

The next owners were Mr and Mrs William Bailey, who remained until about 1930, William playing a significant part on the parish council. Miss Ethel Bailey, shopkeeper here in the 1920s and 1930s was their unmarried daughter, who lived with them at first, until taking up residence in the room behind her shop. At this house, (today known as Resthaven), she set up a large notice over the entrance, inscribed 'S.P.Q.R.' in huge letters, which meant - to the initiated - 'Small Profit, Quick Return'. The Post Office was next door, (now P. O. Cottage), before it moved, much later, to the further end of School Lane, beside the dairy, very near the crossways. Miss Bailey is remembered as a real character, and it was she who had the present stores built, (where John and Barbara Macdonald look after us so well today), and moved her business there.

Kelly's Directory for 1929 shows that Christopher Miles Skerret Rogers was a poultry farmer at Home Farm, but by 1931 the property was on the market again. The asking figure was about £400, - somewhat different from today's prices - and

Herbert Gibbs and his wife Louise Eleanor bought the house and land, living there with their daughter Audrey Vera, who was soon to be married. Mr. Gibbs had served throughout W.W.I., and was very badly wounded at Mons, suffering for the rest of his life from this terrible experience. Their granddaughter, who lives in Norwich, remembers very happy times when she and her sister stayed as young children at Little Melton in the 30s,and 40s, and tells the tale that for some months during the first world war, Mrs. Gibbs had not known whether her husband was alive or dead, until the day that he suddenly turned up on the doorstep, totally unannounced. Much later on, during W.W.II. when David Niven was at 'The Rose and Crown', his army batman was billeted at Home Farm, where he so much enjoyed Mrs. Gibbs's excellent cooking, that the great man himself sometimes came for a meal!

Bernard Dorman celebrating his 80th birthday, with his son and daughter, in 1988

After the Gibbs' departure to be nearer their daughter, Mr Bernard Dorman came to live here with his family. He owned the famous Black Horse Bookshop in Norwich, opposite the Cathedral, and stayed here until his death in 1997, being buried near the Lych-gate at All Saints, whose church he had served in many capacities. His very old grey/blue van, which was once used for book deliveries all over the county, remains embedded in a hedge at his old home, with the branch of a tree growing out of the round hole where the filler cap on the petrol tank used to do duty. Sadly, the Black Horse bookshop had to close in the millennium, due to competition from large scale booksellers and the internet, and one cannot help but be thankful that Mr. Dorman, senior, did not live to see this.

Dr Michael Beeby and his wife Sharon bought the property in 1998, and have done much to modernise the interior, and to preserve the character of a very interesting house.

Pond Piece, School Lane,
(built on the site of Moores).

Mr Frank Marston Gibbs noted in 1975 that *'directly adjoining the garden wall of the Manor House are the 18th century buildings and barns of a 40 acre holding. Its mid-nineteenth century house is confronted by a small pit dug out for clay to make earlier cattle byres and dwelling houses, now and for many years full of water, the farm's cattle watering place.'* The house of today is appropriately named 'Pond Piece', situated at the top of the narrow, often muddy drive that leads to Hospital Farm. It has now been for many years the home of Graham and Liz Tomlin and their family.

The original house dates from the early 17th century, and has an interesting history, traceable through the old court books.

In 1654, Henry Alexander and Andrew Tanner surrendered a messuage called Moores, together with 17 ¼ acres to the use of John Sandell and Henry Capps, gent.

In 1659 Henry Capps had died, his son of one year of age, also called Henry being admitted to the property under the guardianship of John Lambert.

In 1679 Henry Capps junior was admitted, having reached his full age.

In 1695 Henry sold the property to Jacob Alexander.

In 1697 Martin Buck was living at Moores, which *'per infortunium combustum est'* (loosely translated as 'has been unfortunately damaged by fire'). Jacob Alexander was ordered to rebuild the house before the Feast of St. Michael the Archangel next.

In 1700 Mr Thomas Skottowe, lord of the manor, testified at court that Jacob Alexander, Gent, had come before him on 28th February 1699 (witnessed by Andrew Brereton, steward of the manor) and had surrendered all his messuages and lands into his hands.

In 1705 at court, Mr. Seamans, Mr Norman and Mr Colman (Trustees for the Corporation of Norwich) were admitted to two estates, late Mr. Alexander's, including Moores. It should be explained that in 1611 Mr Thomas Anguish, a one time lord of the manor of Great Melton, made provision in his will for a hospital (or school) to be set up for poor Norwich children, encouraging other citizens of Norwich to follow suit. In 1702, Thomas Wisse, a Norwich merchant, gave money with which to purchase land, the income to be used for the upkeep of the Anguish Hospital Schools. It was with this bequest that the land in Little Melton was bought, so giving its name to Hospital Farm.

In 1725 further trustees were admitted for the Boys and Girls Hospitals, Norwich, to 2 messuages & 25 ¾ acres of land (Moores) and 1 messuage and 1 ½ acres, another 5 acres and yet another 2 acres (formerly Harveys).

In 1818 the trustees were admitted through the Enclosure Award of Little Melton to the land and houses as before. (This is designated as No 79 on the Enclosure Map).

In 1841, according to the Census, the farmer there was 70 year old William Forster, but by 1842 the Tithe Award and Map shows 'Hospitals, Norwich' owning 40 acres 2 roods 32 perches of land including a house (here called by the delightful name 'a homestall'), with William Hubbard in occupation.

It was probably shortly after this that 'Moores' was demolished and 'Pond Piece' built in its stead.

In 2001 the farmland is still owned by the Anguish Educational Trust, Norwich, is still called Hospital Farm and is worked by Mr Philip Eagle.

Elm Farm, School Lane.

Opposite the school in Little Melton is a drive leading to Elm Farm. Mr F. M. Gibbs noted that *'this large house and extensive buildings were erected in about 1768 by the Rev. Thomas Starling Buckle, wealthy, but not an incumbent of Little Melton. Its fine brick and pitchpine barn is one of the last of this type to be erected. All corn then, and for another 50 years at least, was carted into the barn ready for threshing by hand flail. Prior to the buildings being erected, Mr. Buckle had purchased 60 or so acres of land from a number of persons. In 1800 he bought the main portion of Hethersett's Beckhythe Common when it was enclosed, thus forming the farm we know today, but much of it has since been sold.'*

Mr Buckle lived in Hethersett, and let Elm Farm. He played a major part in Little Melton affairs, both as a member of the 'Vestry' and from time to time as curate at All Saints.

Thomas Forster was tenant of Elm Farm in 1841.

Goulds.

A copyhold house which used to stand opposite the Manor House near the Green but is probably no longer in existence. Its history can be traced from 1645 to 1760.

Rambler Cottage, Great Melton Road,
(formerly the Town House).

Built on common land by the parish in 1792 to house the poor and sick of the village, this house was originally two cottages. From 1836, with the erection of the huge workhouse at Swainsthorpe, it was no longer needed for its original purpose, the cottages now being let by the year to any parishioner on application. It remained parish property until 1962 when it was sold for private housing, and made into one dwelling. Its full history will be found in the chapter called 'Social Welfare and the Poor'.

Priestes.

A copyhold house whose history can be traced back to 1670. In 1814 *'it was wasted by fire'*, so does not feature in the map accompanying the 1817 Enclosure Award. It seems to have stood in the centre of the village, and may possibly be the property whose old footings of flint and brick were discovered when Gibbs Close was being extended in the year 2000.

Wiltons.

Another copyhold house dating from at least 1613, much altered over the years, and allotted to James Wortley in 1817. The Enclosure Award map shows it as property no. 3, situated some way back from the road, on the left hand side of School Lane, about a quarter of the distance from its junction with Green Lane to today's bypass. In 1842 it was owned by Joseph Wilkinson and occupied by Edmund Eden, according to the Tithe Map and Apportionment.

The art of Biography
Is different from Geography.
Geography is about maps,
But Biography is about chaps.
E. C Bentley

Did you know that...

...**Billy's Loke is the local name for the footpath leading from our modern village hall to the Watton road?** Billy Briggs was a tall, immensely strong, bearded figure, who made his home in the hedge here for more than twenty years in the 1920s and 1930s. Billy used to fill his water bottles at the well behind Sunnyside, Mill Road, the home of Mr. Russell Lofty. His son Maurice (who was born there in 1921) remembers Billy with great clarity, but points out that the original Sunnyside is no longer in existence. It lay beyond the double flint cottage, (the farmhouse, numbers 1 and 2), as you go down Mill Road towards the church, modern brick buildings having been erected on the site in 2001/2.

Billy Briggs had been in the army, (including service in the Boer War from 1899-1902), having qualified as a 'Gymnasium Instructor', and was the proud possessor of a silver-topped walking stick to prove it. It was said that he had been crossed in love by a Bawburgh girl, and was also probably a little shell-shocked as a result of the war, though such a condition was not fully appreciated in those days. Once home in Little Melton, many years later, he found no members of his family left, so he just settled down in the hedge beyond today's village hall, sleeping on straw and two old overcoats, and erecting sacks as walls and roof. Maurice Lofty recalls most vividly the sound of Billy singing and shouting to himself on moonlit nights, as the noise carried over the fields behind Sunnyside. Although he was quite harmless, local children were terrified when he appeared, and ran away as fast as their legs could carry them.

Billy was born in the village in about 1876, and was christened here on 3rd March 1878, together with his younger sister Lucy. He was the sixth of seven children of Barnard Briggs, a farm labourer, and his wife Sarah, who had just moved into the parish from Hethersett. He lived with his parents until they died, his father in 1885 aged 48, and his mother in 1887, aged 49, both being buried in Little Melton churchyard. By 1891 at the age of sixteen, Billy too was an agricultural worker, now living with his elder brother Barnard at the home of their uncle and aunt, James and Carling Briggs. Presumably he joined the army once he was of age, and left the parish, to return nearly a quarter of a century later. His Norfolk neighbours, including the local farmers, doctors and police, believed it was impossible for a human being to survive outdoors in all weathers for more than a *'twelvemonth'* or so, with little protection from rain, cold and wind, but Billy proved them wrong, living in this way for about twenty years. He had just enough money to pay his way, (possibly from a small army pension), and would resolutely refuse any charitable help, doing odd jobs locally for a few days when he was without funds. He kept a timepiece in a tin underneath the sacks that formed his bed, bought bread from the travelling baker, pumped his water from Mr Lofty's well, and nearly always had *'baccy'* in his pocket, as he enjoyed a pipe of an evening.

It was Mr Russell Lofty and Mr James Ringwood who found him one winter's day, lying ill on his sacks underneath his overcoats. They had missed seeing him around, and had taken the trouble to go to look for him. Medical help was summoned, and Maurice Lofty remembers Dr. Maingay's arrival in his big red Rover, which he had to park nearby, before clambering his way along the footpath to get to the hedge.

Billy was then taken to the workhouse at Wicklewood where he was soon to end his days, being laid to rest in Little Melton churchyard on 14th February 1939, aged 63 years. One of his brothers and one of his sisters were also buried here, Barnard Briggs (who had moved to Haddiscoe) in 1945 aged 74, and Lucy Briggs (of Raveningham) in 1948 aged 71. It is interesting that there is a Briggs Field in an 1817 map of Little Melton, (lying beyond and behind Manor Farm, on the right of School Lane as it approaches today's bypass) which shows that the Briggs family once held land here.

Amongst papers about the village owned by Emmanuel College, Cambridge, is a schedule of tithes payable in August 1798, which includes a list of 18 landowners in Little Melton. There are just two large farms, (Mrs Dade of Church Farm owned 172 acres, and Mr William Girling of Manor Farm leased 120), while a further 17 people owned land varying in size from 36 acres to half an acre each. William Briggs is shown as the owner of 8 acres, the ninth largest area, which presumably comprised Briggs Field. There was a great deal of movement from one village to another in the eighteenth and nineteenth centuries – more than many of us imagine - and though they moved about, members of the extensive Briggs family always seem to have considered Little Melton their real home. Samuel Briggs and his wife Harriet (Fox) had four children in Little Melton between 1804 and 1812, while another Samuel Briggs, (probably their son, though born in Bawburgh), was living here in the 1830s with his wife Lucy, (born in Little Melton), and their 9 children, all born here. Robert Briggs and Alice (Pettit) had at least seven children, and went to Hethersett in 1810, later moving to the parish of St. Giles, Norwich. All their children seem to have been baptised and buried in Little Melton, however, and there are sad entries in our burial register in 1827 and 1828, showing that three of them died from a fever in St Giles, Elizabeth aged 9, Alice aged 6, and Lydia aged 16 years, being brought home here for burial. Alice, their mother, died in 1855, aged 67, and Robert, their father died in 1859, aged 71, and they, too, are also buried in Little Melton.

Billy Briggs' story is certainly eccentric, but he had his priorities right. To him, come what may, Little Melton would always be home.

The Mission or 'Gospel' Hall c.1980

...there used to be a Mission Hall capable of seating 200 people on the site of today's bungalow 'Mardi Gras', School Lane? It was opened in 1883 and belonged to 'The Children of God' being still in use for a large part of the 20th century. Many independent, industrious folk attended, but what a squash it must have been! It was particularly renowned for its Sunday School, which was sometimes held at Colney Hall, particularly in its early days.

Maurice and Mina Lofty cared for the Mission Hall on School Lane, Little Melton, from about 1950 until its closure in 1983, when Mr Lofty and Mr Oakes were the two final trustees. The chapel was then pulled down, the site extended, and a bungalow built in its place, known today as 'Mardi Gras'.

The land on which the chapel stood had originally belonged to the Colney estate, which asked a peppercorn rent of a shilling a year from the Christian Brethren who worshipped there. During much of the time that the Barclays were in residence, (1887-1956), the family was most supportive, and allowed a flourishing Sunday School to be held in the Coach House at Colney Hall itself, with many children attending from Little Melton. When the estate was finally sold in 1957, the land on which the Little Melton Gospel Hall stood was given to the Brethren. Mr Lofty and the other Christian members had the old wooden structure removed, and a new one built in its place.

Rather surprisingly, the old building had originally been used to house an engine which drove machinery for weaving cloth, as the tenant at Colney Hall in the early 1880s was in the drapery trade. He is noted in the 1881 census as Mr George M. Chamberlin, a 'Warehouseman', living at the Hall with his wife Emily, 3 children born at Eaton and 5 servants. Many older people may remember 'Chamberlins' on Guildhall Hill in Norwich, a very up-market, and expensive clothes shop, which belonged to this family. It was later taken over by Marshall and Snelgrove, and now is home to a Tesco supermarket.

Kelly's Directories of Norfolk from the year 1896 onwards have interesting entries for Little Melton, with the words: *'Here is a Gospel Mission Hall seating about 200 persons.'* This was a very well-attended place of worship in the early years of the twentieth century, though the number of regular worshippers was probably less than half this figure. But when the time came for most families to own a car, attendance dropped rapidly, more and more people choosing to have a day out on Sundays instead of going to chapel.

Amongst the printed papers held by the Local Studies Library in Norwich, there is an intriguing, tiny green booklet of 16 pages, just 2 ½ inches by 4 inches in size, headed *'Little Melton Mission Hall – Hints and Counsel for the Children of God'* and printed in 1883. Apparently the old weaving shed was no longer needed for its original purpose, and had just been converted for use as a chapel. Worship was held twice on Sundays, with The Lord's Supper being celebrated weekly, and services were also held on Thursdays and Fridays, with a men's writing and reading class on Tuesday evenings. This was probably much needed and well attended, at a time when local children were beginning to learn how to read and write, (following the erection of the school in 1875), an opportunity denied to many of their parents.

So, all in all, the Gospel Hall at Little Melton provided neighbourly support through Christian worship for a full century, 1883 to 1983.

...an eminent nineteenth century doctor, who pioneered research into cancer was the son of a Little Melton farmer? He was HARRY LAMBERT LACK, F.R.C.S., his father tenanting Church Farm from the Great Melton estate from about 1885 until his death in 1897. Henry Lack lived at The Grange at the far end of Great Melton Road and was also a churchwarden, signing the indenture when the local squire, Rev. Henry Evans-Lombe, gave the land on which the Church Room was built as a Sunday School in 1885. The other churchwarden to sign was Mr.Samuel Barrell, the local miller, here for over 40 years from 1861 to 1904. The Church Room was sold for private housing in the year 2000, and what an attractive property it has turned out to be.

Mr Lack's second son William took over in 1897, farming here until 1938. He had the local shooting rights which he much enjoyed, being a keen sportsman, and converted 'Lack's Lake', as it used to be called, into a beautiful water garden, with stone steps leading down to it. The origin of this horseshoe-shaped water feature is unknown. It may have been dug a long time ago as a moat, for in medieval times Little Melton-Hall stood on or near the site of the Grange. The fine house of today appears to have been built soon after the Tithe Redemption Map was made in 1842, and to have incorporated some part of an older building into its construction.

In the autumn of the millennium year 2000, William Lack's grandson, Mr Tony Young and his wife, of Axminster, Devon, visited The Grange, home today to David and Mary Bolton's family, and recalled very happy holidays with his grandparents there in the 1930s. His mother was married at All Saints, Little Melton, and later spent some years with her soldier husband in India, so the farm became a second home to Tony as a boy. He particularly remembered a fine pig named Tom, much to the amusement of the Boltons' young son of the same name.

Mr Young discovered the graves of his forebears in the south-east corner of the churchyard, he and his wife giving a generous donation in their memory, so becoming members of The Friends of Little Melton Church.

...our church tower was floodlit during the Queen's Silver Jubilee week of 1977, thanks to Mr Nash?

Chapter Nine

Little Melton Light Railway

And that's how it all began, my dear,
And that's how it all began!
Rudyard Kipling.

Bob Brett ran his first railway on 22nd April 1989, giving much pleasure to hundreds of children over the years and raising many thousands of pounds for charity. Little more than a decade later, on 8th July 2001, Bob was to die at his home, Vine Cottage, Little Melton, at the early age of 64, after a long battle against cancer, fought with typical, self-effacing courage. It was hoped that the railway could continue, for at least a time, but this has proved impossible without Bob's immense input, few people realising what a huge amount of time and effort he must have given to it. Since his passing, part of the track has been sold, but nearly a mile still remains.

Bob's work at the Heigham Sawmills was widely recognised, as was his great knowledge of wood and woodland preservation. This was his main passion in life, and he was never happier than when sharing this enthusiasm with others. He was much loved and respected throughout the whole of Norfolk and beyond, and this book is dedicated to his memory.

What follows are extracts from a booklet written by Bob himself. This is in four parts, the first written in 1991, the second in 1994, the third in 1997, and the fourth in 1999.

First extract written in 1991:

'The idea of having a railway at Vine Cottage came to mind in 1986. Being more interested in wood than railways at the time, I thought it would be a good idea to build a railway entirely from wood. There was to be a wooden train running on wooden rails and sleepers. This idea was soon abandoned after about 200 yards of 10¼ inch gauge track constructed from 1¼ inch square ash rails on cedar sleepers. The trouble was that variations in temperature caused the ash rails to split along the grain lines and the wooden test buggy scuffed the inside of the wheels causing rapid wear.

Disappointed, but not wishing to abandon the railway idea completely, I contacted Peter Way of Cherry Tree Nursery, North Walsham. I remembered Peter had a well set out 7 ¼ inch gauge railway in his garden centre and had laid his own

Vine Cottage c.1985

line. He agreed to lay a track for me, and work started on an aluminium track in November 1987 and this was finished by April 1988. By then about 5000 feet of track had been laid using keruing sleepers on a bed of granite chippings.

While Peter was laying the track I had been discussing ideas for a railway with a good friend, Matthew Warwick, a skilled wood turner and designer who had an interest in railways. Matthew came up with a brilliant design for a platform, station, and signal box, and made a model of the station.

The model and plans were then shown to another friend, Edwin Peck, a very competent and imaginative self-employed carpenter. Edwin soon became keen on the idea and being free at the time was able to start work on the project in March 1988, completing the job by September of the same year, having added a footbridge of his own design for good measure!

I then contacted the Rimmer brothers who had recently started a business "Garden Pride". They set out shrubs and plants by the station (Melton Wood Junction) and laid flower beds next to other parts of the track.

Edwin then made an extensive study of signals, pestering the staff of The North Norfolk Railway and climbing all over their signals to understand the workings. This thorough examination resulted in the installation of three fine semaphore signals, two on the footbridge and one on the main line, all operated by a very ingenious system of wires, rods and wooden levers. This was all very good, but we still needed a train!

David King, another friend of long standing and a well known steam engineer from Suffield agreed to build me a loco and three carriages. Work started

Thunderbox

on this project in March 1988 and 'Thunderbox' and carriages were completed in February 1989. The engine is powered by a Honda 200cc motor-cycle engine supplied by Paul Clarke, my neighbour, who runs his own motor cycle business. The engines and carriages sit on bogeys as there are several tight bends to negotiate in the circuit. It is a great train and I was able to implement some of my original intentions of using wood wherever possible as Thunderbox is made of sweet chestnut and the carriages are all in elm.

While the train was being built Peter, the platelayer, was laying more track from the engine shed, taking a line towards the house, alongside Green Lane and rejoining the existing line at the end of the orchard. Peter organises several outings for us. These range from N.E.N.T.A. tours on a standard gauge train down to other 7 ¼ inch layouts similar to our own. Here his deft footwork enables him to manoeuvre the smaller locos into a more favourable position.

Everything was now ready for the opening to the public. We had two trains, Thunderbox and Alice. Alice is Peter's train, which he now keeps here. She is older than Thunderbox and more mature, so she is a steadying influence on him, which helps to keep him on the bends as well as the straights and narrows. By this time Peter had laid nearly three quarters of a mile of track and Edwin had completed the buildings and signals.

An opening ceremony with various events was organised for the weekend of 22nd and 23rd April 1989, proceeds to be divided equally between the Little Melton Church Organ Fund and the West Norfolk Seal Rescue. At 2 p.m on Saturday my mother officially opened the railway by cutting the tape in front of Melton Wood Junction and Thunderbox trundled through. Saturday was a fine day and we had a great turnout. Refreshments were served and there were various competitions etc. The next day was not so good, rain setting in during the afternoon. However, having foreseen the possibility of poor weather, brollies had been bought the previous day and everyone on the train was thus protected by a brightly coloured umbrella, adding a bit of colour to a rather drab afternoon. The

Little Melton Light Railway

whole weekend was reckoned a success (apart from Thunderbox coming off the rails opposite Vine Cottage). We raised about £600 for the two charities and since that date have opened the railway every fourth Sunday in the month for a different charity.

In January 1990 we decided to build another line from the station, over the pond to a terminus near the Old Piggeries Tea Room. Work was soon begun on this, Peter laying the track from both ends and Edwin and I constructing a trestle bridge over the pond. The trestle is built on a curve, is over 50ft long and despite the levels going violently haywire for a short distance the bridge was finished in three days.

Old Piggeries Station c.1990

Old Piggeries Terminus Station is now completed. Edwin designed it and built it with the help of our reliable and competent signalman, Reg Ives. It is hoped that this new station will relieve some of the congestion, which occurs during busy times at Melton Wood Junction.'

Second extract from update in 1994:

'Edwin Peck completed his engine 'Sir Matthew Pilgrim' about 3 years ago. It is a magnificent machine built entirely from wood and is modelled on the Shay – an American logging engine with an offset boiler. All eight wheels are powered making it very track worthy and slippery uphill gradients present no problems.

Norman Duffield and Reg, not to be outdone, then decided to build their own loco – 'The General'. This is an electrically driven engine with a 24 volt, 1 horsepower motor, a petrol engine and alternator set to charge the battery. It is modelled on classic small diesel shunting engine design. After some frustrating

191

Sir Matthew Pilgrim

teething problems The General has now come into his own and ranks alongside Thunderbox and Sir Matthew. All three get along quite well and don't mind helping out when one or other is over hot, overtired or off sick. A third set of coaches is under construction, which will allow three trains to run next year (engines and staff willing).

We have acquired an old portable wooden building, which used to be the office for the sawmills. This now houses a Thomas The Tank Engine 00 miniature layout. This is very popular with children and adults alike. At the other end of this building Norman and others are working on a model layout for the L.M.L.R track and buildings. This is a complicated and time consuming job, but progress is being made and when completed it will be very nice for us to see where we've been going for the last 5 or 6 years!

Just finished on Melton Wood Junction platform is the new railway shop. Edwin has made this from home grown Douglas Fir – with Lebanon Cedar cladding. It is an extremely sturdy construction and will house our original W. H. Smith bookstall. This bookstall used to stand on the platform at North Walsham Station for many years. It was rescued by Peter, and we hope to give it a new lease of life at L.M.L.R.

One sad loss to report: Lex, one of the large black pigs has 'passed on' – no, we didn't eat her, she got some nasty piggy disease. Meg, however, is thriving and eats enough for two anyway and she gets

The General

bigger every year. Her pen runs alongside the track and she is fed by the passengers every time Thunderbox or The General go past. Her record at the moment is nine loaves in three hours. She was going for the record as the last train of the day approached, but she just couldn't face another loaf and had to waddle back dejectedly into her sty.

Meg has been joined by Tracey the Bantam Hen. Nobody knows anything about Tracey. She turned up one day with her husband and has stayed since. Unfortunately her husband ran off some time ago, but Tracey and Meg get along fine and often eat and sleep together.'

Third extract from update in 1997.

'Since the last update there have been two major additions at L.M.L.R. The first is a new line running from Melton Wood Junction and the second is a new engine made by Malcolm Cox for his son Alex.

The new line was laid by Edwin during the summer of 1996 and runs from Platform 2 at Melton Wood Junction. Trains run from here through a cutting in a large figure of eight round a paddock and through young woodland returning to Platform 2. The distance is about a quarter of a mile, giving us a total track length of well over one mile.

Melton Wood Junction before the addition of the platform shop in 1994

Malcolm and Alex Cox have built a most impressive new engine. 'Big Ben' is powered by a petrol engine driving a hydraulic pump, which supplies two independent hydraulic motors mounted on bogies. This gives the locomotive eight wheel drive and plenty of power to negotiate the gradients on all routes at L.M.L.R. Both Malcolm and Alex help on running days. Malcolm is either driving Big Ben or guard on one of the other trains and Alex helps with the 101 jobs that always need doing before we run, plus helping out wherever he can every time we run.

Another building to appear at L.M.L.R is the "Gazebo". This is an octagonal construction approximately 10 ft across and made entirely of wood by Edwin. It is situated at the entrance to Railway Wood and acts as an information centre for the wood. Inside there are posters of the various flora and fauna, which can hopefully be seen by anybody during a woodland walk. Apart from the posters there are tree recognition forms. There are 12 numbered trees in the wood and the visitors are welcome to try to identify them.

Railway Wood itself is growing well since planting in 1982. There is a picnic area with a bench seat, stools and a table. All this woodland furniture was made entirely by chainsaw by Chris Sharples of Great Melton. Chris is a forester from Great Melton and helps maintain the woodland in our two plantations. He has recently planted Hornbeam and Birch down Lost Line and hopefully in a few years time this will become a 'green tunnel' for the train to pass through.

Two dates stand out as significant during the last couple of years. On 23rd February 1996 we were honoured by a visit from The Very Rev. Peter Nott, Bishop of Norwich. It was a very cold day but his reverence was not to be put off a ride on the trains. Later he was persuaded to plant a tree to commemorate his visit and it was thought appropriate that the species chosen was a Tree of Heaven! This tree is flourishing well and a brass plaque has been installed in front of it.

Our April running in 1997 broke all records when Musical Keys booked the railway and over 800 rides were given during the afternoon. This was an amazing feat, especially as the Fat Controller was unable to be present that day and so (he says) it just shows what the staff can do if they try hard enough!

A new platform has been laid on the main line between the engine shed and Melton Wood Junction. This has been a useful addition as passengers can alight here if there is congestion at M.W.J. This is especially the case during our Father Christmas Specials in December. It has also proved useful as a boarding platform for the disabled. Spit, the cat, can usually be seen seeking out a bit of fuss and attention on running days (She doesn't get much the rest of the month!) She doesn't like to be picked up but enjoys it if you stroke her forehead!'

Fourth extract from update in 1999.

'During the last ten years, we have run on the fourth Sunday of every month, with just two exceptions. Once, when the weather was so foul that we were forced to cancel – January 1996, and once – May 1997 – we had to postpone for a week due to staffing problems. There have also been numerous occasions when the line has operated for private 'dos' such as birthday celebrations and 'specials' for handicapped youngsters.

To date 47 charities have been supported since opening in 1989, and nearly £13,000 has been raised for the charities (not including such money as they have raised by their own sideshows etc.) The total number of passengers carried is 34,670, the record in one afternoon was 804 (April 1997) which has been run close more than once, most recently, September 1998, with 692. This record however, was broken this April, with a total of 821!

The 'Paddock Line' which was planned and laid down in 1996, opened in 1997. Being rather shorter than other routes, it needed some additional attraction. It was designed with tentative thoughts in mind of fulfilling a long standing ambition, i.e. possibilities of running live steam.

Hotspur

The steam engine was to be built by a firm in Northampton and it would be named "Hotspur", after a B.R. Brittannia class engine, which was regularly driven on the Norwich – London line in the 1950's, by the father of Margaret Duffield and

Reg Ives. So October 1997 saw steam operating properly on the L.M.L.R for the first time.

Since then, Hotspur has run whenever the weather has allowed, driver experience continues to be gained – it's apparent that you never stop learning with live steam! Passengers seem to enjoy it and we hope Hotspur will continue to operate at every opportunity as a fitting running mate for the rest of the shed locos, Thunderbox, Sir Matthew, The General and Big Ben.

During a running afternoon, a cup of tea and a cake or two is very welcome, both for visitors and the slaving away staff! The Old Piggeries Tea Room has had a face lift and looks very smart, thanks to good work by Peter and Barbara Coupland. Sale of refreshments is a good opportunity for the charity of the day to raise money, all profits being theirs.

Father Christmas specials continue to be very popular, usually drawing some 700 or so, over the two days, to ride the trains, visit himself in his grotto and the younger ones to receive a present. These events are a lot of work for all the people involved, grotto, lights, decorations and something like 400 presents to prepare. Thanks are due to Malcolm for the 'improved grotto' construction.

After ten years, some of the track and some of the buildings begin to show their age (some may say so do some of the staff!), but, by and large things still run smoothly. We try to keep a light happy atmosphere consistent with safe and sound operating practice'.

* *

Bob was a member of a large family. His Great-Grandfather was Jonathan Thomas Brett (1841-1921), who fathered 10 children, including 7 sons. The eldest was Bob's Grandfather, John Brett, who started the North Heigham Cabinet Works in Paddock Street, Norwich. John had 6 children, his 3 sons running the North Heigham Cabinet Works until the 1960s, the second son, Bert Brett, being Bob's father. Bert ran the sawmills side of N.H.C.W. and it was from him that Bob learned the timber trade. When the firm ceased trading, Bob took over the sawmills side of the business and developed and modernised the mill, which now specialises in supplying home grown and imported sustainable timbers.

Jonathan Thomas Brett's other sons included Arthur Brett, his fourth son, who started the antiques business in St. Giles, and the reproduction side, where they sell bespoke furniture world wide. The firm is now run by Edward and James Brett, grandsons of Arthur Brett. The fifth son was Albert Brett, one of whose sons was Gerald Brett who bought and developed Looses in Magdalen Street, which is now run by his son, Michael Brett. Albert's eldest son, Reggie Brett, ran the retail furniture store Bretts of St. Benedicts. Bob himself never married, but leaves a married sister Julie Champeney, with a family.

Robert 'Bob' Burton Brett
1937 - 2001

Sir Humphry Davy
Abominated gravy.
He lived in the odium
Of having discovered Sodium.
Edmund Clerihew Bentley.

Did you know that...

...an Inventor lived and worked in Little Melton for fifty years from 1938 till his death in 1989?

He was JOHN RUSSELL CROMPTON MOORE who lived with his wife at the Old Rectory, on the Watton Road. He invented the altimeter, used by Sir Edmund Hilary on his ascent of Mount Everest on May 29th 1953. The tachometer on the BRM racing car was also his work, and he was involved in creating the undercarriage suspension of the Lunar Landing Module. Shortly before his death he was seen on Anglia TV demonstrating a revolutionary bicycle wheel which would ensure a more comfortable ride.

John was born at Holy Trinity Church Rectory, Norwich, where his father was rector, later becoming Archdeacon of Norfolk and Vice-Dean of the Cathedral. At All Saints, Little Melton, John was a Churchwarden for many years, being a regular reader of the lesson, preferring to use the beautiful language of the King James' Bible whenever possible. He is buried in the new part of the church graveyard.

...the Norwich residence of Sir Benjamin Wrench, Lord of the Manor of Little Melton in 1724, was on Exchange Street, just off the Market Place? It was pulled down in the 19th century to build the Corn Exchange, (hence the name of the street), and this in turn was demolished to allow Jarrolds to extend their city centre shop in the 20th century. The name 'Benjamin's' was given to their second floor coffee shop to commemorate Sir Benjamin's association with the site, and a 'Green Plaque' on the side of the store marks the exact location of Sir Benjamin's house.

...Willow Farm, the attractive house, painted pink, standing well back from School Lane near the crossways, **belonged in the 1930's, to Mr. George Woodgett, the great-nephew of the Captain of the Cutty Sark?**

Capt. Richard Woodgett was master of the Cutty Sark between 1885 and 1895 when this famous sailing ship made all her record voyages. Built in 1874 she was the last Tea Clipper to compete with steam power. Richard Woodgett's second wife was a Miss Winkie Parker. When Robert Falcon Scott went to the Antarctic in 1910, Mrs Scott took Miss Parker as nanny to her son Peter, but when the boy was old enough to go to prep school, then it was that Winkie married Captain Woodgett of the Cutty Sark.

Cutty Sark

...for very many years, the Norwich Crusaders Rugby Club has played matches at Little Melton on most weekends during winter? Rousing cheers from both teams can often be heard at the close of play, when darkness is beginning to fall.

...there is a little running stream dividing Great and Little Melton? It rises near Wymondham, and winds its devious way into the Yare at Marlingford. When the Danes first came here in the ninth century, it would have been very much larger than it is today.

Chapter Ten

Little Melton in times of conflict

They shall grow not old, as we are that are left grow old;
Age shall not weary them, nor the years condemn.
At the going down of the sun and in the morning
We will remember them.

Laurence Binyon

On 19th October 1921 a memorial plaque was unveiled on the north wall of the nave of Little Melton Church. It bears the names of the following six men who died as a result of the conflict of the Great War of 1914-1918:

Pte.William Blake
Driver Henry Robert Jeckells
Lance Corp.Albert Joy
Pte.John Newstead
Pte.Baron Archibald Rooke
Pte.Walter Bertie Warr

Six men from our small rural community, (in 1901 the population was only 284), who gave their lives for their country. Were they, in turn, following in the footsteps of other soldiers from the district in earlier times? In 1316 Edward II ordered every rural 'township' or community to provide men at arms to *'help repel the attacks of the Scottish marauders'* threatening the peace of England at that time. We can only speculate, too, as to whether men and women from Little Melton joined the army of Robert Kett and his brother William of Wymondham as they and their followers marched through the countryside in July 1549, to protest against the high-handed repression of Church and State. Their route from Wymondham to the City of Norwich went through Hethersett, and would have passed within two miles of Little Melton Church, as they made their way along the old London to Norwich Road, crossing the River Yare at Cringleford, before setting up temporary camp at Bowthorpe. Surviving lists of supporters do not include the names of any known sympathisers from the parish, and church burial registers did not exist at such an early period. However a 19th Century account of the Rebellion does list two governors of our own Hundred of Humbleyard, amongst many governors who were in sympathy with the Ketts' cause.

The rebels' last camp on Mousehold Heath near Norwich was said to comprise 20,000 men, women and children, if estimates of the time are to be believed. What we do know for certain is that Nicholas Sotherton, a former mayor of the city, rode post-haste to London to inform the young king, Edward VI, and the Privy Council of the danger menacing the City. It is probable that he was the same Nicholas Sotherton who wrote an almost contemporary account of the Rebellion called *'The Commoyson in Norfolk'*, and who was to buy Melton-Hall, Little Melton, a few years later in 1574. He was very far from being a sympathiser with Kett's cause, like most citizens of Norwich of the time. You may remember that the rebels were finally defeated by the Earl of Warwick and his mercenary army, many hundreds of Norfolkmen being killed in the battle, and their leaders sentenced to death. In due course, William Kett was hung from the tower of Wymondham Abbey, and Robert from Norwich Castle, where, many years later, more enlightened citizens erected a tablet to his memory.

Kett's Oak 2002 (B1172 between Hethersett and Wymondham)

During the Civil War of 1649 to 1660, most Norfolkmen were Puritan in outlook, forming part of what was known as 'The Eastern Association' which supported Oliver Cromwell. The gentry, however, though mainly supporting this cause, were sometimes divided in their loyalties, even within the same household. Most of the Anguish family, lords of the manor of Great Melton, supported the king, and lost much of their wealth as a result. Edmund Anguish (who features on the brass in Little Melton church, when his first wife and baby son died in 1604), actually took up arms against parliament later on, and had much of his woodlands rooted up as punishment by the Cromwellian army. The Royalist sentiment is well expressed according to Francis Blomefield's 18th century account of the wording on a family tomb in the then ruinated All Saints church, Great Melton; *'here lieth John Anguish of Great Melton Esq., who after a faithfull Discharge of his Duty to King Charles the first of blessed Memory, in his Wars during the wicked Rebellion, died on the 12 of Febr. Aged 79 years'.*

Members of the Skottowe family, here in Little Melton, seem to have been strong supporters of parliament, even before Cromwell became Protector. Richard Skottowe, (son of Augustine), was granted arms in 1647, the year he followed his father as lord of the manor. His fine monument in the chancel of All Saints depicts these arms, which are described technically as *'Per Fesse or and azure, a mullet of eight points countercharged. Crest, a dexter hand, with the wrist vested holding a mullet of eight points'.* The circumstances of the grant are interesting. A parliamentary committee had occupied the College of Arms and ejected the reigning Garter, Clarenceux and Norroy Kings of Arms, appointing Sir Edward Bysshe as Garter King of Arms instead, and it was Bysshe, the nominee of parliament, who made the grant himself.

Timothy Skottowe, a leading silversmith and goldsmith in Norwich, (Richard's uncle), was entrusted by the parliamentarians with the duty of weighing the plate being contributed to the cause by members of the Eastern Association. His receipt for a consignment from Sir John Potts of Mannington survives, for Sir John chose to pay his contribution of £100 in the form of plate rather than money. How values have changed, when *'6 silver candlesticks, 2 banqueting dishes, 1 preserving ladle and dish, 8 plates, 1 basin, 1 'broath' standing bowl, 1 chafing dish, 1 vinegar cruet, 1 closet candlestick, 1 porringer and 3 trencher salts, (together weighing 371 ounces)'*, were worth less than the cost of just one silver candlestick at today's prices! Timothy, however, was a Royalist at heart, and refused to contribute to the Parliamentarian *'Subscription towards the regaining of Newcastle'* and is reported to have raised a troop of horse for Charles I. His will shows that he died comparatively poor in 1645, and was probably fined as a 'malignant'.

A conflict nearer our own time, that of the Boer War in South Africa (1899 to 1902), is said to have caused the mental deterioration of a man remembered well by more senior village people, Billy Briggs by name. After leaving the army, he lived in a hedge near today's modern village hall, and his sad story is told in *'Snippets 8'*.

It is now too long ago to find many with personal memories of the six soldiers who died in the Great War. We must rely on research in the official records to find out about the part they played, and where their final resting-places are to be found.

Private William Blake was born in Hethersett but at the time he enlisted in the army he was living in Little Melton. He was assigned to the 34th. Battalion

Royal Fusiliers but was later transferred to the Labour Corps, a non-combative section of the army where men who were no longer fit enough to fight were serving. He died of wounds somewhere in 'France or Flanders' - the official record making no distinction between the two - on 15th May 1918 at the age of 34. William Blake was buried in a marked grave in St.Sever Cemetery Extension near Rouen, in Normandy, together with more than 8,000 other British and Commonwealth soldiers. In spite of being less than six months away from the cessation of hostilities, that one month of May in which William died was to see the deaths of 69,000 allied men on the Western Front. Many, like William, died of the wounds they had received in earlier fighting. British hospitals set up in that area, (south of Rouen), were operational for almost the whole of the war.

St. Sever cemetery extension, Rouen, France 1999

The next name on the War Memorial is that of Henry Robert Jeckells. He was a Dilham man who had married a Little Melton girl, Azalear. His parents lived in Tunstead at the time of the War. Robert had a house with outbuildings and land covering half an acre by the old Green in Little Melton, near Manor Farm. After enlisting in Norwich, he became a driver for the 40th Field Ambulance Division of the Royal Army Medical Corps, and was eventually sent to serve in far-off Mesopotamia, (present day Iraq). Fighting had spread to the Middle East with the entry of Turkey into the war in November 1914, on the German side. A small Anglo-Indian force was sent to Mesopotamia to prevent Turkish forces from occupying the oil fields in Iraq and Iran, and also from cutting off the route to India via the Suez Canal. The force secured early victories but was halted by the Turks in their attempt to capture Baghdad in Iraq. They were besieged and forced to surrender in April 1916, and not until March 1917 was the occupation of Baghdad achieved. Driver Jeckells, (his Christian names are transposed in official records), died on 7th August 1916 and is buried in Amara War Cemetery. The town of Amara is on the left bank of the River Tigris and the War Cemetery is situated between the river and the Chahaila Canal. Amara itself had been occupied by the Mesopotamia Expeditionary Force in June 1915 and became a hospital centre there and then, seven general hospitals and some smaller medical units being set up. More than four and a half thousand servicemen are buried in Amara, of whose graves more than a thousand are unidentified. Over the years the appearance of the cemetery has changed. Initially all the graves had headstones, but it was found that salts in the soil were causing severe deterioration, and the stones were regretfully removed in 1933 and replaced by a screen wall on which all the names were engraved. Henry's widow Azalear Jeckells continued to live in the village in the house by the Green.

The third person honoured on our War Memorial, Albert Joy, has eluded our efforts to discover more. Sadly his name does not appear in the official record 'Soldiers who died in the Great War' nor in records from the Commonwealth War Graves Commission. 'Joys' have lived in Little Melton since 1783, and an 'Albert Joy aged 9' appears on the 1891 Census, living in the village with his father William, a County Council roadman, and mother Eliza. This would have made Albert 33 when the War started in 1914, but we cannot be sure that we have the right Albert. Perhaps someone reading this can help.

Norfolk Regiment
cap badge

The fourth name is John Newstead. John was born at Wickmere, Norfolk, and enlisted in the Norfolk Regiment. He died of wounds in 'France and Flanders' on Tuesday 4th July 1916, aged 20 years. He was said to be of Wickmere, the son of Robert and Rachel Newstead of Little Melton, Wickmere, Norwich. He is buried at Abbeville Communal Cemetery, on the Somme in France, Abbeville being the headquarters of the British Lines of Communication during the greater part of the war. (Perhaps, from this, John should be commemorated at Wickmere, which is in north Norfolk, halfway between Aylsham and Holt, but there is obviously some connection with Little Melton). Can anyone throw light on this please?

The fifth name commemorated on the Memorial is that of Pte. Baron Archibald Rooke. He was to die in action in July 1918 on the Somme, in the fierce fighting that went on throughout the spring and summer of that year, in order to capture Bouzincourt village, near Albert, from the Germans. Baron is buried with about 700 other soldiers who died there in Bouzincourt Ridge Cemetery, having served with the 7th Battalion of the Buffs (East Kent Regiment). He was born in Little Melton, and was living here when he enlisted, the son of Horace Rooke, who owned a cottage and garden of just over three-quarters of an acre, with glass houses, on the Hingham Road, the B1108.

Our last man honoured is Walter Bertie Warr, a private in the 1st Battalion the Norfolk Regiment. He was also to die in action somewhere 'in France or Flanders' and is commemorated on the Arras Memorial, Pas de Calais in France, where 35,000 British, New Zealand and South African troops who have no known grave are remembered. He died on St George's Day, April 23rd 1917, the son of Thomas and Rebecca Warr of Lakenham, Norwich, and husband of Ellen Rebecca Warr of Little Melton, who lived at No.1 Parish Cottages, Great Melton Road, today's Rambler Cottage. The day he died had seen the start of heavy renewed fighting at Arras, with little ground gained and huge loss of life. He was 33 years old.

Sadly the war which drew to a close at 11 o'clock on the morning of the 11th day of the 11th month, 1918, which had been thought to be 'the War that was to end all Wars' did not turn out to be so, and little over twenty years later a second great conflict plunged the world into misery. Again men from our small community were to fight and die in far-flung places, and memories of them and of wartime in the village still remain fresh in the hearts and minds of many.

The Second World War of 1939-45 was to leave lasting memories both with former servicemen and civilians in the village. A one-time village resident, Mrs Daniels, now living in Wymondham, remembers people from Norwich leaving their homes at night, to sleep out of doors in the woods between Norwich and Little Melton to escape the bombing in the City. Some village residents had their relatives to stay with them, too, at the height of the Blitz, but the village itself was not immune from the bombing. On May 4th 1943 the solidly built Victorian school received a direct hit and became the only school in East Anglia to suffer serious war damage. Injured in the attack was the young son of the new headteacher, Mrs Barbara Buckton. Mrs Buckton and David were just returning to the building as the 'All Clear' sounded, signifying the end of that night's raid on Norwich, when a bomber flying overhead jettisoned its unexploded cargo onto the countryside. On that same night damage was caused to the Norfolk and Norwich Hospital (then on St Stephen's Road in Norwich), and to Colman's factory in Norwich.

While Mrs Daniels' husband was away on active service, (like many other men from the village), she helped out in the fields topping and tailing sugar beet, as there was a shortage of labour. One day a bomb was dropped in a field she had been working in, fortunately long after 'knocking-off' time and a big hole was there next day. Some of Mrs Daniels' most poignant memories are of the evacuees sent from London with their standard issue of a tin of corned beef, tin of condensed milk and a packet of biscuits. The evacuees were often in a very depressed state on arrival, and families from the village used to go and see whom they felt they could take in. Mrs Daniels offered a home to a young woman from London and her child, *'a very friendly girl'.* Unfortunately she was so homesick for her family and friends in London that she returned there in no time, and was not heard of again, leaving Mrs Daniels to wonder to this day what had become of her.

The war brought other strangers to the village, too. American servicemen came to relax at the dances and shows in the clubroom behind the Rose and Crown Public House, (affectionately known as *'the Cold Blow'*), and the pub was also a temporary billet for the debonair English actor, David Niven, already embarked on a distinguished career in British and Hollywood films. He was serving as an officer in a secret reconnaissance unit called 'Phantom', and together with two other officers was engaged in a training exercise in the area. David Niven went on to become a Major and later a Colonel in the Army, seeing service in France before the war ended. Also in the village were two Italians, interned as prisoners of war, and assigned to work on the land, where no one seemed to be afraid of them. Their fate, when hostilities ended, is also unknown.

David Niven - 'Phantom of the Cold-Blow?'
c.1942

By its nature, conflict in the last century gave no immunity to the most vulnerable members of the community, the very young. Mrs Marjorie Gould, then a pupil at the Blyth Secondary School in New Catton, Norwich, remembers the frightening times when the buses were grounded in the Bus Station during air raids, not being allowed to leave until the All Clear sounded, leaving the terrified pupils wondering how they would get home again. Several men and women from the village worked in factories in Norwich engaged in the war effort, cycling to work in all weathers and in the face of enemy action. Although everyone was frightened during the air raids, and the strictly-enforced blackout made the village lanes very dark places on moonless nights, there was a strong sense of community and all shared in the sorrow and grief of those who lost loved ones.

When peace finally arrived in 1945, the village was mourning the loss of five of its members. Their names are honoured on the Lych-gate at the parish church. This was erected as a memorial to those lost in both World Wars and was dedicated by the Bishop of Thetford on December 13th 1948. On the Lych-gate are inscribed the following names: -

Derek Reginald Bell
Richard Buckle
Maurice Charles Bugg
Louis Hampshire Moore
Carlos Anthony Sewter

Derek Bell was a sergeant in the 76th Squadron of the Royal Air Force Volunteer Reserve in 1943 when he was reported missing at the age of 21. He is commemorated on the Runnymede Memorial which overlooks the River Thames, four miles from Windsor. Twenty thousand Commonwealth and European Allied airmen who lost their lives in the Second World War, and who have no known graves, are remembered there. Sadly Derek's brother, Dick, was to hear the first news of the loss of his brother from a Navy pal he met up with in Hong Kong where he was also on active service.

Richard Buckle was the son of Ernest and Dora Buckle who had lived in Braymeadow Lane in Little Melton in the 1930s. He died of injuries received in the war.

Maurice Bugg was only 20 years old when he lost his life in May 1944, fighting against the Japanese in India. He was a private in the 2nd.Battalion of the Royal Norfolk Regiment, and was caught up in the fierce fighting at Garrison Hill in Kohima. This battle is now regarded by military historians as being decisive in halting the Japanese advance into India. Much of the fighting was hand to hand combat and took place in the garden and on the tennis court of the Deputy District Commissioner's residence. The site of the battle was incorporated into the Kohima War Cemetery, and its remoteness emphasises the far-flung nature of the fighting in this conflict. A stone bears this moving inscription:-

'When you go home
Tell them of us and say
For their tomorrow we gave our today'.

Maurice was the son of Charles Engledow and Gertrude Louisa Bugg of Little Melton, who are buried together in the extension of our churchyard. Mr. Bugg died in 1967 aged 75 and his wife in 1977 aged 76.

The fourth name on the wooden panels of the Lych-gate is that of Louis Moore whose mother and step-father lived in the village. Both Louis and his girl friend, who was also in the services, died in the conflict. Louis was a gunner in the Norfolk Yeomanry Anti-Tank Regiment of the Royal Artillery when he died of wounds on June 7th 1941, at the age of 25. He was buried in the Ismailia War Memorial Cemetery in Egypt.

Left; Gunner Louis Moore and his fiancée, Right; his Egyptian grave. c.1941

The last name on the War Memorial emphasises the part Norfolk civilians played in the Second World War. Mr Carlos Sewter was working at Boulton and Paul's Factory on Riverside Road in Norwich when it was attacked on the sunny late afternoon of 9th July in 1940. No warning had sounded of what was to be the first of forty-four air raids on the City of Norwich between July 1940 and November 1943. Workers at Colman's Carrow Works and at Barnard's Mousehold Factory were given little time to seek shelter. Boulton and Paul's, which had always been involved in aircraft production, was working at that time on wooden fuselages for Oxford Trainer aircraft and nose sections for Horsa gliders. Ten people died as a result of the raids that day. Mr Sewter received severe injuries and was rushed to the Norfolk and Norwich Hospital accompanied by his son, who also worked at the factory. Sadly he died three days later from his injuries and was buried in the Norwich City Cemetery. His name is honoured in the County Borough Register of Civilian War Dead. He was 46 years old, and his widow, Rose, continued to live in Little Melton at Dormer Cottage, School Lane, until her death in the late 1980s. She was to see the village expand out of all proportion after the war.

In 1945, and for many years afterwards, the only buildings on what was then called 'The Street', between Dormer Cottage and the Crossroads, were the Rose and Crown and Willow Cottage! Thankfully although wars continued to rage throughout the world, the village was to see no more conflict in the twentieth century.

****

Mrs. Mollie Loomb was the Licensee of 'The Rose and Crown' at Little Melton during World War II and we are grateful to her for sharing some of her experiences. She says:

I was running the pub in the village from 1940 for nineteen years. We had soldiers now and again staying during the war, those on the gun sites. They used to come to the house with their wives…we never charged them or nothing. My husband had made a very good radiogram, he played it very loud, and I used to run dances in the Clubroom for 9d on Monday nights, a quiet night. They used to do very well. And all these ninepences we gathered together, and when the soldiers came home on leave - the lads from the village, the ones that come in the pub - we gave them 10 Players and 10 shillings. We also started this committee that gave them some money when they come home. I can't remember how much they got – even the girls – they were in the Army, weren't they?

We also used to have fetes on old Clarke's meadow. One August Monday that was thick fog, absolutely thick fog, you couldn't see your hands in front of your face, but it carried on as usual. They all came, and we had different things you played games on. It was quite successful. You know, we got up to all sorts of things, busy times they were.

We had some quaint people in the village. It was a very quiet village, people used to play tennis in the road. That tells you what it was like. There was a big Alsatian. She would lie in the road waiting for the girls – two sisters – to come home. People used to just ride around the village on their bikes. Oh yes, we had some very quaint people.

We used to have black outs in the war, no street lights or anything like that. There was old Hoddy, a tall man with huge feet. He liked to sing and dance in the pub on the brick floor. We used to have lots of entertainment. Hoddy was walking home one night when it was dark and little Jimmy – tiny little man – he came cycling on his bicycle, riding along, but he couldn't see anything, pitch black it was. He just had a tiny little light on the front of the bicycle which showed no light at all. He rode along and went straight between Hoddy's legs, and there he sat, lamp up against Hoddy's back, so he couldn't see a thing. Oh we did laugh, that's a fact! There was old Archie Harmer. There was a lorry being backed into Bobby Eagle's driveway. You know where Bobby used to work, Hospital Farm now. He was backing in there, no lights again you see. Archie couldn't see him 'cause lights were at the back and on the road side of the lorry, and Archie ran into the side of the lorry, and the lorry ran over his foot. And so he just stood there, you see, so the chap says "Get outa the way". So he says "I will when you get off my bloody foot".

Mollie Loomb (left), her 'right-hand person' May and a Pub with no beer! Early 1940s

Oh dear, we used to have some fun…. We had some jolly good dances at Jimmy Nash's farm, (Norman's later on), 'cause we had soldiers on the gunsites all around us, and you bet that the like of some of them could play an instrument. The officers would go round and pick up the men and bring them here, and we'd have a smashing dance – English soldiers. We had American soldiers too, and we used to entertain some of them. Once we invited them to tea in the big tap room. We used to play darts in the afternoon – no beer about, and we drew the curtains 'cause everybody would stand and gawp in the window. So we were playing darts one Sunday. All of a sudden in burst the policeman. "What's going on here...what's going on here?" He got like a set back when he found there was no beer about.

We were just having an afternoon with a game of darts and a cup of tea. When David Niven stayed in the village, he stayed for a fortnight at the Rose and Crown Pub, now the Village Inn. They were there training the men to use these wireless cars. They'd never used them before. They were in the field and the men were in the clubroom, and when they had their exercises you'd see the officers and the men running round the house with gas masks on. Half of them would go down to the coast and send a message as if there were a gas attack. That's what they were here for, they were taught to use these wireless cars. I was David Niven's batman when he was here 'cause his batman was on leave. So I'd take his hot water for his wash, and a cup of tea to him every morning. He was a very nice fellow, Captain Niven. He was made a Major later on. He was well known even then. He went into Public Relations and made all those war pictures. He and his wife came to dinner one night. He made some very nice pictures.

We used to see doodle bugs going up the road. We lay there one night. It was so hot that August in the war, lots of hot days in the war we had. We would take the blackouts down, leave the windows wide open, then you could look at the sky. We used to see some doodle bugs going up the road. Later on, you'd hear the bump and they'd be down. I was always jolly glad when they got past us. There was a German unloaded some bombs, that's when they hit the school. There were some bombs in Clarke's meadow, and that was all soft ground, and so they went in a long way. They all had to be dug out, they were all unexploded, they were. Some fell on the other side of me, on Jimmy Nash's field. They exploded and lifted our roof off, and our ceilings all came down. I got up to have a look, you see. When we got back in the bedroom, we couldn't see all the dirt, and said "Oh leave it, we'll see what it's like in the morning." The school had the roof hanging down. They had to put all the tiles back again, they were all shifted. They had to take it all down in the end. But Norwich got it badly. They had a nasty time all Dereham Road way, and that. They had a nasty time.

There was an old person of Lyme
Who married three wives at a time;
When asked: 'Why the third?'
He replied; 'One's absurd,
And bigamy, sir, is a crime.'

Anon.

Did you know that...

   ...the **Depositions of the Norwich Consistory Court for the period 1449 - 1530 show that a case of Bigamy had a connection with Little Melton?** It came to light when Edward Peretre of Melton Parva petitioned the Norwich court to allow him to marry Audrey Kemp. It appears that although the banns had been quite properly read three times, the curate of Mistress Kemp's parish had refused to marry them on the grounds that she already had a husband! Mistress Kemp agreed that she did indeed have a husband *'in fact but not in law'* as she had *'married'* a Master John Matthew at Acle in Norfolk and borne him two children, believing him to be a widower when they married. Two years later she had discovered that he had a wife still living in Heacham named Margaret Manning, whom John had married fifteen years earlier. Having deserted Margaret, he then 'married' again at Oby, and after the death of this lady had gone through a third ceremony with Audrey Kemp. Fortunately, Edward Peretre and Audrey were able to bring two witnesses to the court who had previously lived in Heacham, Thomas Chapman, now of Norwich, and Thomas Horsebroke of Colney, who testified that the first marriage had indeed taken place, thus proving that Audrey was never married *'in law'* to John Matthew, and was therefore a single woman!

   ...a **Flourishing Band existed in the 1920s called the Hethersett & Little Melton Band,** and that the late Bob Richardson, well-known local farmer and Methodist lay preacher, was leader of it at one time? An account of his life in the two villages can be read in his autobiography *'Some Fell on Stony Ground'*.

   ...the **Norwich Apprentice records show that several village boys served apprenticeships of seven years apiece in the worsted weaving industry** that brought so much wealth to East Anglia in the Middle Ages? Most of them served Norwich weavers, but in 1654 a weaver named Henrie Dawkins was working in Little Melton itself, and he took on Henry Band, son of Robert Band, a husbandman in the village that year. Two boys named Robert and Thomas Blosse, whose father Thomas was a yeoman in Attleborough, became apprenticed to him the following year.

...the Village Hall was opened on the 7th May 1990 by Keith Skipper, the well-known Norfolk writer and broadcaster? It was built at a cost of £180,000 and the facilities included badminton courts, changing rooms, committee rooms and a fully-stocked kitchen for private social functions. Village fund raising allowed the building of the children's play area outside. With money from a *'Commuted Sum'* from the developer of Greenacres, a tennis court was added, and later on as part of the Millennium celebrations in the village, a small garden was built and planted, dedicated in 2001 to the memory of Bob Brett. With the aid of a Lottery Grant in 2002 the car park was surfaced, completing a superb village amenity.

Little Melton Village Hall being opened by Keith Skipper, aided by (left) Marianne Smith (6) and (right) Elspeth Richmond (5).

...the account books of the Surveyor of the Highways show that the winter of 1836/37 was a very severe one? On January 2nd 1837 eight men were each paid 1s 6d (seven and a half pence nowadays) for the five and a half days they had spent clearing the village roads of snow. Later in the same year, the Surveyor of the Highways claimed 2s. 6d. in *'incidental expenses'* for his journey from Little Melton to Hethersett to 'have the books signed'.

...a 'Hundred' was an administrative division of a shire? This probably originated way back in the 10th century. The meaning of the name is obscure, but at first it may have contained a hundred families or else a hundred taxable hides of land. Little Melton was in Humbleyard Hundred, which takes its name from a valley in the parish of Swardeston, where the Hundred Court was held in 'a low yard'. The church Deanery of Humbleyard still exists today.

...each Parish in a Hundred was responsible, in some way, for the maintenance and manning of a Beacon that carried news of important national events, (like the defeat of the Spanish Armada in 1588), across the country? Humbleyard Hundred's beacon was the Brumwell (or Brummell) Beacon in Tunstead Hundred, and responsibility for its upkeep was shared with Tunstead and Forehoe Hundreds. Rates were levied according to the size of the parish, and in 1652 Little Melton's rate was set at 2s. 11d., Great Melton's was 9s. 8d., Hethersett's 12s. 6d. with 2s. 3d. set for Colney. Humbleyard Hundred was ordered by the Norfolk Sessions Court to repair and maintain watch on the beacon in the quarter leading up to Michaelmas each year, and to pay the charge for the pitch, charcoal, powder, brimstone and match used should it have to be lit. All beacons were expected to be maintained in good order so that they could be lit at any time.

...Nurse Edith Cavell was a governess at Colney Hall? She looked after the Barclay children there, in 1889 and 1890, for three days each week. Another three days a week were spent with the Gurney children at Earlham Hall, making the six mile journey from Swardeston by pony and trap. She later left to become governess to a family in Brussels. Her life was tragically cut short, being executed by the Germans on October 12th 1915.

Chapter Eleven

Social welfare and the poor.

Poverty – Death of my Aunt

My aunt she died a month ago,
And left me all her riches,
A feather-bed and a wooden leg,
And a pair of calico breeches;
A coffee pot without a spout,
A mug without a handle,
A baccy box without a lid,
And half a farthing candle.

Anon.

Just beyond the crossways on Great Melton road stands Rambler Cottage, an attractive little building of mellowed red brick with three dormer windows in its pantiled roof, fronted by a lawn, with a red chestnut tree at its centre, and flower beds on either side. Few would guess that this was originally the *'Town House'* or *'Poor House'* of the village.

When Mrs Anne Carter bought the property in the mid 1990s, knowing nothing of its history, the deeds showed that the Parish Council of Little Melton had been the owner until 1962, when it sold the plot of just under a quarter of an acre to Mr William James Chamberlain for £1,000. James Nash and Reginald Percy Garrod were the signatories for the council, and Mr Garrod has since confessed that he was much against the sale! Mr Chamberlain turned the two cottages into one house and sold the orchard land along Mill Road for the construction of two chalets.

In 1962 there were no documents about the property in the possession of the Council, so a statutory declaration was made by William Barley of The Bungalow, Little Melton, in which he stated that he was 76 years old, and had resided at Little Melton for 25 years, had been a member of the Parish Council for 20 years, and knew the property proposed to be sold. He said that it had been in the possession of Little Melton Parish Council for the past 25 years, that the buildings had from time to time been repaired by the Council out of the rents, that the Council had from time to time let the property, and that he had never known or heard of any adverse claim having been made by any person with regard to it. He finished with these words *'I verily believe that no deeds or writing relating to the said property are in the possession, power or procurement of Little Melton Parish*

Council or do exist'. What an irresistible challenge this presented to the new owner.

Visits to the Norfolk Record Office in Norwich proved fruitful, as the 'Little Melton Town Books' (or minutes of vestry meetings) from 1809 to 1831 have been microfilmed and are available for study. Almost the first entry reads as follows: *'On 13th October 1810 it was agreed that the Poor House, lately rebuilt, shall be appropriated to the use of poor widows and not to be let to any person by the year otherwise'.* (*'Very suitable'* thought Anne, a widow). The vestry minutes were signed by Edward Heath, William Lofty, and John Leeder, while six others signed with a cross, John Child, William Davy, William Copeman, Elizabeth Thompson, Sarah Reynolds and Thomas Palmer. In 1814 and 1815 Widow Fox was paying 15s rent a year, but perhaps there were not enough needy widows to fill the house, because by 1817 two men were in residence, Symonds paying 1s. 6d per week rent, and J. Clarke a shilling a week. All sorts of entries relating to the purchase of items for the Town House followed, including candles, sheets and blankets, a chamber pot, a coal skep and several chaldrons of coals, saucepans, a wash tub, a brush, bed mats and bolsters.

In 1826 accounts were shown for the building of a well in the back gardens, which still exists today. 600 Kiln Burnt Bricks for 'Well for Poor House' cost £1. 4s, and carriage of same cost 5s. A new well rope was 2s., and the Blacksmith's bill for Trions for well was 5s, and so on and on, faithfully recorded, week by week. Sadly the provision of coffins for people who had died at the house also features quite frequently, as do payments to the bearers, the grave diggers, the parson and the women who laid out the bodies.

Rambler Cottage, 2002

On 2nd January 1817 the Churchwardens and Overseers of the Poor were discussing how best to raise the sum of £120, with which to pay off 'the remaining part of a Bond due to the Executors of the late William Howlett'. Later that year William Copeman offered the requisite amount, 'for a Bond on the Town House'. What did all this mean? Had the money been borrowed originally to purchase a property for use as a Poor House perhaps, or even to build one? The Centre of East Anglian Studies at the University of East Anglia was approached for advice, and a visit to the Public Record Office at Kew was suggested, in order to search a series of documents called 'MH12', which were said to consist of correspondence between the Poor Law Commissioners of Somerset House, London, and the Poor Law and Local Government Boards of England and Wales, dating from 1834 to 1900.

'MH12' turned out to consist of no less than 16,741 bound leather volumes of every letter ever written between these bodies, filed first under counties and then under Poor Law unions, and without an index! The first three volumes for Henstead Union, Norfolk, were ordered, covering the years 1834 to 1844, and after several hours of scrutinising endless irrelevant hand-written letters, and just as frustration was beginning to set in, the name 'Little Melton' suddenly leapt out of the pages, and what a treasure trove this proved to be.

Here, in all its glory, was nothing less than the original letter written in 1835 to the Commissioners by the Rev. Thomas S. Buckle of Hethersett, the owner of Elm Farm, Little Melton, giving full details of the history of the Town House. Mr Buckle wrote that the Churchwardens and Overseers of the Poor had been much concerned over the lack of accommodation for the aged poor and sick in Little Melton, and in 1792 had built two cottages in which to house them, on common land near the crossways. £200 had been borrowed, of which only £80 had been repaid plus interest, a new security being entered into in 1817, when 'all the then ratepayers were made parties to this. Some signed the bond, but not all. Of those who signed, some are dead, some have left the parish, but the debt has not been further reduced'. Mr Buckle added that he was aware that the recent Poor Law Amendment Act of 1834 had required parishes to sell their village poor houses to help pay for the building of the new Union Workhouses, and asked whether, in these circumstances, the parish might be given permission to sell their poor house, to return the £120 still owing to the bondholder, and to give the money remaining towards the building of the Henstead Union Workhouse at Swainsthorpe.

A lot of correspondence followed, interspersed with page after page of other matters relating to a host of different villages, but eventually another entry was found, in which the Commissioners wrote 'At the time the debt which it is wished to repay was incurred, the Churchwardens and Overseers were not empowered to borrow, but if the £120 can be legally paid, the Commissioners will give their consent to it.' They asked for copies of the Vestry Minutes and the Enclosure Award and Map, and finally, some considerable time and many pages later, decreed that 'the property proposed to be sold by the parish of Little Melton is not parish property, and therefore cannot be sold under their order, but that the property in question is Charity property'.

This meant that the Little Melton Vestry had no alternative but to hold onto its Town House, and was probably none too pleased about it, as the building was said to be in a poor condition at this time, and was costing money. In addition, what was it to be used for, now that the poor and sick of the village were to be incarcerated in the newly built workhouse at Swainsthorpe? Very sensibly, an agreement was reached that 'the village cottages', as they would now be called, were to be let by the year to any parishioner who wished to rent them.

William and Rebecca Alice Burcham were the last tenants of the cottage at No.2, on the left (or Great Melton) side, he dying in 1953 aged 66 and his wife in 1961 aged 70. She is described by her grandson David Goulding of The Bungalow, Little Melton, as having very long, dark brown hair, ('almost black'), and liking a glass of stout daily. Peter and Clara Gould lived in the other cottage, and are the grandparents of Herbie Gould who today runs the fruit and vegetable store towards the end of Mill Road. Both David and Herbie used to visit their grandparents frequently when they were teenagers, and are full of tales of 'the old days', when the occupants kept themselves 'very much to themselves' and didn't speak to each other. Each house had its own steep stairway in the corner of the front room, (now replaced by a central staircase). water was drawn

Peter Gould and his Whippet outside one of the two cottages. c1960

from the well or dipped out of the rain butts, and of course there was no indoor sanitation. The well and the old brick privy still remain in the back garden today, the latter now in use as an excellent toolshed.

Further research has shown that years ago when the cottages were built, Mr William Howlett, (the original bond holder) lived at Hockering, where he died in 1814, and was the well-to-do uncle of Mr Edward Heath of Church Farm, Little Melton. William Copeman, who lent £120 in 1817, lived in the village at Dowes, (today's Dormer Cottage on School Lane), and was a yeoman, and unmarried, leaving all his property in 1834 to his nephews Edmund and William Fox, his personal estate being sworn at under £1,500. He is buried in Colney churchyard.

How much poverty was there in rural Little Melton at the time the Town House was built? One clue can be found in the parish registers, for throughout England, from 1783 to 1794, a duty of 3d had to be paid on each christening, marriage and burial at the parish church, the only people exempted being paupers. Clergy were instructed to enter every detail in their registers, and were given a 10% commission for their trouble.

Sixty-nine baptisms took place here during those twelve years, fifty-eight families paying the tax when their babies were christened, and eleven being exempted as too poor to pay. Of these children, who now all had to be at least partially supported by parish relief, four had been born to penniless single mothers, and seven to indigent couples. Of the twenty-eight people buried, no less than eleven were paupers, nearly half the total, a truly staggering figure. Fortunately, the sixteen couples who got married all managed to scrape together the three obligatory pennies demanded.

From way back in 1598, each parish had been made responsible for the care of its own poor, and three years later the Poor Law Act of 1601 was to become the 'Bible' as it were of Poor Law administration for many centuries to come. Overseers were appointed in each parish to collect the poor rate and to carry out the necessary care of those who would not, or could not, help themselves. Later, by the Settlement Act of 1697, newcomers were only allowed to settle in a parish providing they held a 'Settlement Certificate' from their 'Parish of Settlement' (sometimes the parish of their, or their parents' birth if they had not gained a certificate by any other means), guaranteeing to take them back if they became in need of poor relief.

Most of the Poor Law documents for our village date only from the early to mid nineteenth century, but give us a glimpse of what life must have been like then for ordinary people. At this period, the most usual way to gain a settlement certificate in a particular parish was to complete a full year's residential work there, or, much less commonly, to serve an apprenticeship, to rent a property worth £10 per annum, or to hold parish office. Without this treasured piece of paper, however, should someone fall on hard times, he or she and the whole family were more than likely to be returned, *willy-nilly*, to their original place of settlement, whether or not work or accommodation was available for them there.

Fortunately, no less than ten Settlement Examinations and eleven Removal Orders for Little Melton still survive in the Norfolk Record Office, where they can be seen on microfilm.

One interesting examination is that of John Blyth *'of the parish of Melton Parva*, (or Little Melton), *labourer'*, taken on oath before Jehosophat Postle Esq., the Justice of the Peace who lived at Colney Hall nearby. This was held on 26th February 1816, *'touching his last legal settlement'*. John said that he was about 22 years of age, and was born in the parish of Wymondham where his father resided, whose legal settlement was in the parish of Twyford. A fortnight before Michaelmas (Sept 29th) 1811 he had let himself to John Girling, a farmer of Melton Parva, starting to work for him at Michaelmas. He had worked as a living-in labourer for Mr Girling for one whole year, continuing until the end of the following February.

This proved a satisfactory examination for John, who was granted a settlement certificate for Little Melton, having completed a full year's work for his employer there. This was just as well, for his further statement shows that he was by now unemployed. In March 1813 he worked *'as a barrower of bricks'* for Mrs Watson, a widow and brickburner of Wymondham, *'being hired by the piece for his said work'*. By Michaelmas 1813 Mrs Watson's nephew engaged him for a whole year to drive the team of horses for the business, at the weekly wage of 15s, but by Lady Day (25th March) 1814, Mrs Watson had disposed of her brickmaking business to her son Thomas, and he had been out of work ever since.

19th century cooking utensils

On 20th May 1826, William Fox of the hamlet of Heigham, weaver, was examined, giving us an example of how someone who had not gained a settlement certificate for himself was forced to take the legal settlement of his parents. William said he was 32 years old, and was born in the parish of St. Benedict's, Norwich. He was the son of William Fox, weaver, whose legal place of settlement was Little Melton, as was his paternal grandfather's. He said that his father had been relieved by the Overseers of the Poor of Little Melton on many occasions, that he had learnt the weaving trade from his father, without an apprenticeship, and that he had never done anything to gain a legal settlement elsewhere. He added that he had married Martha Spaden nine years ago, and had two children, William aged 7 and James aged 5, Little Melton was therefore found to be his parish of legal settlement and he was returned here.

Another examination of 20th March 1816 shows us how the settlement system often worked in practice. This time it was John Coker of the parish of East Dereham, husbandman, who appeared before Mr. Postle, the Colney magistrate. John said he was about 29 years of age, and was born in Gressenhall where his father resided as a legal inhabitant. At the Dereham Quarter Sessions about a fortnight before Michaelmas 1808, he let himself to Edward Heath of Melton Parva, Yeoman, for the whole year, but after completing that period of service 'he had never been let since for a complete year in any one place'. He added that he had been married to his wife Jane for about six years and had three children. The outcome was that although his home was East Dereham, and although he had not lived in Little Melton for the last eight years, his service with Mr. Heath gave him a legal settlement here. It was therefore the responsibility of the Overseers of the Poor of Little Melton, and not the Overseers of Dereham, to support him and his family, and to bring him back to Little Melton, where they had to try to find him work and a place in which to live.

Some years later, on 12th April 1831, William Gould of Hethersett, husbandman, was examined. He said he was about 26 years of age, and was born at Ashwellthorpe where his father resided, whose legal settlement was the parish of Great Melton. At Michaelmas 1824 he let himself to Thomas Hubbard of Little Melton for one whole year, at the live-in wage of £5, and at the end of that year had never been let for one whole year since. He had been married to Rebecca for four years. Little Melton was adjudged his parish of legal settlement.

Removal Orders are distressing documents, showing the harshness of the system whereby whole families were uprooted without redress, and transported bodily from one place to another. For example, an order was made on 10th October 1830 by which George Brand, weaver, aged about 33, his wife Susanna aged 26, their children Mary Ann aged 7, John aged 4 and Sarah aged 18 months were removed from Wymondham to Little Melton, which was George's father's place of settlement. Similarly, on 27th March 1821, the order was given that Benjamin Tuttle, husbandman, Elizabeth his wife, and their children Elizabeth aged 11, Harriet aged 7, and the twins William and Maria aged 2, were to be taken from Little Melton to Great Ellingham, their legal place of settlement.

Some slight compassion in carrying out such orders was shown occasionally. On 5th January 1830, the Overseers were ordered to remove Robert Mortar and his family from Little Melton to Earlham, but as Robert's wife Mary had given birth to baby James only ten days previously, this was postponed until 9th February, when Mary was no longer *in childbed*. Meanwhile, Little Melton charged Earlham nineteen shillings for the upkeep of the family *due to the suspension of the order*.

Illegitimate children provided many a headache for the powers that be at this period. On 21st May 1833 sixteen year old David Reeve was examined by Mr. Postle, the magistrate. He was described as *a male bastard child, born of the body of Susannah Edwards, wife of Christopher Edwards of Attleborough*, and chargeable to the parish of Little Melton, where he was now living without a settlement certificate. Susannah Edwards was then interviewed, but we know nothing of her testimony, though David was eventually removed to the parish of St. Paul's, Norwich, presumably because this was the parish where he had been born.

A few months later, on 3rd December 1833 Charlotte Rayner, a singlewoman, was deported to Hethel. It was stated that *she is now with child,*

'Swainsthorpe Union' workhouse. c.1930

whereby she is deemed to be actually chargeable to the parish of Little Melton'.
This removal must have been made either because the alleged father lived there, or because Hethel was her or her parents place of birth.

Following the big Poor Law Amendment Act of 1834, when workhouses were built to accommodate the poor of many parishes, the same removal system remained.

In April 1845, Edward Bacon of Little Melton was in the Swainsthorpe workhouse, as was Charlotte his wife, and their children Thomas (8), Philip (6), David (3) and Solomon (1). When examined, Edward told a very complex story, saying that he had been born in Easton, and was now 42 years old. Twenty three years ago last Michaelmas, he had let himself to Mr. Drake who lived at Hevingham. That same day Mr Drake moved to Colton and he went with him, and served him there. Mr Drake stayed at Colton only seven weeks before moving to Morningthorpe, where Edward also worked for him. Mr Drake then went to Fritton, where he lodged with him again, serving him there until the old Michaelmas day. After a full year, he collected his wages and left his service. At that time Edward was unmarried, and said that he had never worked for anyone for a whole year since, nor obtained a settlement certificate in any other way. On 1st July 1835 he was married at Little Melton Church, and while living there he went to Hempnall to see the Overseer to ask for relief, who gave him half a crown (2s. 6d.) on two separate occasions. The Master of the Swainsthorpe workhouse, Mr Thomas Faulkner gave evidence that the Overseers of the Poor for Little Melton had been maintaining the Bacon family over the past month. Finally Mr Samuel Hipperson, Churchwarden, Messrs. Thomas Forster and Thomas Dove Aldred, Overseers, all of Little Melton, made application for a Removal Order for the whole family to Hempnall, which, (somewhat surprisingly), was duly granted.

Two findings that emerge from these documents are the degree of movement from one place to another experienced by our forebears, and the lack of stability in their lives. Nostalgic statements like 'the good old days' are nothing but a load of nonsense, for people did not 'stay put' for life in the 'idyllic' village of their birth. Work had to be found wherever it was available, often many weary miles away, and there were no welfare handouts in times of distress. To cap it all, particularly from 1834, there was the ever present fear of ending up in the workhouse, where husbands were separated from wives and parents from children, and where an *'idiots yard'* catered for the misfits of this world.

Many people now visit the Rural Life Museum at Gressenhall, built as a workhouse in 1777, and from the displays there, one can begin to gain some idea of how terribly frightening it must have been to be uprooted from home, and taken miles away to live with strangers in a huge *'pauper palace'*. In its early days, Gressenhall was a reasonably benign institution, where families could spend at least part of the day together, and it was not until much later, after the 1834 Act, that the regime everywhere became really harsh. Wicklewood was also one of Norfolk's very early 'Houses of Industry', which was where our neighbours from Bawburgh were sent when they could no longer support themselves. Bawburgh was in the Forehoe Union, while both the Meltons and Hethersett were in the Henstead Union, our poor having no centralised workhouse to go to until 1836, when the house at Swainsthorpe was built.

Great Melton had also tackled the problem of homelessness, Sir John Lombe having sold ten acres of High Common to John Thomlinson and Clarke Stoughton in 1791 for the building of a poor house. The history of this has not been fully researched, but by 1803 *'Great Melton Workhouse'* had been officially listed in the British Parliamentary Papers. It was the only registered parish workhouse in the whole hundred of Humbleyard, and must have been quite small. In 1803 it had just seven permanent residents, their labour earning £6. 9s. towards their keep, while in 1814 and 1815 it had ten occupants, and was probably sold before 1836. Hethersett, too, had its poorhouse, later converted into the Queen's Head Public House and now a restaurant, though this, like the cottages at Little Melton, was never officially registered as a workhouse.

The poor rate was fixed by the Overseers every quarter according to need, Little Melton parishioners frequently being charged ninepence, one shilling or even one shilling and sixpence in the pound on the rateable value of their property. A few Rate Books survive for Little Melton, and show the name of the ratepayer and the owner of the property, the rateable value and the amount paid. The cost of caring for the poor was enormous, and fell not only on the shoulders of the well-to-do, but also on those of the majority of parishioners who had little to bless themselves with in the first place. The 1834 Poor Law Amendment Act was passed by a worried government in an attempt to alleviate part of this burden, which would now be shared by all parishes in the union. The Swainsthorpe Workhouse served no less than 37 parishes, and Mr John Girling of Manor Farm was the first Poor Law Guardian for Little Melton to be appointed to the board.

The Minutes of the Henstead Union house are still kept at the Norfolk Record Office, but the Admission and Discharge Books, that would have told us so many interesting details, were apparently thrown away after use, as being of no value. The Archivist's comments about this were chilling in the extreme, and give some insight into the general attitude of that period. *'The paupers really didn't count at that time'*, she said, *'their names didn't matter, they were almost non-persons, just a burden on society, and few admission books survive for this reason, the Wicklewood ones being an exception'*.

In 1782 the weekly bill of fare at the Wicklewood workhouse was as follows, and one wonders how long anyone could have survived on such a diet.

	Breakfast	Dinner	Supper
Sunday	Bread & cheese	Beef & dumplings	Beef broth
Monday	Beef broth	Peas	Bread & cheese
Tuesday	Milk broth	Thick milk	Bread & cheese
Wednesday	Bread & cheese	Beef & dumplings	Beef broth
Thursday	Beef broth	Peas	Bread & cheese
Friday	Onion gruel	Baked puddings	Bread & cheese
Saturday	Bread & cheese	Thick milk	Bread & cheese

A list of 'Payments made by the Little Melton Overseers for the first quarter of 1836' survives at the Record Office, and may be worth quoting. (Do remember that the tiny 5p coin of today replaced a whole shilling of 'old' money, though values have changed enormously).

Jan. 18.	William Parrish. Sick.	5s.
	Mary Barnes & family	5s.
	George Brande	1s.
	[He can't have found work after the removal order of 1830]	
Jan 25	M. Barnes & family	5s.
	George Brande	1s.
Feb 1	Wm Parrish. Sick.	5s.
	George Brande	1s.
Feb 8	Wm Parrish. Sick.	7s.6d.
	M. Barnes & family	5s.
	Geo. Brande	1s.
Feb 15	M. Barnes	2s.6d
Feb 22	M. Barnes relieved with bread	2s.6d
Feb 29	M. Barnes relieved with bread	2s.6d.
Mar 3	John Mitchel. Sick.	3s.
	Robert Pellet lost time	5s.
Mar 7	John Mitchel. Sick.	3s.
	M. Barnes & family	2s.6d
Mar 14	J. Mitchel. Sick.	3s.
	M. Barnes & family	2s.6d
Mar 21	J. Mitchel. Sick.	3s.0d.
	M. Barnes & family	2s.6d
	Pair of Highlows for lad Wm Mitchel	11s.0d
	[These are high boots]	
	Pd for ½ yr's washing for him	10s.0d

	Coat for same	*10s.0d*
	Calico for shirts for same	*3s.4d*
	Making up same	*1s.6d*
Apr 16	*Paid 13 wks maintenance & clothing*	
	For Eliz. Hurdy	*£3.1s.9d*
Apr 17	*Removal Order for Martha Wisseman*	
	& 3 children to Wymondham	*15s.0d.*

One man who took a most unusual and very positive attitude towards the poor was the Rev. John Barkley, vicar of Little Melton from 1839 to 1883. Within a year of his arrival, he had visited all his parishioners and was horrified at the poverty he found, particularly among the sick, so he decided to visit Swainsthorpe with a complaint. The Henstead Poor Law Union employed a number of medical men, who also had their own private practices, their duty being to look after the paupers at times of illness. The system was that the Overseer or Poor Law Guardian of the parish would issue a Medical Order to a really sick family, who then had to walk the five miles to Norwich to take it to Mr. Gowing's surgery, (he being the doctor who looked after Little Melton), before treatment commenced.

It was the family of William Gould that worried Mr Barkley most, the same Gould who had been subjected to a settlement examination ten years earlier. He was an agricultural labourer, now living with his wife and seven children in a cottage on Mill Road, one room up, and one room down, and with a toddler of 2 years 3 months very ill with fever. The Medical Officer was sent for, but did not attend for several days, only prescribing medicine, after having had the symptoms described to him. Mr Barkley felt this to be very wrong, as the doctor had not seen the patient first, and this formed the substance of his complaint. Mr. Gowing maintained, however, that this was how he treated all his patients, whether private or public, first dispensing medicine, and only visiting if told the next day that the illness had not abated. Other children also became ill in Gould's family, but the doctor did not visit. They were luckily a hardy lot, and all survived.

Mr. Barkley received no satisfaction from the Henstead Union officials, so he decided to complain to the Poor Law Commissioners in London, with the result that pages and pages about the poor of Little Melton still survive in his flowing hand among the voluminous MH 12 documents at Kew. In all, they describe no less than twenty-two cases where he felt that the medical treatment had been inadequate.

The story told about Robert Bailey was particularly distressing. Bailey had a wife and four children, and had lived for several years in the village, though his settlement certificate gave Hempnall as his legal parish. He was ill about a month before harvest in 1840, and obtained an order for medical relief from the

Relieving Officer of Little Melton. He was too ill to take it to Norwich himself, and the Medical Officer never visited, just sending him medicine from time to time, over a ten week period. At last medical assistance was procured for him, at the private expense of a neighbour, and later he was sent to the workhouse for some weeks, together with his family. On returning home, he received outdoor relief once more, on account of being ill again.

One of his children died shortly afterwards, but he never applied for medical help, either for himself or for his child, because he was told by the Guardian of Hempnall parish not to take any relief from Little Melton. The child suffered a great deal over a long period and died in a very bad state. He did then apply to the Overseer of Little Melton for help to bury the child, but was told to apply to his own parish. He took it upon himself to procure a coffin, in the hope that the Poor Law Board would give him the means of paying for it. His wife walked all the way to Pulham St. Mary and back, (as Hempnall is in the Depwade Union, its workhouse being at Pulham), a total of sixteen miles, but was refused help, because neither she nor her husband had applied to the Relieving Officer of Little Melton. The body was very offensive by this time, and his cottage was only one up and one down.

The Poor Law Commissioners seem to have taken the vicar's complaints seriously, and eventually in 1844 a full enquiry was held at Swainsthorpe, all the cases that Mr. Barkley had complained of being looked at in some detail. Unfortunately, two or three years had elapsed since the illnesses had occurred, memories were unreliable, and entries in the Medical Officer's Day Book were given greater weight than any verbal testimony remaining from the families involved

The chairman remarked in his summing up that *'the uncertainty which must ever prevail upon all questions of date that depend on the recollection of the labouring classes render it all but impossible to discover the real facts of the case'*, and glowing reports were given of Mr Gowing's care of the sick poor. However, the Medical Officer was slightly admonished over the Gould case, the doctor being told that the Commissioners did not approve of the practice of prescribing medicine before a visit was made to a patient.

This is a grim tale indeed, but even here humour often lies just beneath the surface, in this case provided, quite unwittingly, by the courageous Rev. Barkley in person. He solemnly told the Board that to save the doctor trouble, he himself often prescribed medicines to his sick parishioners, as he felt it to be part of his duty as a Christian minister. No comment was made but the mind boggles!

Another even more exceptional man who did an enormous amount to improve the working life of the agricultural labourer was George Edwards. He was one of seven children born and brought up in a two-roomed cottage, his father's wage being seven to eight shillings for a full seven days labour each week, supplemented by four shillings earned by his mother's work on her hand loom. George had no schooling, though he went to Sunday School, and later his wife taught him to read and write. Rent of a two-roomed cottage was between 1s. and 2s. 6d. a week, leaving little money for food. When George was six, his mother used to give him a little bread soaked in boiling water for breakfast, and two slices of bread with a small piece of cheese and an apple or onion for dinner, as meat was rarely eaten. For a few unhappy weeks the whole family was lodged in the workhouse, but at six George was scaring crows from the fields, at ten he had learnt to plough, and once adult he became a team-man in charge of the horses, earning 2s. a week with board and lodging. Many years on, and against all the odds, Mr George Edwards was to found the Union of Agricultural Workers and to become a Member of Parliament, one of the most respected members in the House, who was later given a knighthood. His home was Martham, not Little Melton, but the early part of his story was that of very many families in very many rural parishes throughout Norfolk at the time.

Poor Law administration did not finally come to an end until the Local Government Act of 1919, while our modern *'welfare state'* was to grow, of course, from the all embracing Beveridge Report of 1942.

'Washing day in Little Melton' unknown date, but the cottage still stands at the junction of Braymeadow Lane and Colney Lane

The greatest bore is boredom,
The greatest nuisance known,
Is he who talks about himself
And his affairs alone,
When you want him to listen
While you talk about your own.

Anon.

Did you know that...

...**an old retired Teamman of the 1930's** used to deliver milk round the village, telling many a tale in the process? His habit, like that of most country folk, was to wash outside winter and summer on a table near the back door. He simply dipped the bowl into the soft rain water tub. One frosty morning there was a tinkle and a voice; *'Water's hard this morning.'* It was the dry humour of a typical Norfolk farmworker.

...**in 1929 there were only four people with telephones in the whole of Little Melton?** They were Charles Ernest Bilham, nurseryman at Vine Cottage (Hethersett 25X); Edwin Alfred Clarke, J.P., farmer at Elm Farm (Hethersett 25Y); William Spencer Diaper, farmer at Manor Farm (Hethersett 29), and Wm Lack farmer at The Grange (Hethersett 12).

...**the Little Melton Village Sign was given by our local Womens Institute,** designed by Miss Philippa Miller and unveiled by Mrs Patricia Batty Shaw, the National President, on 28th July 1981?

The sign shows the parish church with its bell, (said to be the second oldest in the county), above a horse and ploughman and the village windmill. It was worked in metal by the head of metalwork at Norwich School, Mr. Paul Moore. The post and name plate were given by Mr Bob Brett and the base by Mr. J. Symonds.

...**Little Melton's Womens Institute was founded** in 1965 and remained very active for over twenty-five years. When low numbers made it no longer viable, the sad day came when it had to be officially disbanded by the Norfolk Federation of Women's Institutes. This was on Thursday 21st November 1991, and was much regretted by its few remaining members, who had particularly fond memories of their many drama productions.

'Opening' of the Village sign 28th July 1981

1, Jean Durrell; 2, Marjorie Greenwood; 3, Vera Cole; 4, Phyllis Tobyn;
5, Mrs. Neale; 6, Ellen Heather; 7, Alice Plummer; 8, Elsie Miles; 9, Pauline Clarke;
10, Dorothy Broughton; 11, Vera Browne; 12, Barbara Robinson;
13, Angela Saunders; 14, Emmeline Flower; 15, 'Nan' Adam; 16, Enid Jarvis;
17, Patricia Batty Shaw W.I. National President; 18, Marion Broughton; 19, Bill
Tobyn; 20, Mrs Juby Secretary of the Norfolk Federation of Womens Institutes

Little Melton Womens Institute Drama Group
Performing 'At Home and Abroad' in the Church Room 1973

1, Daphne Eagle; 2, Elsie Miles; 3, Dorothy Broughton; 4, Sarah Broughton;
5, Ivy Day; 6, Annie Adam; 7, Stevie Rigby; 8, Jacqui Perrin; 9, Peggy Jakes;
10, Jean Chamberlain; 11, Jenny Botwood; 12, Margaret Broughton; 13, Vera Cole;
14, Doris Schay; 15, Doris Herwin.

Chapter Twelve

Little Melton and its neighbours

COLNEY, BAWBURGH, GREAT MELTON AND HETHERSETT.

Beneath this slab
John Brown is stowed.
He watched the ads
And not the road.
Ogden Nash.

Over the porch at the little round-towered church of Colney is a plaque in memory of John Fox who died on 20th December 1806 in the 79th year of his age, *'killed near this spot, having been thrust down and trampled on by horses of a wagon'.* John worked for Mr Jehosophat Postle of Colney Hall, who must have thought a lot of him, as it was he himself who had the memorial erected. From the Colney burial register, we learn that John lived in Little Melton, as have many of the Colney Estate workers over the years. One wonders what John would think of Colney today, the peace and quiet of the pretty rural backwater he once knew now engulfed by roaring vehicles on a busy dual carriageway, serviced by traffic lights,

John Fox's plaque above Colney church doorway c.2000

where the old turnpike has been widened to give access to the newly built Norfolk and Norwich University Hospital, and its near neighbours the BUPA hospital, the Research Park and the University itself.

Colney was a small estate or 'closed' village, nearly all land and houses owned by the lord of the manor resident at the Hall. This had been built by Jeremiah Norris some time between 1767 and 1781, before being sold in 1791 to John Patteson of Norwich, brewer and wool merchant. Four years later it was tenanted by Jehosophat Postle and his family, who bought it in 1797. During the

Colney church c2002

latter part of the 18th and throughout the next two centuries, Little Melton has had no resident manorial lord, so Mr Postle as the nearest Justice of the Peace, and his successors, were important figures locally. It was to them that the Little Melton Churchwardens turned for the annual approval of their Vestry Minutes, and from them that the Little Melton Overseers of the Poor sought permission to carry out their work.

In 1834 Colney Hall was sold to Joseph Scott, farmer and magistrate, who rebuilt and extended the mansion. He was apparently not much liked locally, but he did improve the living conditions of his estate workers and servants, and in 1880 sold to the trustees of John Nigel Gurney of Sprowston. John was under age, so the Hall was first let to Mr Chamberlin, whose family later owned a fine draper's store on Guildhall Hill, Norwich, and then in 1887 to Mr Hugh Gurney Barclay, who was able to buy the property in 1900. The Barclays built Hall Farm (a model in its day) and

Colney Hall c.1957

houses for the estate workers at Colney Park, and their enormous interest and involvement in the school at Little Melton, which served the children of both villages, is described elsewhere in this book. When Mr Hugh Barclay died in 1936 at the age of 84, he was succeeded by his eldest son, Evelyn Hugh Barclay and his wife Phyllis. Evelyn lived there for the next 20 years, buying Manor Farm, Little Melton in 1939, then tenanted by Mr Jimmy Nash. On Mr Barclay's death in 1956 his widow moved to Herringfleet Hall on the Somerleyton Estate, and the following year Colney Hall and its 1,474 acres were sold in 41 lots, the Nash family buying Little Melton Manor Farm, its land and cottages.

In 1957 Colney Hall had four reception rooms, twenty bedrooms and no less than seven bathrooms, in an age when internal plumbing was still something of a luxury. Since then much of the house has been pulled down and partially rebuilt, and much of the woodland felled and replanted. A hundred years earlier, in 1851, when Joseph Scott Esq., J. P. was owner, the census shows that he had as many as ten resident servants, a coachman, footman, cook/housekeeper, ladies maid, young ladies maid, housemaid, laundry maid, kitchen maid, under laundry maid, and school room maid. In the early 21st century, Mr James Boddy and his wife Sharon live there with their family, and without a single resident servant of any kind!

Great Melton has also been an estate village for many years, in the ownership of the Lombe and Evans-Lombe families. It was money made from the manufacture of silk in Derbyshire that originally contributed to the setting up of the Marlingford, Great Melton and Bylaugh estates, to which 200 acres in Little Melton were added after 1817, being sold by Edward Heath. Earlier, from 1575 to 1609, the Downes family were resident lords of Great Melton Manor, as were the Anguish family who followed them.

The fact that there are two churches in Great Melton is because they once belonged to two different manors. There were two main manors in Great Melton -

Great Melton Hall in the mid 19th century

Ladbroke Lithograph of All Saints church, Melton Magna 1822

Peverell's and Hacon's - each with its own church, standing side by side in the same churchyard. The manor of Peverell's had the patronage of the church of All Saints, with the chapel of Algar's Thorpe. When Blomefield wrote his 'History of Norfolk' in the 1740s, All Saints was a ruin. The nave was 20 yards long and the chancel 9 yards, and it had a south porch but no aisles. (There were several memorials to the Anguish family in All Saints. They had held Peverell's manor and did much to beautify this church in the 1630s when it was in constant use).

Ladbroke drawing on stone of St. Mary's church, Melton Magna, 1828

The manor of Hacon's had the patronage of the church of St. Mary. The tower was built in 1440 with three bells. The church was 27 yards long and 6 ½ yards wide. It was thatched, as was the south porch, but the chancel was tiled, and there were no side aisles.

In 1713/14 a sensible act of parliament was passed by which St Mary's and All Saints were consolidated and made one rectory, advowson and parish. The church of All Saints was pulled down and the materials used to repair St. Mary's, which was then used for worship instead of All Saints. The advowson was sold to Gonville and Caius College, Cambridge in about the 1720s.

Then, in the 1880s, there was a complete change of plan. All Saints was now restored, rebuilt and enlarged, its only original features said to be the tower and an Early English lancet window, taken from St Mary's, which now became a ruin. All Saints is the church in use today.

The ruined tower of St. Mary's and the complete All Saints church Great Melton c.2002

It is an extraordinary story of the swings and roundabouts that can affect two medieval churches in the same small parish. There were probably enough people to fill one church on Sundays, but not two, so perhaps it was inevitable that one building should be allowed to disintegrate. But why was All Saints pulled down in the eighteenth century, when it had been such a beautiful church, and St Mary's built up in its stead, only to make way for the rebuild of All Saints and the ruination of St. Mary's in the late nineteenth century? The mind boggles at the expense and labour involved.

Wallpainting depicting the Annunciation of St. Walstan - Gisleham, Suffolk

In medieval times Great Melton was a centre of much importance, King Henry III having granted it a weekly market and fair in 1250. For very many years after this it became the place for a great day out - the shopping and entertainment centre of the local area – with many pilgrims making a detour here after visiting Bawburgh to worship at the holy shrine of St Walstan.

St. Walstan is the patron saint of farm workers, and in the middle ages, hundreds came to pray at his final resting place, the village church of Bawburgh today being dedicated to St Mary and St Walstan. He was the son of a prince, but chose a life of poverty, taking a job working on a farm at Taverham. After many years of faithful labour, his master wanted to make him his heir, but Walstan asked instead for a cart and a cow in calf. He trained her progeny of two young bulls to pull his cart, and one day in old age, he is said to have received a divine visitation which foretold his death. Walstan died peacefully soon afterwards, while working in the fields he loved, so his body was placed on the cart and his bulls harnessed to it, being allowed to wander at will without a driver. They paused at Costessey, where a spring sprang up, and at last came to Bawburgh, (said to be Walstan's birthplace), where they finally stopped. Here they left behind them yet another spring, known as St Walstan's Well, whose pure waters were famous for centuries throughout the kingdom and beyond. Though the shrine was destroyed at the Reformation, St Walstan is very much part of Bawburgh's history, and he is still remembered with much affection in the twenty-first century.

Today Great Melton has only a small population and is intensively farmed, happily managing to retain its old rural charm and character. Peacocks roost in the trees adjoining the two churches, and walkers may well be rewarded with the sight of pheasants aplenty, while green and great spotted woodpeckers, yellowhammers and the occasional little owl can still be glimpsed by the observant passer by. Great Melton Hall no longer exists, but in its heyday in the mid 19th century, Mr. Edward Lombe kept a magnificent collection of stuffed birds there, (preserved by the celebrated taxidermist Leadbeater), which

Bawburgh church - St. Mary & St. Walstan 2003

eventually found its way to the Castle Museum in Norwich, forming the basis of the original natural history displays.

Little Melton, in contrast to both Colney and Great Melton, was an 'open' village, with a number of different people owning its freehold and copyhold acres, and without a resident lord of the manor for many years.

In early times each rural parish was responsible for the upkeep of the roads and tracks within its boundaries. A Highway Act of 1555 ordered every village to elect two parishioners, known as highway surveyors, whose job it was to inspect roads three times a year. In addition, every person holding land with an annual value of £50 or more was required to provide two men, a team of horses or oxen, and all tools with which to repair the roads for eight hours on four days each year, as instructed by the surveyors. The only people in Little Melton with land of this value would have been the farmers at Melton-Hall (where the Grange now stands at the end of Great Melton Road) and Manor Farm (at the Colney end of the village), so most roads probably continued to be little more than muddy, rutted tracks.

In 1663 the first Turnpike Trusts were created, under another Act of Parliament, the earliest Norfolk road built under this scheme being from Wymondham to Attleborough in 1695. These were metalled roads with rammed gravel or stones, and tolls had to be paid for each man, beast or cart using them.

Celia Fiennes wrote in 1698 *'Thence I went to Windham....mostly on a causey, the county being low and moorish and the road on the causey was in many places full of holes, tho' it is secured by a barr at which passengers may pay a penny a horse in order to the mending of the roads, for all about is not to be rode on unless in a dry summer...'* Half a century was to elapse before the Norwich to Hethersett road was built in 1746/47, while 1770 saw the completion of the Norwich to Watton Turnpike, today's B1108, cutting through the northern part of Little Melton, Colney and Earlham. The local Tollhouse stood where Colney Parish Room is today.

What were these villages like years ago, when shanks's pony was the main means of transport and when agriculture was the dominant way of life? Parish boundaries have not changed much since 1845, when White's Directory tells us that Little Melton had just 666 acres of land and Colney 917, while Bawburgh had 1,362 and Great Melton 2,477, being only a fraction smaller than Hethersett with 2,635 acres.

Ekwall's Dictionary of English Place Names describes Melton as meaning *'a middle farm'* in Old English, so husbandry has been carried on in Melton Magna and Melton Parva (the original Latin names for Great and Little Melton) since earliest times, as it has in Colney (meaning *'the Place on the Yare'*), and Hethersett (*'a fold for deer'*). Bawburgh is said to be derived from a nickname, identical with the Old English *'beaw'*, meaning Gadfly.

How many houses were there in each village in the seventeenth century, for instance, and what sort of buildings were they? The Hearth Tax of Michaelmas 1664 is now in print, and goes at least some way towards answering this question, but must, of course, be considered in the context of its time. For some years after the restoration of the monarchy, when the royal coffers were short of money, people were taxed on the property they occupied, provided they were parish ratepayers and their house was worth a minimum of £1 per annum, all paupers being automatically excluded. The majority of villagers seem to have lived in buildings worth less than this and so escaped the tax, which was much resented by the better off, two shillings per year being the sum demanded on every fireplace. From these returns we find:

Village	No. of houses taxed	No. of houses untaxed
Colney	4	22
Little Melton	18	53
Bawburgh with Bowthorpe	29	102
Great Melton	33	111
Hethersett	75	197

In Colney, Richard Browne, gent, had 8 hearths, and Allexander Burnett, clerk had 7, while Nich Reckham had 4 and John Sadd 3 (The Rev. Burnett was also serving Little Melton parish church at this period, and Nich was probably a member of the well-to-do Rackham family of Little Melton).

Unfortunately, many names are missing or illegible in the tax return for Little Melton, but Thomas Rackham stands out as having had 9 hearths, by far and away the largest number. He may have been living at the Manor House, or possibly at Greycot, as described in the chapter called **'House Histories'**. Two families had only one hearth each.

In *'Bawburgh cum Bowthorpe'* Sir Robert Yallop, Knight, had 16 hearths, Richard Harvey, gent. had 9, while two people named William Humerston, gent. had 6 apiece, and 10 villagers are shown as only having one hearth.

In Great Melton, Edmund Anguish, gent. had 10 hearths, (and was presumably living at Great Melton Hall), but Henry Humerston, gent. had no less than 16, which presents something of a mystery. Where did he live? Four of those taxed had just one hearth apiece.

Hethersett was the largest village then, as it is today, Ann Flowerdewe having 11 hearths, the greatest number listed, and twenty seven having one hearth each.

The truly staggering feature to emerge from these figures is how many people were exempted from payment, and must have been living in what would be called 'sub-standard' housing in today's jargon. Most people listed had two or three hearths in their homes, which implies a central chimney, with at least one chamber above it. It was not until 1801 that the first census was taken, and from then on we have a better picture of village structure. The figures for the following fifty years are given below;

Village	Year 1801	Year 1811	Year 1821	Year 1831	Year 1841	Year 1851
Little Melton						
No. of houses	22	24	32	37	76	76
No. of people	189	178	210	292	330	379
Great Melton						
No. of houses	58	59	65	75	82	80
No. of people	329	319	386	406	429	393
Hethersett						
No. of houses	90	94	183	219	246	264
No. of people	696	692	927	1080	1138	1209

St. Remigius church, Hethersett 2003

Statistics can be a bit boring on their own, but these figures show that at the start of the nineteenth century, there was an average of as many as 8 to 9 people living in every house in the 'open' villages of Hethersett and Little Melton, while there were less than 5 ½ people per dwelling in the 'closed' village of Great Melton, maybe because Sir John Lombe, the resident lord of the manor there, was keeping a benevolent eye on the needs of his workers.

The other interesting fact to emerge is that Hethersett had greatly increased its number of houses between 1811 and 1821, while Little Melton did much the same between 1831 and 1841, and one cannot help asking why this happened. The answer is quite straightforward, as the building boom in both villages was the direct result of land enclosures in Hethersett in 1800, and in Little Melton in 1817. It was then that the commons were sold into private hands for use as arable or pasture, and allocations of land (in lieu of former holdings) were made to all individuals who could prove their claim to them. The enclosure movement led to far reaching changes, and is described much more fully in the chapter **'Farming'**.

One result in Little Melton, after 1817, was that several smallholders now found themselves the owners of small blocks of land, often adjoining the roadside, and soon realised their building potential. Population was rising, and with it a shortage of houses, so what did the new landowner do? He erected cottages, of course, mostly just *'two up and two down'*, or even *'one up and one down'*, which he let to newcomers at a profit. The deep hollows scattered round the village fields today bear witness to the clunch digging that must have gone on, when these clay-lump or wattle and daub buildings were erected.

Wealthier men also had an eye to the main chance, one of them being Thomas Hubbard, a butcher of Wramplingham. In 1817 he had bought six acres of common between Hethersett's Beckhythe and Great Melton Road, meaning to build on it later. In due course, he erected a fine flint and brick double cottage here, fronting Burnthouse Lane, (later greatly extended and divided into Crossway Stores, - one of the oldest businesses in the village - and Crossways), while further along towards Great Melton he built another two. The white, flint-fronted house lying along the roadside, now divided into 'Su Cottage' and 'Stone Cottage', and its brick-built neighbour, (the South Norfolk Council properties, 1–3 Great Melton Road), which stands at right angles to it, were built by Mr Hubbard and date from about 1821. It is likely that he and his wife Elizabeth lived in the white flint building from about 1823 to 1827, when they had four children baptised in the parish church. A curious feature of this house is the scarcity of windows overlooking the road. Was this due to a need for privacy, or, as seems much more likely, because the dreaded window tax was not finally abolished until 1851?

Later, after Mr Hubbard's death in 1858, sale particulars show that each of these 'two freehold substantial buildings', (as Su and Stone Cottages and the Council Houses were described) was now divided into three parts. The first was occupied by George Brand, James Woods and Abraham Simons, and the second by Samuel Bailey, Robert Bailey and George Bishop, agricultural labourers, of whom Robert was an invalid, previously resident in the Union Workhouse at Swainsthorpe, and Samuel was a rat and mole destroyer. One well supplied all six families with water, and there were good- sized back gardens for growing vegetables.

Earlier in June 1832 Thomas Hubbard had bought part of the lands allotted to Mr William Howard in the Enclosure Award, selling one piece to Robert Lovett, a miller of Besthorpe, who wasted no time in erecting both a dwelling house and a brick tower mill there. In its heyday this had 4 double-shuttered sails, a boat shaped cap and petticoat, a 6-bladed fan, gallery and five floors. (A petticoat is a timber skirt extending down below the cap of a tower mill to protect the track, curb and top of the tower. The gallery is the access platform at cap level). The mill was sold in 1904, its most famous miller being Samuel Barrell who ground corn here for over forty years from 1861 to 1904. He was a major figure in the locality, for many years being farmer, baker, tax-collector and churchwarden, as well as miller, dying in 1910 aged 86. Today only the stump of the mill remains, its metal superstructure having been donated during world war two to provide material for munitions.

By 1836, Hubbard had converted part of a house, buildings and double cottage into a blacksmith's shop, being property he had also bought from Mr. Howard, establishing William Hubbard as smith. This was located halfway from the crossways to the mill, but on the opposite side of the road. There is still a mention of a smithy here in the census of 1861, but not in later years, so perhaps it was a short lived venture, farmers preferring to take their horses to be shod in Colney or elsewhere.

Once upon a time we used to think that our forebears travelled about very little, but nineteenth century statistics have disproved this. The 1851 Census was the first to show where people were actually born, and the results proved to be very unexpected. This table gives the birthplace of heads of households in six of our local villages, showing that more than half of the population had moved in from elsewhere. They may not have moved all that far, but population was very far from being static.

Name of Parish	Total Number of households	Born in parish	Born Elsewhere in Norfolk	Born outside Norfolk
Colney	14	0	10	4
Ketteringham	42	16	20	6
Great Melton	76	26	46	4
Little Melton	82	20	58	4
Bawburgh	92	28	58	6
Hethersett	277	101	163	13

In the old days there seems to have been a great feeling of community among local people, when everybody knew almost everybody else in the small villages in which they lived, but as we have seen, this was frequently not the village of their birth. Of course landowners usually 'stayed put' for long periods, but the rest of us 'up-sticked' and moved from place to place as opportunity offered.

Throughout these pages we have tried to tell the story of the development of Little Melton and its neighbours from the time of the Old Stone Age to the start of the twenty-first century. Although population growth will almost certainly continue (possibly at a considerable rate), let's hope that our rural communities will still be able to retain at least some of the caring spirit that has always been part and parcel of the fabric of village life. Perhaps, fifty years on, others may wish to continue the tale from where we have had to leave off, so let's end this volume with yet another brief quotation, this time from the pen of Lewis Carroll.

"Where shall I begin please your majesty?" he asked
"Begin at the beginning" the King said gravely, "and then go on
till you come to the end: then stop"

Appendix A

LORDS OF THE MANOR OF LITTLE MELTON AND MELTON-HALL

There were originally two manors in this parish, the larger being known as the Manor of Little Melton, and the smaller as the Manor of Melton-Hall, (Hertford's or Hereford's Manor). Francis Blomefield in his 'History of Norfolk' gives a complicated list of its owners. In 1228, Will. de Bek held it of the heirs of Montchensy.

Four points of interest relating to the Manor of Melton-Hall are that:

(a) Melton-Hall used to stand on the site of 'The Grange' near the church, at the far end of today's Great Melton Road.

(b) It was probably the Lord of the Manor of Melton-Hall who built the church.

(c) Thomas Batchcroft was lord here, and lived at Melton-Hall before his death in 1501. He is buried in the Lady Chapel of All Saints, Little Melton.

(d) Nicholas Sotherton purchased Melton-Hall in 1574, and from that time the manors became joined as one.

Lords of the Manor of Little Melton include:

1066 Edwin, who gave the manor to the Abbot of St. Benet's. (Blomefield)

1086 Godric, one of King William's Norman Stewards. (Blomefield). Godric and his wife gave the land in Little Melton that had been Edwin's to the Abbey, *'for their souls after their death'*, agreeing that their son Ralf de Montchensy should hold the manor during his lifetime. (Records of St Benet's Abbey).

1101-1134 **Ralf de Montchensy**, (Godric's son), gave 10 shillings each year *'for the monks table'*, but his heirs were to give 40s. In the time of Abbot Anselm, the land was granted to **Basilia**, 2nd wife of Ralf, she paying one mark of silver as rent each year. (Records of St Benet's Abbey).

Hubert de Montchensy, (Ralf's brother), inherited after Basilia's death. During King Stephen's chaotic reign, (1135-54), when he and Matilda were fighting over the right to the throne, Hubert claimed the manor for himself alone. In 1155-56 he reluctantly agreed to give back the land, and to hold it *'of the abbey'* for 10s a year. He was also fined 20 marks. (Records of St Benet's Abbey).

The Montchensy family seems to have continued to hold the manor over at least the next 125 years. (Blomefield).

1285 **William**, (son of Sir Warine de Montchensy), was lord. (Blomefield).

In 1381 members of the **Argentein family** held the manor, with a complex descent. (Blomefield).

1445 **Will. Wymer** and Margaret his wife settled it on John Alyngton, junior, Esq., and Mary his wife. (Blomefield).

1469 **John Alyngton** and Mary his wife held the manor. (Blomefield).

1534 **Elizabeth Marsham** purchased the manor from Giles & Mary Alyngton. She was widow of John Marsham of Norwich. (Blomefield).

1557 Elizabeth's son, **Thomas Marsham**, held the manor, and by will left half to Elizabeth, his wife, and half to Ralph Marsham, his brother.

1567 **Ralph Marsham** of Norwich, grocer, was sole lord. (His mother is said to have given it to him, rather than to another of her children, because he had married a daughter of Hamon Claxton of Livermore, Suffolk, his mother's family). (Blomefield).

Robert Marsham, Ralph's son and heir was next lord. He left the manor to

Edward Marsham, his eldest son, who died 1612. (Blomefield).

The manor was sold about 1620, when by sale particulars, it was let at £125 per annum, and contained above 320 acres. The freehold rents belonging to the manor were £3.12s.2d per annum, but there is no note of the income from the far greater number of copyhold rents. (Blomefield).

Before 1623 **Thomas Sayer** and **Will Barker** had the manor, and settled it on:

Laurence Sotherton, Gent, who was lord in 1623. (Blomefield). He was grandson of Nicholas Sotherton, Gent, of Norwich, who had bought Melton-Hall in 1574. (Laurence's father, Henry Sotherton, son of Nicholas, died intestate in Little Melton 1618. His inventory shows his house possessed 5 main rooms, almost certainly Melton-Hall. (Sotherton pedigree from Norfolk Genealogy, Vol. 13).

Augustine Skottowe, Alderman & Sheriff of Norwich, purchased the Manor of Little Melton before his death in 1636, when his eldest son Richard was only 10. He married Elizabeth, daughter of Henry Bacon. (Blomefield).

Richard Skottowe (Augustine's eldest son) was lord from his majority in 1647 until his death in 1656. He married Bridget, daughter of Sir Charles le Gros of Crostwick, and had two daughters who died as infants. (He was a parliamentarian who was granted arms in 1647). (Blomefield).

Bridget Skottowe, (Richard's widow), was Lady of the Manor in 1656. (She held court on 20th October that year). (Manorial Court books).

Thomas Townsend Esq. and Bridget his wife held the manor in 1657-8. (Bridget had presumably re-married). They held courts on 19 Oct 1657 and 16 Oct 1658. (Manorial Court Books).

Augustine Skottow, (Richard's brother) was lord from about 1659 to 1683. He married 3 times, his third wife, Susan, daughter of Robert Wells of Rougham, providing him with 2 sons. (He was a Captain of Trained Bands in 1664, so, though originally a parliamentarian, had prudently become a Royalist after Charles II's accession in 1660).

Thomas Skottowe (Augustine's eldest son) followed his father as lord from about 1696. He married Elizabeth, daughter of Christopher Coulson, Esq., of Thorpe, heir to Great Ayton Hall in Yorkshire. Thomas released the estate to Mr Lombe on 20 June 1705, following the expiry of the 39 year lease from his grandfather Augustine Skottow. (Evans-Lombe papers). Apparently he still presided as manorial lord for some years, before moving to the Cathedral Close, Norwich. (Manor Court books). Thomas and Elizabeth's eldest son, Thomas, became Lord of Gt. Ayton, Yorks, through the right of his mother.

Benjamin Wrench, knight, became lord of the manor on 27 May 1724. He was a notable Norwich physician, who died in August 1747, aged 82 years. (Dictionary of National Biography and Manor Court Books).

Edward Bacon Esq. bought the Manor from Sir Benjamin's executors, and held his first court at Little Melton on 18 Oct 1749. (Manor Court books). The family, (also lords of Earlham), later changed its name to **Frank**, and held the manor for nearly 200 years, until 1939. In 1895 **Bacon Frank** Esq was lord, as was Rev. **Edward Frank** in 1811. **Frederick Bacon Frank** Esq. held the manor from about 1845/96.

Later, **Mrs. Mary Frank** held court here, and was still alive in 1937. (Manor Court books and Kelly's and White's Directories of Norfolk).

The last court hearing for Little Melton Manor seems to have been in 1845.

ppendix B

INCUMBENTS OF LITTLE MELTON

Sir Rowland the Priest

VICARS PRESENTED BY IXWORTH PRIORY

1275	WILLIAM
1301	WILL de WIPET
	WILL de IXWORTH
1316	WALTER de EWSTON
1322	WILL le BAILIFF (OF NORTON)
1323	ALAN (Son of Stephen de Lavenham)
1349	During the Great Plague
	THO. COSSE
	WALTER BATE
	JOHN GILBERT
1371	SIMON de HORNINGTOFT
1375	GILBERT de HETHERSETE
1388	JOHN FOWLER
1395	HENRY STORK
	JOHN ARTEYS
1401	RIC. MANGER
1410	SIR ROBERT BERNAK
1419	JOHN JOSSE
1426	THO. DRAWSWERD
1430	JOHN de AYLESHAM
1457	JOHN JOSSE (Re-appointed)
1502	WILL GODRED
	THURSTON BROWNE
1554	THOS. HEWE (Presented by Richd. Coddington Esq.)
1555	WALTER SPARRY
1555	RIC. WHEATLEY (Presented by the Bishop)
1567	EDW. REED (Presented by Fran. Chamberlain Esq.)
1587	ROBERT HOWSE (Also Vicar of Baburgh)

VICARS PRESENTED BY EMMANUEL COLLEGE, CAMBRIDGE.

1608 ALEX. WIXTED

1611 JOHN FAWETHER

1612 WILL. MERRICK

1613 THO. ROBINSON

1618 RIC. YOUNGS

1640 THO. BULBEK

GAWEN NASH (Deprived for not taking the Oaths to King William III)

1691 JOHN BRANDON (Also Rector of Wramplingham)

1743 JOHN FREEMAN

1746 ROBERT POTTER

1771 GERVAS HOLMES

1796 WILLIAM COOKE (Presented by the Bishop by lapse)

1810 JAMES DUNN

1830 ADOLPHUS AUGUSTUS TURNOUR (Presented by the Bishop by lapse)

1832 THOMAS CURRIE

1839 JOHN CHARLES BARKLEY

1883 JOHN JORDAN SODEN

1894 ARTHUR GORDON GREEN

1898 JOHN LANE MORLEY

1910 CHARLES STANTON GRAY

1911 EDWARD SPARKE UPCHER

1919 NIGEL WOOD PAINE (Sequestrator)

1926 NIGEL WOOD PAINE (Vicar, also Rector of Gt Melton. Presented by the King by lapse).

1939 THOMAS ALBERT FROST (Also Vicar of Bawburgh)

1948 H. LLEWELLYN DAVIES   (Also Vicar of Bawburgh)

1956 CLAUDE HUGH PALFREY (Also Vicar of Bawburgh)

1958 LEWIS ERIC H. GRIFFITHS (Also Vicar of Bawburgh)

1959 PERCY STURDY   (Also Vicar of Bawburgh)

1963 FREDERICK WILLSON

1975 ROBERT A. LOVELESS

1982 JOHN WATSON

1983 MICHAEL B. SEXTON (Also Rector of Hethersett & Great Melton)

1987 BRIAN M. LLEWELLYN (Also Rector of Hethersett & Great Melton)

1995 DIANE BEVERLEY LAMMAS (Also Rector of Hethersett & Great Melton)

Appendix C

List of Wills, Administrations and Inventories studied:
Date of probate is given and reference number wherever possible

Proved in the Prerogative Court of Canterbury

MARSHAM John of London & Little Melton, Gent.   1601 - PROB 11/98

MARSHAM Robert of Little Melton, Gent   1614 - PROB 11/125

JERNINGHAM Edward of Little Melton, Gent   1659 - PROB 11/294

JOHNSON Thomas, of Norwich, Gent   1661 - PROB 11/303

JOHNSON Robert, of Little Melton, Gent   1680 - PROB 11/364

SKOTTOWE Thomas of Cathedral Close,Norwich,Gent   1766 - PROB 11/154

SKOTTOWE Katherine of the Cathedral Close, Norwich   1769 - PROB 11/950

HOWLETT William of Hockering, Gent   1814 - PROB 11/1553

Proved in the Norwich Consistory Court

BACHECROFT Margaret wife of Thomas   1489 - 41/42 Wolman

ROSE John of Little Melton   1493 - 38 Norman

BACHECROFT Thomas of Little Melton.   1501 - 20/23 Popy

ROSE Robert of Little Melton   1555 - 278 Walpoole

DAINES Thomas of Little Melton - (inventory only.)	1599 - DN/INV 16/50
ABELL William of Little Melton, husbandman, (inventory only)	1606 - DN/INV 21/69
ROSE Thomas, the elder, of L.M. & inventory	1613 - 203 Coonney & DN/INV 26/187
ROSE Jeremy of Little Melton, yeoman	1615 - 71 Angell
SOTHERTON Henry of Little Melton - (inventory only)	1618 - DN/INV 29/267
ALEXANDER George of Little Melton, yeoman	1619 - 145 Mason
ROSE John of Little Melton, yeoman	1643 - 67 Alston
ROSE Robert of Great Melton, yeoman	1648 - 81 Purgold
MITCHELLS Thomas of Little Melton, yeoman	1706 - 801 Piddocke
RACKHAM Bridget, of Norwich, widow	1712 - 222 Dawson
RACKHAM Nicholas of Great Melton	1718 - 147 Bigot
RACKHAM Hester of Great Melton, widow of Nicholas	1718 - 149 Bigot
CARTER John of Little Melton, yeoman, & inventory	1725 - 449 Gregson & DN/INV 76B/109
MILLS John of Little Melton, woolcomber, (inventory)	1729 - DN/INV 78A/13
RUDD Thomas of Little Melton, husbandman	1730 - 31 Widdoson
BRANDON John of Little Melton, Clerk in Holy Orders	1743 - 43 Withers
GIRLING Elizabeth of Little Melton, widow	1842 - 531 Canler

Proved in the Norfolk Archdeaconry Court

RACKHAM Elizabeth, widow, of Little Melton   1661 - W25 1

RACKHAM Nicholas of Bawburgh, yeoman   1678 - W4 264

RACKHAM Thomas of Little Melton   1678/9 - W147 172

RACKHAM Joseph of Little Melton, (administration only)   1706/7 - A18

BUCKE Martin of Little Melton   1710 - W74 57

FOLKE William of Little Melton, singleman   1711 - W80 190

FOX Thomas of Hethersett, maltster   1727 - W129 503

RACKHAM Nicholas of Little Melton, worsted weaver   1728 - W172 667

RACKHAM Simon of Norwich, yeoman   1739 - W19 145

JOHNSON Sarah, spinster of Colney   1741 - W79 195

RACKHAM Elizabeth of Little Melton, widow   1744 - W106 346

BAWD Thomas of L.M. worsted weaver, (administ'n only)   1745 (No 52)

BUCK Martin of L. Melton, husbandman, (administ'n only)   1747 (No 176)

DADE Henry of Little Melton, farmer   1793

GIRLING William of Little Melton   1805 - W89 128

COPEMAN William of Little Melton, farmer   1808 - W18

COOPER William of Little Melton, farmer, (administ'n only)   1823 - A18

COPEMAN William of Little Melton, yeoman   1834 - W46 645

FORSTER Thomas of L.M. gentleman, (administ'n only)   1846 - A16

GIRLING Mary of Little Melton   1852 - W32 243

Proved in the Norwich District Probate Registry

HIPPERSON Samuel of Little Melton, farmer   1864

FORSTER Thomas of Little Melton, farmer   1868

ALDRED Thomas Dove, of Little Melton, farmer   1870

ALDRED Joseph Miller of Little Melton, farmer   1875

Appendix D

Grateful acknowledgement is made to the Norfolk Record Office for permission to reproduce pages 10 and 11 of the Manorial Record Book for Little Melton, 1652 (MC 1861/23 865X9) on pages 24 and 50 of this book, and for the following extracts from documents;

Inventory of William Abell, 18th June 1606. (DN/INV 21/69) below, referred to on page 62 of this book, in the chapter on farming.

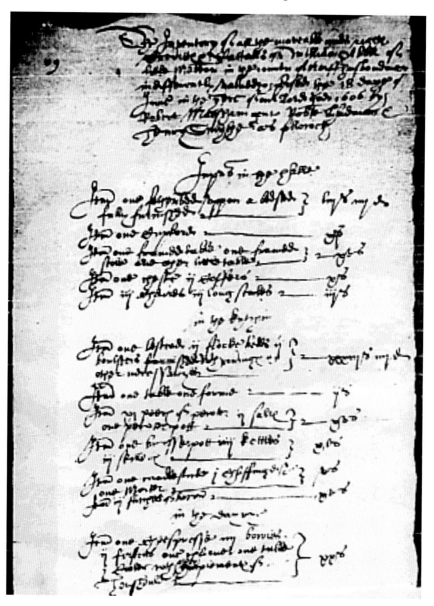

Transcript of section shown left;

The Inventory of all the moveable goods and chattells of William Abell of Little Melton in the county of Norfolk, husbandman, indifferently valued and prised the 18 daye of June in the year of our Lord God 1606, by Robert Marsham, gent, Robte Hadman (?) & Henry Smythe as followeth:

Imprimis in the halle

Item, one fetherbed uppon a bedsted fully furnished	53s 04d
Item, one cupbord	11s
Item, one framed table, one framed stoole, one other little table	15s
Item, one cheste, 2 coffers	10s
Item, 3 chaires, 3 long stooles	3s

In the kytchin

Item, one bedstead, 2 flocke bedds, 2 boulsters, ? With coveringes & other necessaryes	33s 04d
Item, one table and forme	2s
Item, 11 peeces of pewter, 2 saltes, one pewter pott	15s
Item, one brasse pott, 4 kettles, 3 skellettes	15s
Item, one candlesticke, 1 chaffing dishe, one morter	5s
Item, 3 flitches of bacon	15s

In the dayrye

Item, one cheese presse, 4 bowles, 2 ferkens, one .... ?, one table, one cooler with other implements of househould	20s

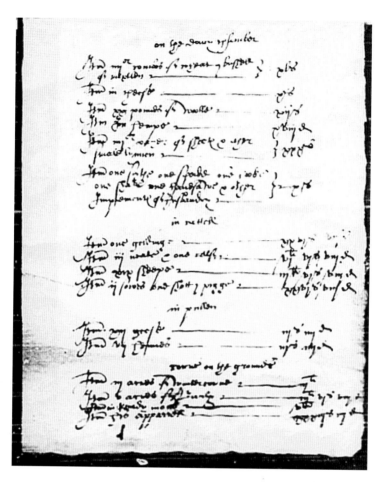

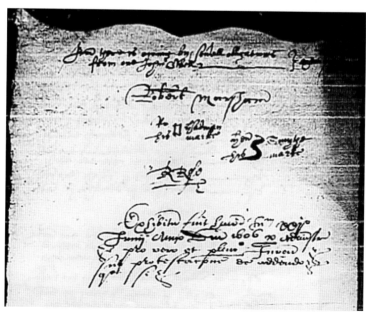

Continued transcript of section shown left;

In the dairy chamber

Item, 4 (**?**) combes of wheat, 2 bushels of mexllen	15s
Item, in cheese	10s
Item, 20 (**?**) poundes of woolle	12s
Item, in hempe	18d
Item, 4 payer of sheetes & other smale lynnen	30s
Item, one scythe one spade, one rake, one shatie (**?**), one handsawe & other Implements of husbandry	10s

In Cattell

Item, one gelding	26s 8d
Item, 3 neates and one calf	£6 6s 8d
Item, six sheepe	£3 6s 8d
Item, 2 sowes, one shott, 1 pigge	26s 8d

In pullen

Item, 12 geese	3s 4d
Item, 6 hennes	3s 4d

Corne on the grounde

Item, 3 acres of Winter corne	£3
Item, 6 acres of Barley	£3 6s 8d

Item in Ready money	5£
Item his Apparrel	32s 6d

Item there is owing by rentell obligated (**?**) from one John Clarke (**?**)   10s

Robert Marsham

Ro Hadman, his marke

Hen Smythe, his mark

R. Rose.

Exhibited 22nd June 1606

DN/INV 21/69 Wm Abell. (N.R.O.) Norwich Consistory Court

Wm Abell died intestate. Administration was granted to Robert Abell 21st June 1606 MF 172 Folio 278

Inventory of John Mills, Woolcomber, 21st April 1729, (DN/INV 78A/13) reproduced in this appendix, and referred to on page 28 of this book, in the chapter on Village Government.

Transcript of Inventory shown left;

A true and perfect Inventory of all and singular the goodes, chattles, and credittes of John Mills, late of Melton Parva, in the County of Norfolk, Woolcomber, deceased, & the same were viewed & apprized by us whose Names are hereunder subscribed, the one and twentieth day of April in the year of our Lord 1729

	£	s	d
Imprimis, His wearing apparel & Linnen	06	-00	-00
*Item, **In the Kitchen**, a Fire Range with Irons thereto belonging, two firepans and tongs.*	01	-00	-00
Two pair of brass candlesticks	00	-04	-00
A warming pan & copper pot	00	-08	-00
Two brass Boilers two old Sauce-pans	01	-00	-00
12 pewter plates dishes & a bason	00	-12	-06
Six woodden chaires, 2 rush bottomes & 3 old stooles	00	-07	-00
A Deal-table & an Oval table	00	-07	-00
*An old ironing-board & tables, smoothing iron & heats (**?**) a pair of bellows*	00	-05	-00
A cupboard with glasses, earthen ware, two tin boxes & other trifles in them.	00	-07	-06
A Marble Motar & Pestal, & two Slates	00	-07	-00
An old Tea-Kittle & tin ware	00	-05	-00
Six Knives & Forkes	00	-03	-00
*Item, **in the Dairy,** 3 Milk bowls, an old churn & 3 shelves*	00	-09	-00
Two sieves, a frying-pan & two earthen Meat-pots	00	-05	-00
*Item, **in the Parlor**, an old Stove & an Oval Table*	00	-11	-00
Six leather chaires, a Couch & five cane chaires	01	-06	-00
Two little tables & a stool	00	-04	-00
A Tea-table & Corner Cupboard	00	-10	-00
A Chest of Drawers & Dressing-Box, & a Cabinet	01	-03	-06
A Clock & Case	02	-00	-00
A Bed as it stands	03	-10	-00
Small Pictures & Sconces, a pair of Bellowes & brush	00	-05	-00
*Item, **in the Cellar**, Glass & Stone Bottles, & a powdering Tub*	00	-07	-00
A Box of Candle	00	-15	-00
*Item, **in the Parlor Chamber**, a bed as it stands*	04	-00	-00
Another Bed	02	-15	-00
A chest & nursing cradle	00	-04	-00
*Item, **The Household Linnen**, viz. Two new pair of Sheetes, & a further pair of old ones, & two pair of better sheetes, with two pair of pillow beeres, & four board-cloathes, & half a dozen Napkins*	05	-04	-06
Two Cradle quilts	00	-04	-06

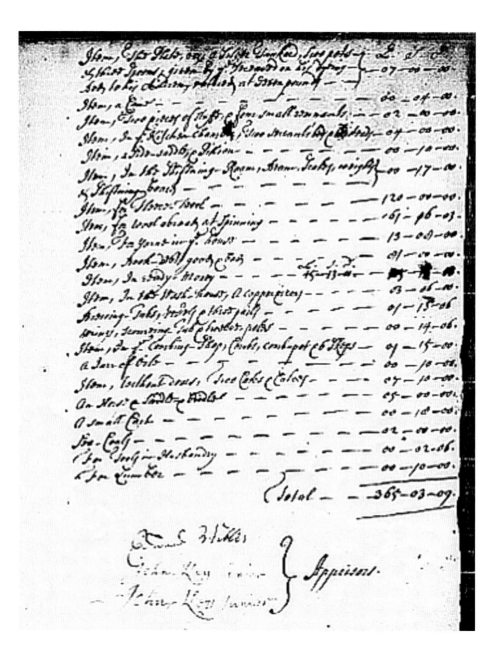

Continued transcript of section shown left;

	£	S	D
Item, **The Plate**, viz. A Silver Tankard, 2 pots			
& three spoons, given by the deceased on his dying			
Bed to his children, valued at seven pounds	07	00	00
Item, a Cane	00	04	00
Item, Two pieces of Stuffe, & four small remnants	02	00	00
Item, In the **Kitchen Chamber**, two servants' beds & bedsteads	04	00	00
Item, a side-saddle, & Pillion	00	10	00
Item, **In the Shiftning-Room**, Beam, Scales, weights	00	17	00
& Shiftning board			
Item, for Fleece Wool	120	00	00
Item, for Wool already at Spinning	161	16	03
Item, for Yarne in the house	13	08	00
Item, Book-debts good & bad	81	00	00
Item, in ready Money	15	13	00
Item, In the Wash-house, a copper & iron	03	06	00
Brewing-Tubs, Vessels & three pails	01	13	06
Strings, scouring-Tub & twelve poles	00	14	06
Item, in the Combing Shop, Combs, comb-pot & 6 skeps	01	15	00
A Jarr of Oile	00	10	00
Item, Without Doors, two Cows & Calves	07	10	00
A Horse & Saddle & bridle	05	00	00
A small Cart	00	18	00
Sea-Coals	02	00	00
For Tooles in Husbandry	00	02	06
For Lumber	00	10	00
Total	365	03	09

Edward Willis (?)
John Hey Senior (?) } Apprisors
John Hey Junior (?)

Note: John Mills died intestate, leaving widow Letitia. Administration was given to Letitia on 3rd April 1729. (She signs Letticia Mills) MF 125, N.R.O. (Latin) (Little Melton Registers do not survive before 1734. No mention of any Mills).

A PPENDIX E

APPENDIX – NAMES 1650 TO 1765
FROM MANORIAL COURT BOOKS

As no church registers exist for Little
Melton before 1734, the following
names have been extracted from the
Manor Court Books 1650 to 1765, in
the hope that they may be of help to
frustrated family historians. Surnames
are spelt in a variety of ways and many
tenants, who held land here, did not
reside in the village. (Reference
865X9 MC 1871/23, 1871/24, 1871/25
& 1871/26, all at the Norfolk Record
Office).

Alexander George 1652 dies 1691
Alexander Henry (son of Geo) dies 1694
Alexander James (son of Geo) alive 1704
Alexander Joseph (bro of Hy & Francis)1691/1700
Allen/Allin Thos 1686/90
Amyas Wm 1684/5
Amys Thos 1649
Andrewes Henry 1684 3rd son of Henry
Andrewes John dies 1670
Back John 1740
Bailey Wm 1745/46
Baker Benj 1717/1733
Baker Wm 1705/17 father of Benj
Baned John 1650
Barker Jacob 1661/70
Barker James 1655/64
Barker Richd 1660/65
Barker Thos 1660
Barker Wm 1659
Barnes Edward 1689 dies c.1712
Barnes Robert 1656/63
Barnes Wm bro of Edw 1712/51
Battele/Bately Richard 1663/67
Baxter Robt 1658/70

Baxter Thos & Margt 1634/53
Bawde Edward 1659
Bawde Henry 1653/63
Bawde Henry jnr 1663/82
Bawde John 1650/69
Bawde Rbt 1650/84
Beale Wm 1665
Beaumond John c.1668
Beaumond Wm & Alice 1653/67
Beaumont Wm jnr 1665
Bennett Chas/Hannah 1679/1701, son of Rbt jnr
Bennett Rbt 1650 dies 1664
Bennett Rbt jnr, son of Rbt senr 1654, dies 1679
Betts Francis & Diana 1707
Betts Thomas 1748
Beverly Wm 1706
Bloom Christopher 1709 dies c. 1731
Bloom Christopher, 1740/42 son of Felix
Bloom Felix brother of Chris senr 1731/40
Blye/Blyth/Bloy John 1692/1702
Blyth John 1705/07
Bolden (?) Henry 1714
Brand Reg son of Thos 1710/35
Brandon John, clerk, 1728
Brasnett Francis 1658/61
Browne Marie wife of John 1653
Browne Wm 1684/90
Brumstead Wm 1709
Buck Henry 1696/1725
Buck Henry junr 1725/40
Buck John 1683/96
Buck Joseph 1708/32
Buck Martin 1705
Buck Martin 1733/49 eldest son of Rbt. Jnr
Buck Martyn 1655, d. 1695, father of Rbt
Buck Rbt 1684/1704 son of Martyn
Buck Rbt jnr 1705, dies 1733,
Buck Thos 1678/1705 when lived Old Hall Farm.
Buck Thos 1705, dies c.1719 bro of Rbt
Bush Nathaniel 1730
Bussey John 1650/80
Cabborn Edward 1656
Cannell Peter 1746/48
Capps Henry 1654
Capps Henry jnr 1659/95
Carter Anne (nee Reiner) (wife of Jn) 1682
Carter Edward 1752
Carter Gilbert 1706 dies c.1743 (Mary 1st wife)

Carter Gregory 1687/99

Carter John dies 1670, dies 1725 wife Anne

Carter John jnr 1699/1712, son of Jn & Anne

Carter Thomas 1689 dies 1696, bro of John

Carter Wm 1659

Carter Wm 1725/50, son of Jn & Anne

Carver John 1655

Cawsey John 1684/5

Chambers Matthew 1667-70

Chambers Matthew/Margt 1667/70

Chambers Susanna dau of Matt 1670

Chambers Samuel 1721

Chesson Wm 1743

Clark(e) John 1702/50

Clark(e) Rbt & Alice 1650 –53

Clarke Thos 1712/51

Clarke Thos junr 1751

Clarke Wm 1650

Cobb John 1665

Coleburne Edw 1714/30 after death of Edw his father

Coleburne Wm 1730/62 after death of bro Edw

Condley Chas 1697 dies 1702, father of Thos.

Condley Thos 1702/09, succeeds father Chas

Cooke Thos 1685 d. 1703, nephew Thos succeeds him

Cooke Thos 1703, dies 1746, nephew of Thos

Cooper John 1687/96

Cowell Edward 1650-52

Cowsell Wm 1665

Crake Jonas 1741

Cullyer John 1659

Cullyer Rbt 1652

Custance Hambleton succeeds father John 1752 dies 1757

Custance John 1743 dies 1752

Custance Press yst son of Hambleton 1757

Dade Henry 1764

Dade Robert 1743

Dade Rbt jnr 1757/61

Dade Wm 1734/51

Dale/Deale Wm 1710/50

Daniel Rbt 1743/49

Davey Jehosophat 1666/67

Dav(e)y Thos 1659/1703

Davy Peter 1699/1705

Davy Thos 1782

Dawkins Hy & Ann 1653. Hy dies 1680

Dawkins Hy jnr 1654/61

Deale Thos 1650/64

Deale Wm 1678/91

Denny Wm died c.1652

Denny Wm son of Wm 1655

Dowe Hy 1650/70

Drake Rbt 1744

Drake Wm 1751

Dunham Richd 1650/68

Dunham James 1658/59

Dunham Nicholas 1664/67

Edmonds Henry 1690/1714

Ellis Eliz wife of Richd 1757

Ellis John, clerk, son of Eliz 1764

Ellond Thos snr 1650, dies 1663

Ellond Thos jnr 1650, dies 1659

Elwyn Thos 1657

Evans Jeremiah, clerk, 1707

Fiddeman Joseph 1683/87

Field Wm 1679

Fisher Thomas 1663/65

Flynt Roger,clerk, & Margt 1653/82

Fowler Thos 1667

Fox Benj 1736/51

Fox John 1707/28

Fox Rbt 1729/31

Fox Thos 1701/11

Fox Wm 1713/21

Fox Wm jnr 1714/34

Frances John 1714

Freeman Clement 1650, dies 62

Freeman John 1657, dies 60

Freeman Robert son of Clem. 1662/1704

Freeman Thomasina 1664/5

Freezer John 1717

Freezer John 1742/51

Freezer Joseph 1744

Fuller Thomas 1662/91

Fulton Thos 1678

Gallant John 1742

Galyard Stephen 1709/10

Garrard/Garrett Edw/Philippa 1650/81

Gavell Benj 1680/91

Gay Richd 1724

Ginbon/Gaburn/Gibbon/Guibon Edw 1650/85

Girling/Girland John 1737/43

Gooch Ann 1730

Gooch Francis/Ann 1712/16

Goodwin/Gowin/Gowing Thos 1735/46

Goward Richd/Thomasina 1679/85

Green Wm 1681

Greene Rbt 1655/57

Griffen Rbt 1650/55

Hadnam George 1650 dies c.58

Hamond Thos 1650/67

Hare Matthew 1667

Harris John 1667/68

Harrold Chas son of Peter/Philadelphia 1729/32

Harrold Peter 1719, dies c.1728

Hart Rbt 1748/51

Haylettt John 1711/51

Heand Thos jnr 1654

Heyhoe Jacob 1718/24

Hill Wm 1684

Hobart Thos 1667

Hooke Jn 1686, dies 1695

Houlden/Holding Edw 1650/52

Howard Daniel 1712

Howarde Thos 1655/56

Hudson Chas 1681/94

Ireson/Iverson John 1697/1712

Ireland Wm 1727/38

Jermy Thos 1670

Jernegan Edw Gent 1632/52

Jernegan Ellen widow 1632/52

Johnson John 1706

Johnson Robert 1678, dies 1680

Johnson Thomas 1689 son of Robt

Kalham Wm 1739

Kirby John 1683/86

Levick John 1655, dies 1668

Lighten Hy 1719

Lighting/Lighton/Lightwyn Jacob 1696/1731

Lighton James 1733/42

Lock Henry (mother Honoria) dies 1765

Lock Honoria 1724

Locke Anne 1688

Locke Jeremiah 1685, dies 1724

Loftey Edward 1662/64

Lofty Wm 1697

Lovett John/Thomazina 1660/63

Lovett John son of Jn/Tmzina 1679

Lovett Thomazina sister of Jn 1679

Lowe Joseph 1714

Lowe Philip 1707/32

Machin John 1747/49

March Thos 1660

Marshall Francis 1678

Martins Thos 1741/42

Middleton Wm 1667

Miller Rbt 1716/20

Mitchell Edmund 1692

Mitchell(s) Daniel 1711/25 heir of Thos

Mitchell(s) Matthew 1654/69 father of Thos

Mitchell(s) Thos 1682/1705

Mollett Geo (son of Rbt/Mary) 1658/64

Mollett/Mallett Rbt 1650, dies 1657

Mollett Rbt 1657/1666

Mollett Wm, dies 1659

Moore John 1725, dies 1754, father of Mary

Moore Mary 1755, dau of Jn

Neale Wm 1679/83

Newman John 1741/46

Nicholas Robt/Maria 1670

Norman John 1738/44

Norman Wm dies 1724

Osborne Nicholas 1704/6 yst son of John

Osbourne John 1651, dies 1700 dau Anna

Palgrave Sir John 1650/65

Palmer John 1724/51

Parmer Andrew 1656

Patteson Henry (son of Hy.S.P. 1730)

Pawling Henry 1667

Payne Richd 1685/88

Peele John, dies 1686

Pettiman/Pittiman Susanna 1681/82

Pickering Margt widow of Wm 1645/53

Pickering Robt son of Wm 1653

Pickering Thos son of Wm 1653

Pickering Wm dies 1644

Pickering Wm son of Wm 1645/51

Rackham Bridget, d. 1712, moth of Jacob/Nich/Thos

Rackham Chas, 1723/46, son of Nich/Eliz

Rackham Eliz, 1707

Rackham Eliz, wid of Nich, mother of Chas, d.1744

Rackham Henry 1684/5, son of Nich/Bridget

Rackham Jacob 1678, son of Nich/Bridget

Rackham Jacob 1728/30

Rackham John 1661/67

Rackham Joseph/Diana 1655, she d.1701, he 1706

Rackham Nicholas/Bridget 1650, he d.1678.

Rackham Nicholas 1679 son of Thos/Anne

Rackham Nicholas 1681 son of Nich/Bridget, d.1729

Rackham Nicholas jnr 1718/36

Rackham Richard 1684

Rackham Richard jnr 1723

Rackham Robt 1703

Rackham Thomas/Anne 1653, he d.1678, father of Nich

Rackham Thomas 1683

Rayner/Reyner/Rayneham Mary 1656, dies 1695

Rayner Samuel 1734

Raynham Thos 1670

Reeve Rbt 1650/52

Revans Jeremiah, clerk, 1706/28

Reyner John 1742, dies 1745

Rix Henry 1770/80

Rix Robert 1667/69

Roberts Richard 1735/43

Rookwood Thos 1719, dies 1727

Rookwood Thos 1729/48 son of Thos

Roper Philip 1632/1650

Rose Isaac, clerk, 1643, dies 1652

Rose John/Merrye, bro of Isaac, he dies 1643

Rose Wm 1651/60

Rowland Edward 1656/88

Rowland Edward jnr 1665

Rowland George 1684

Rowland John 1650/63

Rowland John jnr 1665

Rudd Thomas 1700/29

Rushbrooke Edward 1665

Russell Eliz 1724, dies 1729, wife of Rev John.

Russell John, clerk of Postwick, 1729, dies 1746

Sabborne Edw 1651/64

Sadler Anne 1714, dies 1724, dau of B. Tooley

Samon/Seaman George 1652/60

Sandell John 1654

Schaberne (?) Wm 1659

Scott/Skott Thos 1651/56

Sheen Richd 1670

Sheene Wm 1689

Skeet Thos 1667

Scottow / Scottowe Augustine 1664, dies 1683

Skottowe Thos 1683 son of Aug, 1683/1705

Skottowe Wm 1667

Smith Diany 1655

Smith Edward 1737/64

Smith James dies 1701

Smith James 1738 dies 1740, yst son of Samuel

Smith John 1740/43 yst bro of James

Smith Samuel 1732, dies 1737, father of Jas

Smith Thos 1738

Smyth Henry 1681

Smyth John junr 1654/55

Smyth Thos 1650, dies 1666, son of Thos

Smyth Thos of Hethersett 1660/68

Smyth Thos 1683/96

Starling Robt/Marie 1649, he dies 1660

Starling Samuel 1660 son of Robt

Starling Thos/Barbara 1762/90

Steele Thos junr 1665

Stocking(e)/Stockton John 1684/1709

Strickland Walter 1712/13

Strickland Wm 1682/1718

Sutton Stephen 1650/52

Tanner Andrew/Frances 1649/61

Tooley Bernard 1714 to dau A. Sadler

Tooley Wm 1688

Turner Thomas 1653

Turner Thomas junr 1654

Vynn Honor 1730/36

Vynn(e) Jeremiah son of Honor 1736/48

Vynn Layer 1730/34

Walters Thos/Mertia (nee Rose) 1649/50

Watts Peter 1667

Weldon Thos/Eliz 1747

Wenn Charles 1728/43

Whall John/Martha 1749

Wiffen Wm/Susannah 1739/40

Wiffen Rbt 1750 son of Wm/Susannah

Wiffen Wm 1719 post mortem Robt

Wiffen Wm/Sarah 1750

Wilcox Alice widow 1682 dies 1697

Wilcox Marie dau of Alice 1682

Willy Daniel 1682

Woods John 1650

Woods Thomas 1652

Woollard/Woolland/Woolward 1688/94

Wright Richard 1736

Wright Samuel 1738/43

Glossary

A

Acres, roods or rods & perches. There were 40 perches to the rood, and 4 roods to the acre. An acre was 4840 square yards.

Advowson. The right to appoint a clergyman to a benefice.

Altar. The raised structure consecrated to the celebration of the Eucharist, (or Holy Communion), or the 'holy table' of the English Prayer book after the 1549 Reformation.

Archdeacon. The bishop's deputy in a diocese, with a duty to visit each parish regularly, to inspect the fabric of the church and to assess the general running of parish affairs.

Archdeaconry. A division of a diocese, which can itself be sub-divided into Rural Deaneries.

B

Backhouse. An outhouse, or lean-to building, used for brewing and baking.

Barnack stone. A kind of hard limestone, originally from Dorset, often called marble.

Bishop. A priest having jurisdiction over a diocese.

Bishop's Transcripts. Copies of entries from parish registers sent to the diocesan bishop each Easter.

Brick - English bond. A method of laying bricks, with one course showing long faces of the bricks, while the next shows narrow faces, continuing in alternate layers

Brick - Flemish bond. A method of laying bricks in which each course consists of alternate long and narrow faces of the brick.

Buttery. A store room for food and drink, occasionally used as a kitchen.

C

Canon (of Cathedral). A priest on the staff of a cathedral.

Capital. The decorated and ornamented top of a column or pillar, from which springs the arch which the pillar supports.

Chalice. The cup or goblet used in the celebration of Holy Communion.

Chancel. The eastern part of a church, often separated from the rest of the building by a screen.

Churchwarden. A parish officer, responsible for keeping the church in good repair, and representing the people in parochial matters.

Clay-lump. Unbaked brick.

Clunch digging. Digging for stiff clays, from which clay-lump may be formed.

Coffer. A box or chest.

Combing Shop. A building in which wool is combed.

Copyhold. Tenure of lands being parcel of a manor, by copy of court roll.

Corbels. Supports, set firmly into the wall, to carry a weight from above.

Deacon. A clergyman without the full status of a priest.

Deanery. The group of parishes over which a rural dean presides.

Demesne. Land devoted to the Lord of the Manor's profit. Peasants were obliged to work on it in return for the protection of the Lord.

Diocese. An area with a cathedral under the jurisdiction of a bishop, usually divided into archdeaconries.

Domus. Latin for a house or home.

Driftway. A lane or road along which cattle are often driven.

Enclosure Act. An act of parliament to enclose common land by law.

Enclosure/Inclosure. The action of enclosing common land.

Faculty Books. Books in which the licences (or authorisation) to carry out work on church building or repairs are recorded. These are held in diocesan or record offices.

Feudal. The system based on the relation of lord and vassal in medieval times.

Flint-Knapper. A skilled craftsman who 'knaps' flint, shaping it into tools by striking one flint against another, using a variety of techniques.

Flitch. A 'side' of bacon, salted and cured.

Font. A receptacle, usually of stone, for the water used in baptism.

Freehold. A land tenure which was not subject to the customs of the manor or the will of the lord, and which could normally be disposed of without restriction.

Gelding. A horse which has been castrated.

Glebe. Land assigned to the incumbent of a parish as part of his benefice and the endowment of the church.

Haft. A handle, especially that of a cutting instrument.

Hayward. An official who supervised farming matters, (particularly the repair of manor or parish fences), and who had the care of the common stock of animals and the duty of impounding stray cattle.

Hundred. Administrative unit. Subdivision of a shire county based on the grouping together of estates

Husbandman. A tenant farmer.

Incumbent. The holder of an ecclesiastical benefice, usually the parish priest.

Intestate. Without making a will.

Lancets. The slim, pointed windows which characterise the beginnings of Early English architecture from about 1200.

Ledger stones. Dark slabs of stone in the floor of the church, often with interesting epitaphs of those buried there.

Leet Court. Frequently held at the same time as the Manor Court, its main purpose being to deal with petty offences.

Lych-gate. The gate at the entrance to the churchyard, which provides shelter and a resting place for the coffin on the way to the church.

Manor Court. The court held by the lord of the manor.

Manumission. An act to liberate people from bondage or slavery.

Mensa slab. In pre-Reformation times, the altars were of stone, topped with a heavy slab, often of Purbeck marble. 'Mensa' is Latin for table.

Messuage. A house and the ground around it.

N

Nave. The main body of a church, from the Latin 'Navis' a ship.

Neate. A cow.

Nethergreene. Lower green.

P

Papacy. Referring to the office of the Pope.

Paten. The shallow dish, usually of silver, on which the bread is laid when Holy Communion is celebrated.

Pews. The benches with backs, to seat the congregation in church or chapel.

Piscina. A stone basin near an altar, usually set into a niche in the wall.

Polygonal single shafts. Many sided shafts.

Porch. An exterior structure, forming a covered approach to the entrance of a building. Porches were often added on to medieval churches later, from the 14th century onwards.

Pound. An enclosure maintained by the manor to confine stray animals.

Pulpit. A raised structure from which the preacher delivers the sermon.

Purbeck marble. Not marble, but a hard limestone, originally from south east Dorset.

Q

Quoins. The outside corner stones at the angles of buildings.

R

Religious Gilds/Guilds. Associations of people living in the same neighbourhood who had common obligations to keep the commandment 'to love thy neighbour as thyself'.

Removal Orders. When the legal place of settlement for a pauper was in dispute, the matter would be heard before a Justice of the Peace, and a Removal Order issued.

Rood Loft. In pre-Reformation times the church would have been separated into two parts, the chancel for the clergy and the nave for the people, with a carved wooden screen as a division between them. Above the screen there was often a Rood Loft, with a Crucifix in the middle, and figures of the Virgin Mary and St John on either side. This was approached by a stairway let into the wall.

Rosary beads. A string of beads used to assist the memory in the recitation of a set of devotions, including the Paternoster and the Gloria, known as the Rosary.

S

Scratch dials. Small patterns of radiating lines centred on a hole, carved into the outer stonework of a church. In the hole was a small peg (known as a 'gnomon' - Greek for indicator), whose shadow moved round with the sun. Each time the shadow touched one of the radiating lines, it was time for Mass.

Sedilia. Seats on the south side of the chancel, usually carved in stone.

Settlement Certificates. The 1697 Settlement Act debarred strangers from residing in a parish unless they provided a Settlement Certificate showing that they would be taken back by their home parish if they became in need of poor relief.

Sherd. A broken fragment of pottery.

Shot(t). Young, half-grown pig.

Stipend. Salary, particularly that of a priest.

Subscription Books. Books showing the signatures of those who had declared assent to the 39 Articles of the Church of England.

T

Terrier. A register of landed property, (often Ecclesiastical or church property).

Tithe. Theoretically a tenth part of income which went towards the upkeep of the incumbent of the parish church.

Thegn. Pre-Norman Conquest nobles who were usually local estate owners and administrators.

Torcs. Circular neck ornaments of the Bronze and Iron ages. They were usually formed of twisted or plaited rods of metal and were richly decorated.

Undercroft. A crypt or underground vault.

Villeins. The highest class of dependent peasantry. They held their own land which could be as much as 100 acres.

Visitation of Norfolk 1664. From 1529/30 the College of Arms made visitations all over the country to see if coats-of-arms were being used correctly. The last visitation of Norfolk was in 1664.

Wattle & daub. Interwoven twigs plastered with clay or mud as a building material.

 ources

SOURCES USED IN THIS HISTORY

PRINTED BOOKS AND PAPERS

Alumni Cantabrigienses (Cambridge University graduates).

Alumni Oxonienses (Oxford University graduates).

Apling Harry. Norfolk Corn Windmills, p.236. Norfolk Windmills Trust.

Arthur V.J. Colney, The Story of a Norfolk Village. (7 Church Farm, Colney).

Barratt Nick. Tracing the History of Your House. P.R.O. 2001.

Bevan A. and Duncan A. Tracing Your Ancestors in the Public Record Office. HMSO 1991.

Blomefield Francis. History of Norfolk, Vol 5. 1805.

Brown P. Domesday Book. Norfolk (Part II), Vol 33. Phillimore 1984.

Bryant's Map of Norfolk 1826. Barringer J.C., editor. Larks Press 1999.

Burke. Landed Gentry.

Burke and Saville. Guide to Country Houses. Vol III.

Campbell-Kease John. A Companion to Local History Research. Guild Publishing, 1989.

Chapman Colin R. How Heavy, How Much and How Long? Lochin Publishing, 1995.

Charity Digest "The Red Book". Report of the Commissioners for enquiries concerning charities, 1834. Clarke Z. Norfolk Charities.

Cox J. & Padfield T. Tracing your Ancestors in the Public Record Office. HMSO 1991.

Cox J. & Colwell S. Never Been Here Before? The Family Records Centre. PRO 1997.

Crockford's Clerical Directory.

Dictionary of National Biography.

Digby Anne. Pauper Palaces. Routledge & Kegan Paul. 1978.

Directories of Norfolk, particularly White's Directory 1845.

Dorman Bernard E. Norfolk. Batsford 1972.

Dymond David. The Norfolk Landscape. Hoodder & Stoughton 1985.

Ekwall Eilert. Concise Oxford Dictionary of English Place Names. OUP 1980.

Elvery Dowers. The Return of Owners of Land, Norfolk, 1873. Elvery Dowers 1990.

Farrer E. Church Heraldry of Norfolk, parts 1-4.

Finn R.Welldon. Domesday Book. A Guide. Phillimore 1986.

Gibson J.S.W. Wills and Where to Find Them. Genealogical Publishing Co. Inc., Baltimore. 1974.

Green Barbara and Young Rachel. Norwich, The Growth of a City. Norfolk Museums Service 1981.

Halliwell J.O. Dictionary of Archaic Words. Bracken Books 1850 (reprinted 1989).

Hammond J.L. and Hammond B. The Village Labourer. Longman (reprinted 1978).

Hethersett Society. Hethersett Heritage. Hethersett Society 1999.

Kennett D.H. Norfolk Villages. Robert Hale 1980.

Ketton-Cremer R.W. Norfolk in the Civil War. Faber & Faber 1969.

Laslett Peter. The World We Have Lost – further explored. Routledge 1988.

Margeson S., Seillier F., Rogerson A. The Normans in Norfolk. Norfolk Museums Service 1994.

Mortlock D.P. and Roberts C.V. The Popular Guide to Norfolk Churches No 2. Acorn Editions 1985.

Muir Richard and Nina. Fields. Macmillan 1989.

Munby Lionel. How Much is That Worth? Phillimore 1989.

Needham A. How To Study an Old Church. Batsford 1948.

Norfolk & Norwich Genealogical Society. Monograph 28. Little Melton Church Registers 1734-1837.

Norfolk Archaeology, published by the Norfolk & Norwich Archaeological Society.
 Vol 16 - Church Plate in Humbleyard Deanery.
 Vol 31 - Inventory of Church Goods 1552.

Norfolk Family History Society. Norfolk Ancestor, Sept 1998, p.567 re 'briefs for Little Melton' Pinchbeck, Lincs.

Norfolk Genealogy, published by the Norfolk & Norwich Genealogical Society.
 Vol 1 - Index.
 Vol 13 - Norfolk Visitation of Norfolk 1664 and Pedigrees for Sotherton and Skottowe.
 Vol 15 - Norfolk Hearth Tax Assessment at Michaelmas 1664.

Norfolk Record Society.
 Vol III - Register of the Abbey of St Benet of Holme.
 Vol XLII - Faden's Map of Norfolk 1797.

Ordnance Survey Maps.

Pevsner Nikolaus. The Buildings of England, S.W. and South Norfolk Penguin 1962.

Poll Books of 1702 and 1802.

Richardson John. The Local Historian's Encyclopedia. Historical Publications Ltd. 1989.

Richardson R.C. Some Fell on Stony Ground. George Reeve 1978.

Robinson B. & Rose E J. Norfolk Origins, 2: Roads & Tracks. Poppyland publishing 1983.

Rogers Alan. Approaches to Local History. Longman 1977.

Rose Michael E. The English Poor Law 1780-1930. David & Charles 1971.

Rouse E. Clive. Medieval Wall Paintings.

Skottow Philip F. The Leaf and the Tree.

Solomons Gerald. Plaques of Norwich. Capricorn Books 1981.

Steer F.W. Farm and Cottage Inventories of Mid Essex 1635-1749. Phillimore 1969.

Tate W.E. The Parish Chest. Cambridge University Press 1979.

Trotter Eleanor. Seventeenth Century Life in the Country Parish. Cass Frank 1968.

Wade-Martins Peter. An Historical Atlas of Norfolk. Norfolk Museums Service 1993.

Wade-Martins Susanna. A History of Norfolk. Phillimore 1984.

West John. Village Records. Macmillan 1962.

Williamson Tom. The Origins of Norfolk. Manchester University Press 1993.

Woodforde James. The Diary of a Country Parson 1758-1802. Canterbury Press 1999.

ORIGINAL MATERIALS

Cambridge Archives (Emmanuel College, Cambridge).

Boxes 20, A122, A123, A127, B9, B10, B11, C1, C8, C12.

(Emmanuel College, Cambridge, has a large archive department, including both Great and Little Melton and some adjoining parishes. It is essential to write for an appointment before visiting).

Hethersett Library.

Sale particulars of properties, 19th century.

A few wills of residents of Great and Little Melton.

Local Studies Library, Norwich.

Little Melton Mission Hall. Booklet published 1883. MEL 289.9 REFHB.

Good News – Parish Magazine 1977-82.

Census Returns for Little Melton and adjoining parishes, 1841-1891.

Norfolk Record Office, Norwich.

Church Registers of Baptisms, Marriages & Deaths, Little Melton. PD 269.

Enclosure Award and Map for Little Melton 1817. C/Sca 2/197 & 2/198.

Evans-Lombe Papers. EVL 251/1-18 457X6, 251/2 1-14, EVL/3 1-11, EVL/4 1-22, EVL/5 1-11. (Nos 33, 35, 40-43, 76 and 78 also refer to Little Melton and are interesting).

Forehoe Union Workhouse at Wicklewood. C/GP 8/3-28.

Gravestones at Little Melton. SO/WI/94 521 X3 with map of graveyard.

Henstead Union Workhouse at Swainsthorpe 1835-1851. C/GP 11/1, 11/2, 11/3.

Little Melton Church Faculty Books. PD 269/33.

Little Melton Church Terriers 1801,'13,'45,'72,1901,'33,'41,'47,'55,'67. PD 269/17.

Little Melton Manorial Books covering years 1650 to 1845. MC/1871/23-35 865X9.

Little Melton Poor Rate Books 1836-1850. PD 269/49-'51,'53,'57-'60.

Little Melton Settlement Examinations and Removal Orders 1816-1833. PD 269/51 & 269/53.

Little Melton Town Book 1809-1817. PD 269/49(S).

Little Melton Town Book 1817-1831. PD 269/50.

Map Little Melton & Bawburgh. Estate to be sold by auction, not dated. DS 172 (26).

Map Little Melton by Wm Butcher, Surveyor, not dated. DS 170 (31).

Map of Mr Girling's Estate in Little Melton Dec 1822. DS 171 (261).

Notes re Skottow Family of Norwich & Melton 1936. PD 269/65.

Register of Parochial Electors 1920 amended to 1945. PD 269/40.

Tithe Apportionment and Map for Little Melton 1842. DN/TA 628 Tithe.

Vestry Minute Books & related matters 1865-1919. PD 269/38-56.

Wills and Inventories. Wills and inventories proved in the Norwich Consistory Court, the Norfolk Archdeaconry Court or the Norwich District Probate Registry (See Appendix C).

Public Record Office, Kew.

> MH 12. Vol 1, 8415, (years 1834/1837) 3259 to 8416. Vol III, (years 1843/46) 56728 & 59920.
>
> Pre-1858 wills and inventories proved in the Prerogative Court of Canterbury (See Appendix C).

Deeds & other papers relating to Little Melton properties, kindly lent by their owners.

> 1924 Rate Book for Little Melton (from Mr Norman Nash).
>
> Assorted papers (from Mr and Mrs Maurice Lofty).
>
> Casetta deeds.
>
> Dormer Cottage, assorted papers.
>
> Grey Cottage deeds.
>
> Historical Notes on Little Melton from the late Mr. F. M. Gibbbs (kindly lent by Mrs D. Broughton).
>
> Little Melton Light Railway, from the late Mr Bob Brett.
>
> Little Melton Mill House deeds.
>
> Manor House deeds.
>
> Minutes of Little Melton Social Club founded 1 Oct 1936 (kindly lent by Mrs Dorothy Broughton).
>
> Papers of historical and church interest from the late Mr Joe Day.
>
> Rambler Cottage deeds.
>
> Rose Villa deeds.

With grateful thanks for all their help to the inhabitants of Little Melton, and neighbourhood, and to:

> Jan Allen and Andrew Rogerson of the Norfolk Landscape Archaeology Unit at Gressenhall.
>
> Mr George Gleadhill for permission to quote from his comparison of conditions at Little Melton and Colney School in the first ten years as a Board School 1875-1885 and under LEA control 1904-14.
>
> Mrs Clements of Little Melton First School, for permission to examine the Admission Register 1884-1934, punishment Book 1900-1966 and Managers' Minute Book 1942-1978.
>
> Mrs. Morris, Archivist, Emmanuel College, Cambridge.
>
> Mr Bill Reekie of Hethersett Library.
>
> The staff of the Norfolk Record Office.
>
> The staff of the Norwich Local Studies Library.
>
> The staff of the Public Record Office at Kew.

Index of Names

B

M

Sharp	Charles	34, 35		**Sowter**	George	168
Sharples	Chris	194		**Spaden**	Martha	221
Shaw	Miss	92		**Sparke**	Charles	141
	Patricia Batty	159, 229, *230*		**Sparkes**	C.	36
Sheen	Mary	127			John	147, 175
Sheldrake	Walter	140			Thomas	34
	William	140		**Sparrow**	W.	20, 32
Simons	Abraham	242		**Sparry**	Walter	247
Simpson	Charles	139		**Spaul**	Rose	49
Sinclair	Richard	45		**Stanley**	Rosie	97
Skerrit	C.	37		**Starkey**		76
Skipper	Keith	47, 212, *213*		**Stork**	Henry	247
Skottowe		154		**Stoughton**	Clarke	224
	Augustine	145, 150, 151, 156, 157, 246		**Sturdy**	Percy	248
	Bridget	245		**Swann**	Mr. & Mrs.	67, 126
	Elizabeth	11, 151, 245		**Symonds**	Arthur	139, 141
	Katherine	112, 152, 249			Betsy	126
	Richard	151, 202, 245			George	139
	Timothy	202			Hannah	40
	Thomas	11, 26, 29,151, 152, 156, 180, 246, 249			Henry	126
					James	40, 126, 140
Smith	Ann	130			John	126, 229
	Edward	170, 177			Joseph	39, 140
	Jonathan	130			Sarah	133
	John	135			Susan	126
	Ken	72			William	133
	Maria	130				
	Marianne	*213*				
	Mary	170		**Tanner**	Andrew	175, 180
	Rosina	138			Frances	175
Smyth	Thomas	24, 156, 169, 172		**Thurtle**	R.	*55*
				Thomlinson	John	224
Soden	Rev. John	114, 248		**Thompson**	Alan	129
Sotherton		154			Edward	174, 175
	Henry	150, 156, 157, 250			Elizabeth	61, 174, 175, 216
	Lawrence	150, 245			James	129, 175
	Nicholas	150, 155, 202, 244, 245			Priscilla	174
					Sarah	129
					William	170, 177

ndex of places

Page numbers in italics are illustrations or photographs and numbers in bold type are chapters about a specific place.

Places associated with Little Melton

Photograph/Illustration Credits

Whilst every effort has been made to give credit to the actual photographer/illustrator, some of the following credits can only be given to the lender of the photograph. If the originator can be proven the publishers will give full credit in subsequent issues.

Apling Harry: 138.

Archant, Norfolk: 4, 74, 96, 97, 145, 148, 179, 213, 228, 230 (top).

Aslin Christopher: 45, 132.

Beeby M. & S.: 176.

Cable Stewart: 10, 12, 18, 21, 25, 27, 52, 59, 61, 64, 89, 107, 123, 141, 152, 158, 164, 201, 230 (bottom), 231 (bottom), 236.

Bolton Mary: 29.

Carter Alan: 170, 172.

Carter Anne: 16, 49, 77, 220, 238, 241.

Day Joe: 105, 151, 199.

Duffield Norman: 189, 190, 191, 192, 193, 195.

Ellarby Studios: 70.

Evans Annetta: 197, 203.

Goldsmith R: 37.

Goulding David: 208, 218.

Hambling R.: 144, 146.

Hammond R.:169.

Hickling Jack & Irene: 79, 88, 126, 136.

Imperial War Museum: 41.

Institute of Archaeology, Oxford: 8.

Jarvis G: 134.

Loomb Mollie: 143, 206, 210.

Ladbroke Engravings: 102, 235.

Lofty M.: 185.

McDonnell Mark: 173.

Mace Violet: 83, 121.

Margaillan J.: 57, 65.

Marshall T.: 237.

Mayor of Bayeux & Director of Gallerie Reine Matilda: 14.

Mitchell J: 6 (based on photograph).

Nash Norman: 129.

National Portrait Gallery: 33.

Norfolk Record Office: 24, 50, 234, 253, 255, 257, 259. (Please also see acknowledgements in Appendix D, and on pages 253-260 inclusive).

Perrin David: 100.

Pickles S: 35.

Plunkett G.A.F.:98.

Postcards by unknown photographers: 68 (bottom), 72, 85, 139, 156, 159, 178, 222.

Public Record Office/Crown copyright: 19.

Rowe Larry: 160, 162, 166.

Royal Norfolk Regimental Museum: 204.

Sheriff Photography: 53, 54.

Swann Kenneth: 68 (top).

The Times: 39.

Wilkins K: 73, 135

Woods Keith: 2, 47, 76, 103, 104, 109, 111, 113, 115, 117, 124, 127, 131, 153, 194, 216, 232, 233 (top), rear cover.

Young Tony: 159.